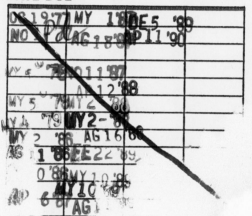

LOBBYING AND THE LAW

EDGAR LANE

LOBBYING
AND THE LAW

BERKELEY AND LOS ANGELES

1964 UNIVERSITY OF CALIFORNIA PRESS

UNIVERSITY OF CALIFORNIA PRESS
BERKELEY AND LOS ANGELES, CALIFORNIA
CAMBRIDGE UNIVERSITY PRESS
LONDON, ENGLAND
© 1964 BY THE REGENTS OF THE UNIVERSITY OF CALIFORNIA
LIBRARY OF CONGRESS CATALOG CARD NUMBER: 64-16059
PRINTED IN THE UNITED STATES OF AMERICA

For Ruth

Preface

This book is the result of an extended (and probably quite common) process of gestation. It began as background material for a study of federal regulation of lobbying, gradually assumed first separate and then equal identity, and ended as a more ambitious effort than the piece of which at first it was a minor part. The reasons seem simple enough now. The states have, after all, been regulating lobbying for nearly a century; the nation, for less than twenty years. Beyond historical abundance, one could argue that lobbying has been a more complex, difficult and corrosive problem in the states than it has been in Washington, although proof of the point might be elusive. The states' efforts to deal with lobbying have also been treated neither thoroughly nor well in the literature, and this, in the end, accounts for the book.

I should like to acknowledge gratefully the aid, comfort, and counsel that many people have given me. Particular obligations are recorded in the text and notes. Research funds generously provided by Princeton University and the University of California have contributed materially to the completion of the work.

For somehow managing to make the children observe the sepulchral silence that I apparently regard as essential to my labors, and for many other things, my wife Ruth is due a very special note of thanks.

E. L.

Goleta, California
June, 1963

Contents

THE SETTING AND THE PROBLEM

It should no longer be necessary to argue the proposition that men's diverse interests define their real political existence. We may be vaguely awed and flattered by public rhetoric that makes of government a distant monolith, greater somehow than the sum of its human parts, a shadowy repository for all the convenient ambiguities of the public interest. But our response to these conventions is neither deep nor durable, and our collective life actually builds on the unstated premise that government is precisely what it seems to be: a specialized apparatus for the achievement of those ends we choose to regard as within our public competence to achieve. Once grant that men have the right to disagree, within the polity's limits of toleration, and it could not have been otherwise.

Since this concession lies close to the heart of our experience, there should be nothing startling about the fact that from colonial times on, men and groups of men have sought both to prompt and to prevent the exercise of governmental power. This fact involves what Willard Hurst called "if not the fundamental object of government . . . at least an aspect of government's main purpose," which is simply "that men should come to it, all the more so because what they want may be against the general welfare."[1] One need not choose among warring conceptions of "the general welfare"—or even concede that there is one—to erect as a fundamental article of faith men's right to assail it and seek preferment for their own vision of the good life.[2]

The recognition that men are stubbornly dissimilar, and that the peaceful adjustment of their differences provides government with one of its principal tasks, is woven firmly through our ordained political theory. Consider, for example, the argument of the tenth of the Federalist Papers—themselves a classic defense of an interest less than total. We recall Madison's dour strictures on the "latent causes of faction," which he saw as "sown in the nature of man." Men persisted in their differences, largely economic in origin, and these "divided mankind into parties, inflamed them with mutual animosity, and rendered them much more disposed to vex and oppress each other than coöperate for the common good."[3] How could these diversities be sufficiently reconciled to allow the definition and achievement of the "common good"? Madison was democrat and politician enough to realize that even the most enlightened head-knocking could not resolve fundamental conflicts of interest. Let conflict, rather, spend itself against a sturdy institutional wall; allow maximum freedom to the play of interests, but build a governmental structure of sufficient strength and flexibility to absorb the shock of their collision. The principal feature of this structure was, of course, a large federal republic, and the safety it promised was mainly the safety of sheer numbers. The more inclusive the frame of government, the more interests it could envelop; their multiplicity would minimize the danger that any one of them might assume such proportions as to threaten the larger community.

Madison's theoretical defense of federalism was not wholly based on the assumption that a multiplicity of interests promised easy cancellation of their claims upon the state. He also foresaw that groups would not always stand alone, that they would coalesce as the exigencies of discrete situations might demand. But these would be "brief coalitions," destined only to dissolve. Man's combative nature would assure their dissolution, and secure the republic against lasting danger of factional imbalance.

In some respects, Madison's conception of the political process was marvellously prescient; in others it has failed to mature. He was right about the number, variety, and political relevance of economic interests; he was wrong in assuming that they could not be permanently conjoined. National political parties have from the beginning been relatively stable and long-lived interest alliances, but the dispersive tendencies of a political system of continental dimensions have easily prevented them from becoming the "tyrannical majorities" of Madison's dark vision. Our parties, indeed, stand as the readiest exemplars of the humble but honorable process of social accommodation, and it is to their loose-jointed continuity rather than to any fine balance of contending interests that we owe the largest part of our political stability. For these interests have never been in equipoise, and, short of reconstruction unimaginably heroic, they never will be. In a very real sense, the society should not hang together as well as it does. The survival of democracy in the United States has been a continuing triumph of mutual restraint and institutional flexibility.

This is only to say that Madison was more diagnostician than prophet. The inevitability of diverse interests in a free society and the need to construct a system of government that could adjust the differences that would inevitably arise between them bulked large in the intellectual structure of which he was the principal architect. It bulks no less large today.

The Meaning of Lobbying

Lobbying is not an American invention. Every democratic system worthy of the name includes a variety of formal and informal means by which men can come to government with their needs; lobbying, or something like it, has long been one of them. If in this sense lobbying is not a uniquely American phenomenon, however, there are others in which it is. The American experience is unique in the degree to which diverse interests have proliferated and sought political expression. It is unique in the degree that our institutional arrangements were intended to conduce—and have conduced—to this end. And it is unique with respect to the legal devices that are the principal concern of this study. We did not import the laws that, with more optimism than accuracy, we call "regulation of lobbying"; they are strictly home-grown barriers that have been casually erected against the demonstrated or presumptive evils of unrestricted political action by, or on behalf of, private interests. They are also part of a distinctively American approach to a universal problem of government. The problem is that of maintaining an optimum distance between private interests and public power; the American approach has been to provide a setting in which the problem might somehow solve itself.

What precisely do we mean by "lobbying"? Definition is difficult because the word has been so largely separated from the contemporary behavior and relationships that might define it. It is a word that summons conflicting images. On the one hand, it is part of the vocabulary of political abuse; on the other, it is part of the symbolic equipment by which men seek to justify themselves. It is the paunchy fixer and the legislator who came from the country and came to be bought. It is the bane of patriots. It is the $300 bribe offered to a Maryland legislator in 1963 to "take a walk" on a vote to bar slot machines.[4] But it is also living reaffirmation of a free people's highest rights. It is education by those whose predilections we share, evidence of our genius for social orchestration, and the American answer to the deficiencies of geographic representation. But it is also sabotage of the legislative process, the majority principle, and representative government by special interests and selfish minorities. It is what prompts Governor Brown of California, frustrated by an unresponsive legislature, to declare that the people of the state "are having a distinct problem with the lobbyists," an observation rather milder than some of his counterparts in other states have been heard to utter under roughly comparable circumstances.[5]

Lobbying is all these things, yet they do not satisfactorily define it. At bottom, lobbying can only be defined by its ends or its means, neutrally described, and there are difficulties in each approach. The end of lobbying is to influence what government does, but this can apply to most political activity. Men join parties and run for office for essentially the same reasons that other men pay lobbyists to inform, entertain, cajole, pressure, or threaten legislators: so that they can influence the choices that public men make. When lobbying is defined by its means, the problem is to keep the formulation narrow enough so that every act of intended political influence is not included, yet broad enough so that every substantial or consequential act of intended political influence will fall within it.

The term "lobbying" has been in common use for more than one hundred years. Throughout the nineteenth century, it meant face-to-face efforts by paid agents to influence legislators to vote in their clients' behalf, often by corrupt or covert means. Although outright corruption is no longer common, lobbying still means direct persuasion, a fact of which the annual registration of several thousand admitted lobbyists in thirty states would appear to offer obvious and adequate proof. But it may also mean very much more. For example, a station editorial broadcast over a CBS affiliate in Los Angeles urges listeners to write their legislators to repeal a tax on bunker oil that has been driving tramp steamer traffic away from Southern California ports.[6] Is this lobbying? Or Florida Chambers of Commerce pay

"expense money" to local legislators during the session in Tallahassee, and small-loan companies threaten to withhold future campaign support from legislators who do not vote "right," a technique
known locally, according to Havard and Beth, as "turning a blow
torch on the navel of the blue hens."[7] Is this lobbying? Functionally,
the answer in each case is probably "yes"; legally, however, it is
probably "no." There are in every state situations in which techniques are equally indirect, or in which there is no paid agency in
a legal sense, or in which the target is an administrative agency rather
than the legislature, but in which the efforts to influence policy may
be no less intended and effective.

The point of this dilation is only to suggest how difficult it is to
draw lines around one segment of a continuous spectrum of political
persuasion and call the enclosed area "lobbying." Where there are
lobbying laws, however, these lines have got to be drawn. Lobbying means men acting to influence governmental decisions, but
whether what they do can be called "lobbying" and held liable to
the requirements of a registration and reporting statute—and, apart
from whatever general values there may be in verbal precision, this
should be the main purpose of definition—hinges on fluid political
and juristic usages. In this sense, lobbying is always what the times
make it. If it means no more than it did eighty years ago, then
Congress and the legislatures of thirty states have been straining at
gnats and swallowing camels.

Although unvarnished corruption is obviously less common than it
was, lobbying methods have otherwise expanded as much as they
have changed, and this is no less true of the identity and structure
of the interests that resort to lobbying before state governments to
advantage or protect themselves. In the third quarter of the nineteenth
century, lobbying was mainly an individualized and grossly acquisitive business. The lobbyist typically represented an entrepreneur
seeking something of value from the state—charters, franchises, loans,
banking privileges, and the like—against the competing claims of
other equally good and ambitious citizens. These were the years that
have been called the "railway period" of our legislative history, and
it was the railway builders who set the tone for the interest politics
of the era, who engaged in it the most extravagantly, and who reaped
the richest benefits. Political solidarity and the recognition of mutual

interests had not yet replaced costly individual competition, and the railway barons and their lobbyist intermediaries fought savagely among themselves for the grants and privileges that the state legislatures had within their power to bestow. Later in the century, other interests—utilities, manufacturers, insurance companies, and the like —emerged from the corporate cocoon to wage further convulsive struggles for political dominance, and once again lobbying figured prominently in their exertions.

Today, by contrast, the central tendency of American interest politics is collective rather than competitive, associational rather than entrepreneurial. Political interest groups, typically multipurpose membership associations representing virtually every variety of significant common interest, have become the main vehicles by which men seek to prompt government to reward them, recognize their needs, or simply leave them alone. For every rail tycoon or land syndicate bent on buying up a legislature in 1870, there are now a dozen trade and professional associations, labor and agricultural groups, Chambers of Commerce, tax leagues, or other voluntary organizations of interested citizens, sharing dominance when they do not compete for it. Eighty years after Gould and Vanderbilt vied ruinously with each other in debauching the New York Legislature, their troubled corporate legatees find joint action through the New York State Association of Railroads or the Eastern Railroads Presidents Conference more attractive than guerrilla warfare. Indeed, the New York Central System no longer maintains separate legislative representation in Albany, although its voice is obviously still heard there. The example is in no sense unique; few sectors of American life have been unaffected by a similar collectivization of political effort.

Two generations ago, the formation of political interest groups was to Robert Luce one of the "perils of the time,"[8] but they have by now become established, accepted, and, on the whole, useful participants in the political process. The origins and structure of these groups have been exhaustively treated elsewhere, most notably in Truman's *The Governmental Process*.[9] It is enough to say here that such groups develop when and because men perceive the interests they hold in common. These interests, in turn, flow naturally and in great quantity out of the social and economic differentiations that are characteristic of a maturing open society. Groups form and proliferate, moreover, only when the political system does not discourage their growth—and may thereby encourage it. Every American legislature has more to do than its predecessor, and the growing volume and complexity of legislative business reflects not only new group demands but also new threats to established interests around which groups have formed, or from which they can develop. Under conditions of political freedom, active government both mirrors and generates a politically active group sub-structure. Since all of these conditions of growth have been fulfilled to an extraordinary degree in the United States during the past half century, the American group complex has also assumed extraordinary proportions.

We have no more than an approximate idea of how many groups seek variously to impose their claims on agencies of government. On the national level, a Department of Commerce compilation in 1949 listed over 4,000 national associations, and referred without listing to 16,000 other organizations of businessmen alone.[10] More than 600 of these national organizations have been active enough before the Congress to concede their obligation to comply with the limited reporting requirements of the Federal Regulation of Lobbying Act, and a comparable number of groups of firms that have not complied have been represented by registered agents.[11] Although one can only guess at the total content of what Schattschneider has called "the unknown associational universe," one could probably locate between 1,500 and 2,000 significant national associations or concerns with substantial and continuous political interests and an organizational structure to support them.[12] Perhaps eight-to-ten times this many are located, or are principally active, in the fifty states. In the larger states, as many as 400 associations or concerns may register as employers of lobbyists during a typical legislative session. Local groups and firms with more than occasional active interest in state legislation are numerous beyond the best-educated guess.

We know even less about how much it all costs. Reports filed under the Federal Lobbying Act have at times indicated annual group expenditures of $10,000,000, although it is safe to assume that this is no more than a dim reflection of what is actually spent on private activities relating to national legislation. Group political expenditures are obviously smaller in individual states and virtually impossible to estimate in those states without registration and reporting laws, but the aggregate of annual group expenditures in the states probably exceeds the national figure. In California alone, reported expenditures have exceeded $3,000,000 during recent general sessions, and this amount is generally confined only to those costs attributable to the hiring and maintenance of registered lobbyists. While there may have been more than a trace of sanguinary hyperbole in a congressional committee's assertion that "lobbying in all of its ramifications" was a "billion dollar industry," no one has yet disproved it.[13] The tangled web of interest politics resists more precise delineation. This much is clear: It involves thousands of diverse organizations, tens of thousands of men and women, and millions of dollars. It is equally clear that on no level of government is public policy conceived, adopted and applied—nor can it be understood—apart from the groups of men whose interests are somehow touched by it. We still have our entrepreneurs impatient of success, but they have typically made common cause.

In the same sense that interest groups have supplemented rather than replaced the individualized interest politics of the nineteenth century, so too have lobbying methods been augmented more than they have changed. Eighty years ago, "lobbying" meant personal solicitation of legislative votes, usually but not always through the agency of hired lobbyists, of whom there were relatively few. These men traded on their privileged entrée to committees, their personal relationships with influential legislators, their specialized knowledge of the legislature's procedural lacunae, their skill as hosts, and, not infrequently, their adeptness at honest argument. And when all else failed, they were prepared to buy their clients the legislation they needed. Overt corruption was common enough to justify De Grazia's general comment that "lobbying methods were unscrupulous."[14]

Tactics are still personalized to some degree. Group representatives, often former legislators who find that their experience and contacts have brisk market value, still confront members of legislative bodies to argue for their votes and buy their dinners. Personal relationships and "privileged access" still count in politics. But corruption in the nineteenth-century sense is less frequent and spectacular than it was, not so much because standards of public probity are more exacting (although they may at least be more sophisticated), than because a watchful press and suspicious competitors have forced up both the risks and the costs of detection. As the Maryland slot machine interests discovered in 1963, it has become virtually impossible to buy up an entire legislature. The relative circumspection of our politics is in curious counterpoint to the distended competence of government, so ripe with the promise of reward.

The real distinction, however, is not that methods are cleaner but that the role of the hired agent has changed. Personal solicitation still has its uses, as the continued presence and prosperity of thousands of lobbyists across the country attest, but less direct approaches may be more productive, and the main thrust comes from the parties at interest or their associational legatees. Tactics vary with the resources, membership, competitive position, skills, and interests of the groups concerned. For one group, this may mean external public relations directed toward the development of broad public support for, or acquiescence in, the group's long-range objectives; for another, the neutralization of competing propagandas; for a third, organized political action, or the threat of such action, on a statewide scale; for a fourth, the exploitation of research and bill-drafting services; for a fifth, the development of joint strategy with other groups. The combinations are limitless. Overall, the emphasis is clearly away from the conventional modes of personal address. The contrast is between lobbying and a true group politics, between the lobbyist and the group bureaucrat, between the insider and the technician. The shift is not, and probably never will be, complete, but it has already drained some of the color from the traditional picture of the lobbyist-for-hire. That this picture still has sentimental appeal to those who should know better does not alter the fact that it is increasingly peripheral to the main design.

Finally, the operational meaning of government to those who would come to it for protection or support—and this in the end means almost all of us—has broadened to the point where a conception of lobbying in purely legislative terms is no more than a semantic convenience. While lobbying has customarily been regarded in both the literature and the law as involving only efforts to influence the legislature, interest groups have been under no obligation to bend their activities to the abstract verities of separation of powers. These groups are active, rather, wherever significant decisions affecting their interests are made. This has inevitably involved them in the politics of administration; for longer than we realize, political interest groups have treated statehouse and state office building as inseparable parts of the same political architecture.

The concern of these groups with administrative structure and decisions has been variously expressed. Demands for the organization of administrative agencies around clientele services reflect one approach. The statutory assignment to professional associations of wide authority for policing professional entry and standards—common in the states—reflects another. Formal requirements or informal expectations that administrative personnel or advisory bodies be recruited from sectors of interest affected by agency operations reflect a third.[15]

More generally, the development in this century of a distinct administrative process has served to multiply and regularize the points of contact between private interests and public administration. Operating under general legislative charters, administrative agencies have been increasingly charged with the formulation and application of rules having the force of law; it should occasion no surprise that those whom the rules affect should try to mold or mitigate their terms. Their right so to do, moreover, has been legitimized and safeguarded in such enactments as the Federal Administrative Procedure Act of 1946 and its counterparts in the states. Although they serve other purposes as well, laws of this kind can be taken as measures of the depth of group involvement in administrative policy-making, and at least in part as an effort to inject into the latter some of the assumptions of accessibility that are usually associated with group-legislative relationships.

This does not mean that groups have turned their attention away from the legislature; they act, rather, on different stages at different times, or on several stages simultaneously. At the risk of oversimplification, one might contrast Collis Huntington's single-minded purchase of early California legislatures with the subtle and complex activities of the California Railroad Association, which might at any time be maintaining a conventional lobbying operation in Sacramento, conducting or subsidizing research on railroad problems, contesting abandonments before state agencies, coöperating with its national counterpart (the Association of American Railroads), participating (quietly) in election campaigns, and contributing to efforts to "educate" the electorate to the evils of publicly supported highways.

These tactics are not unique; they demonstrate only the extent to which interest groups, if they are to be effective, must conform to changing distributions of political power. It is less a question of their having so much energy to expend than it is of their somehow finding enough additional energy to participate tellingly in an ever-widening political process. Groups must constantly attune themselves to the working competence of government, which their own demands have inevitably tended to enlarge.

In sum, the political process has expanded and matured, and lobbying in the nineteenth-century sense no longer looms quite so large within it. There are still thousands of lobbyists in state capitals across the country, no doubt doing many of the things that their forebears used to do. And there are still restless loners, no doubt willing to do whatever they must to make things go their way. In most respects, however, the group politics of today bears no more than a rough familial resemblance to the lobbying of three or four generations ago. In modern perspective, lobbying is one aspect of the efforts of men, characteristically organized in groups, to influence the making of public policy wherever it is made, by means ranging from personal persuasion and entertainment of public officials, through formal representations before legislative committees and administrative agencies, to educational public relations in the broadest sense. To keep this formulation within reasonable bounds, we can restrict it to include only reasonably substantial, direct, and relevant private efforts to influence legislative decisions, but the restriction is only a convenient artifice, and it should be so understood.[16] The group political system is a seamless and staggeringly complex web of inter-relationships; if a word like "lobbying" is inadequate to describe them, we should simply find a better one. As we no longer define an airplane as what the Wright brothers flew at Kitty Hawk, we can no longer define lobbying as what Sam Ward did during the Grant administration.

The relevance of definition to the subject matter of this study should be obvious, for "lobbying" laws restricted to the face-to-face relationships historically associated with the word are likely to become rootless gestures. But this is precisely the price that most state lobbying laws have paid. Narrow in origin and approach, they have for the most part been enacted in haste and allowed to atrophy in leisure—and all the while the little world they seek to capture goes

right on changing. There may be abundant reason why laws so con-
ceptually imprisoned might not be worth the effort to preserve. They
might indeed be dangerous to preserve if they were to help perpetuate
whimsical images of a time that is past, or if we were to impute to
them more curative powers than they actually possess.

The "Lobbying Problem" and the Nature of Regulation

The prevailing view of lobbying can best be described as of the
"yes, but . . . " variety. The literature bulges with earnest discussions of the representative, educational, social, and political values
that interest groups can serve ("Interest groups are necessary and
essential elements in our policy-making process"), often coupled
with other-handed concern about the direction in which "government by pressure" is taking us (" . . . but at the same time they can
impair the effective operation of representative democracy").[17]

Although the indictments are variously drawn, a few dominant
themes recur. In the first place, "pressure politics" is endlessly expen-
sive. As a troubled senator wrote, "Not only do groups ask for more
than they expect to get, but the sum of all their bed-rock demands
is far more than the country can afford."[18] A respected columnist
saw government "engulfed in an obscene grab for the almighty
dollar," and concluded: "These pressure groups are running wild."[19]
Obviously groups do not always get all that they demand, but "the
costs of 150 years of relentless raiding of the Public Treasury" have,
in the judgment of a congressional committee, been "staggering" and
"beyond estimate." Further, "The people must bear the costs of lobbying as well as pay for its end results." Encouraged by tax exemptions
and generous deductibility provisions, interest groups have often
succeeded in adding hidden political expenditures to the ordinary
costs of producing goods and rendering services. In this sense,
"Pressure groups are quite free-handed with both their own and with
other people's money."[20]

And more than economic costs are involved. A widely aired report
counts as one of the "social costs" of lobbying the "ideological conflict and public confusion which has already begun to result from
the use of charged public opinion as an instrument of pressure." Men
live by slogans, but when they allow the latter to become a substitute

for thought, "they have lost the first part of their ability to govern themselves."[21]

Beyond its tendency to contort our political dialogue, a presumptive surfeit of "pressure politics" reinforces the interests that divide the society rather than the common threads that hold it together, and confers special advantages on those interests that are best organized or financed, or that command special skills, media access, mass memberships, or prestigious symbols.[22] Disadvantaged interests, or "the public interest," go unheard, or are heard but dimly. Chief Justice Warren stated the part-whole dichotomy in more or less classic terms when he observed:

> Yet full realization of the American ideal of government by elected representatives depends to no small extent on their ability to properly evaluate . . . pressures. Otherwise, the voice of the people may all too easily be drowned out by the voice of special-interest groups seeking favored treatment while masquerading as proponents of the public weal.[23]

For all the hard questions that it skirts (what, for example, if the "voice of the people" is a discordant babel, or if our legislators take affirmative action not to hear it?), the view that interest groups are disruptive elements is, and has been, widely held.

There are also said to be political costs attached to a "dispersive" system which replaces broadly based government with unstable coalitions of irresponsible and acquisitive minority interests.[24] While some observers find the costs of this "mild chaos" within the range of the tolerable and the chaos itself as a fair reflection of the society's "diversities-within-unity," a somewhat larger (or at least more vocal) complement argue that it is destructive of "party" or "responsible" government.[25] For when the parties cannot or will not govern, "the pressure groups move in by default."[26]

Group tactics also figure prominently in the indictment. Schattschneider's description of "the first rule of successful pressure politics—to make a noise like the clamor of millions but never permit an investigation of the claims"—suggests one common concern.[27] Another can be inferred from Representative Celler's delineation of "bad lobbying" as that in which the message is "cryptic, deceptive, and obscure."[28] Justice Jackson was working similar terrain when he observed that lobbyists' "conflicting claims and propaganda are confusing, annoying, and at times, no doubt, deceiving and corrupting."[29] The theme echoes in the recent general reference by a California legislative committee to "the possibility that influence can be exerted [by lobbyists] in an improper manner," as, of course, it has been throughout our history, and from time to time still is.[30]

In sum, interest groups are whittling away at democracy's underpinnings. If they are not somehow by-passed, balanced, or controlled, we can look forward to such grim consequences as "a conflict between them which bodes ill for our kind of society."[31] Or, in Stuart Chase's more specific vision of Armageddon, it will only be a matter of time "until somebody comes riding in on a white horse," at which point the legislature "becomes a memory and the pressure groups go underground for an indefinite stay."[32]

Now these alarums, if not necessarily the large institutional prescriptions that they support, have been too chronic and often too perceptive to be airily rejected as part of the "peripheral data of politics."[33] That they may rest on highly questionable assumptions as to the role and preferences of the individual legislator, or the technical non-partisanship of major groups, or the nature of "the public interest" does not argue for their cavalier dismissal. That they may also spring in some measure from an almost aesthetic revulsion against the disorderly tugging and hauling of the system does not mean that they are significant only as expressions of intellectual malaise. For our politics *is* disorderly, complex, and chaotic, and it could conceivably destroy itself. As there is a limit to the hurt which a human organism can sustain, so too may there be a limit to any society's ability to feed upon itself. To say that conflict is the essence of politics does not make the battlefield indefinitely fit for habitation.

There may, in fine, be reason to conclude that interest groups and lobbying have gotten so far out-of-hand as to endanger the continued existence of the political system in anything like its present form. Groups are natural elements in the American political process, but they may already have induced more profound changes in its structure and operation than we might recognize or wish. If they have, then surely serious consideration of remedial measures is appropriate. It should not be necessary that needless and unwanted upheaval be imminent before concern with remedies is felt to be timely. Institutional renovation in the United States has almost always required long periods of gestation, and in this sense concern with remedies is always timely. That the system seems to work does not assure its indefinite survival, nor should it argue for a placid moratorium on change.

Proposals purporting to deal with "the group problem" are endemic, but they differ widely in their content, in the diagnoses that underlie them, and in the values that they reflect. They also differ with respect to their availability and realistic prospects of success. Those proposals that would impose serious restraints upon the formation or activities of political interests groups are basically at odds with our tradition and, in any case, stand almost no chance of being consciously adopted in the foreseeable future. Those which argue that a "civilized morality," or "drastic" legislative reform, or "responsible and disciplined" political parties would be the most effective counters to excessive group influence are usually unaccompanied by detailed road-maps leading to this undeniably attractive destination, and they often studiedly ignore the large impediments that appear to bar the way.[34] While the laws with which this study is concerned may not be ultimate solutions, at least they are presently at hand.

In the strictest sense, they are not solutions at all. At bottom, state lobbying laws involve no more than the casual application of a wholesome general principle to some of the more visible aspects of group-legislative relationships—primarily those that can be described as "lobbying." This principle has been called "disclosure." It rests on the old-fashioned belief that, in a democracy, the public interest is always served by the widest possible diffusion of information about matters of public consequence or interest. It further holds that when such information is wanting, withheld, or otherwise unavailable, government should require that it be disclosed. The disclosure principle is as simple as that. It assumes no benefits or uses in advance. It assumes only that if men have access to the facts, they will seek them out and put them to whatever use their preferences and needs dictate.

This general principle has been variously applied in statutory form to campaign finances, foreign agency and propaganda, media ownership, security issuance, and several other areas. Since 1890, it has been the dominant principle in state regulation of lobbying, and more than half the states have now enacted statutes that embody it. These laws proceed from the premise that substantial organized efforts to influence legislative action are of obvious concern to both the legislature and the public; such efforts should, therefore, be publicized, typically through requirements that lobbyists identify themselves and the interests for which they speak, and periodically reveal how much it all has cost.

In these terms, the disclosure idea is very nearly unexceptionable. It is direct, simple, and undemanding. It does not prevent anybody from doing anything. In seeking to promote open dealing and informed public judgment, it is in obvious and natural accord with basic democratic values. All this, however, has had relatively little to do with the "real" reasons that have impelled American state legislatures to enact lobbying disclosure laws. As we shall point out in detail below, these laws have not typically been enacted as affirmations of democratic values, nor as devices for informing public judgment, nor even as means of making the legislative process more visible or protecting the integrity of the legislature itself. They are better understood as carefully controlled responses to potentially damaging evidence or allegations of legislative partiality to particular interests. In short, most state lobbying laws have been enacted by embarrassed or compromised legislatures. They have been crutches more than weapons, tactical incidents more than intended remedies. One of the major purposes of this study will be to examine the origins of these laws, and to seek to unravel the influence that their beginnings have had on their requirements and subsequent operation.

Although there is a wide gulf between the formal rationale for political disclosure and the objective situations that have usually produced it, this rationale still has powerful appeal. There are more ambitious panaceas for the "group problem" but most of them involve some measure of institutional tinkering, seldom an easy process and often a disappointing one. The genius of state disclosure laws—and there is a certain genius in them—is that they involve no tinkering at all. Whatever the intentions of the men who wrote them, disclosure laws provide at least partial measures of our ability to live by some of the principles that we profess. In a sense no less real for being inadvertent, these laws can put a central aspect of the democratic thesis to the test: Do citizens in a democracy care enough about "the facts" to seek them out and use them well? The question does not answer itself.

Beyond whatever function they may serve as exercises in political theory, however, disclosure laws are integral parts of state political systems, and this will be the main perspective of the pages that follow. We will be concerned with the origins, language, and requirements of these laws. We will be particularly concerned with their operation. What level of official effort supports them? To what extent have disclosed data moved into the mainstream of opinion, and what uses have political participants found for them? In sum, where does state regulation of lobbying fit into the political process, and what does it accomplish there? Does the disclosure idea have major values and a useful future in a system such as ours, or is it only a diversion from the need for more fundamental political reconstruction? After seventy years, it should be time enough to ask these questions. If the answers are unpleasant, we do ourselves no service in blinking them away.

Chapter 2

THE ORIGINS OF REGULATION

With his customary long perspective, Robert Luce once observed: "Doubtless ever since representative assemblies began, citizens have visited them for purposes of persuasion."[1] Certainly this has been true of the American experience. Lobbying, in one form or another, has been with us from the beginning, and will probably remain with us so long as the political system continues to conform to broadly democratic values. It has, indeed, been so deeply woven into the American political fabric that one could, with considerable justice, assert that the history of lobbying comes close to being the history of American legislation.

Although a fully detailed account of how men have sought to get what they wanted from government—and this is ultimately what lobbying is about—is beyond the reach or purpose of this study, a general understanding of the meaning and historical development of lobbying in the states is obviously relevant to a study of regulatory devices. Where did lobbying come from, and why has it taken the distinctive forms that it has? What evolutionary factors have purged lobbying of some of its grosser elements and added others more appropriate to the needs and conduct of a complex group political process? With what kinds of problems has lobbying confronted the state legislatures, and how have these bodies responded to them? Of these questions we may briefly treat.

Lobbying Before the Civil War

Luce, whose judgment in such matters is usually reliable, denotes Andrew Jackson's "war" with the United States Bank as the starting point for professional lobbying. This reference mark in national history, although probably accurate as to time, is somewhat misleading, for, as Crawford put it, "the fine art of lobbying was developed in state capitols" and only later transplanted to Washington.[2] Mencken also notes that the first use of the term "lobby" in its political sense was recorded in 1829, when it was applied in the phrase "lobby-agent" to the hired privilege-seekers who had begun to frequent the legislative corridors at Albany. Soon thereafter, Thurlow Weed and others gave to lobbying professional status, established method, and a persisting notoriety.[3]

More significant than verbal origins were the economic alterations underlying the development of political advocacy as a profession. Even before the Civil War, the mushroom growth of the corporate form had far outstripped the ability of a colonial legal system to keep apace. General laws of charter, franchise, and incorporation had not yet been written, and banks, bridges, turnpikes, and virtually all other types of corporation had to be created by special legislative acts, the competitive demand for which had begun to generate great pressures on the bodies which enacted them. In point of time alone, it has been estimated that the granting of corporate charters con- sumed three-quarters of most state legislative sessions in the decade preceding the Civil War.[4]

How were these rich gifts to be got? Honest argument worked for some of the petitioners, but there were no double-locked guarantees that it would. Particularly where there was competition for grants of privilege, or where the terms of the latter were so offensive as to be unable to withstand the possibility of public scrutiny, the purchase of the required legislative votes was often quicker and more certain, and time was always short. The bolder tycoons had no qualms about handling the details themselves; others found it more convenient to entrust their ambitions to a knowledgeable and influential practitioner of the lobbying arts—a capitol lawyer, perhaps, or a former legislator, or what used to be known as "a gentleman of parts." His methods centered on his personal entrée to the legislature; that this might be pressed to a client's advantage by covert means was something that the most righteous entrepreneur could take affirmative action not to know.[5]

The professional lobbyist was one of the natural products of an expanding economy, but he owed part of his existence to changes of another order. The years after Jackson were marked by the solidifi- cation of party machinery, by the final ebbing of the old political dynasties, and by the rise to power of men for whom politics was less a matter of class responsibility than a business. The professional lobbyist and the professional politician were logical counterparts; they sprang from the same soil; they knew how to talk to each other. Indeed, their outlook and their methods might, in the person of a Weed or a Sam Ward, merge altogether.[6] The lobbyist and the politician differed in the stability of their allegiances and in the postures that their roles required; the politician was at least technically the sought, while the lobbyist and those for whom he spoke were the seekers. But they were as one in harnessing the primitive machinery of what was still a predemocratic polity to the special needs of a rapidly expanding economic order. Their spectacular success in this joint enterprise worked to their eventual detriment, but not before they had left their imprint—in many ways ineradicable and in few benign—on our political institutions.

The Railroad Era

Although, as Brogan has observed, the halcyon days of the "pure" (in the scientific sense) lobbyist followed the Civil War, the gilded age of American lobbying began not with the Civil War and Reconstruction but with the building of the railroads.[7] As early as the 1830's, the eastern and north central states suffered the first attacks of the speculative fever that was later to burn and debilitate most of the states lying in the rails' westward path. Their minds awash and pockets stuffed with rail debentures, state and local legislators proved eager to grant virtually any privileges that the promoters might require. Monopoly rights-of-way were not infrequently bestowed, and, when they were contested by shippers or competitors, were often retained by judicious admixtures of simple bribery and complicated wit. Legislatures of the period were also not averse, when properly stimulated, to authorizing the rail companies to finance construction through the issuance of bank notes, sole security for which was usually the proposed road itself.[8] That these concessions had illustrious antecedents did not render their ultimate effects the less serious; these effects would have to include at least partial responsibility for two financial panics, and the infusion of such quantities of liquid into the rail's financial structure as would require heroic efforts during the balance of the century even partially to desiccate.

When in the forties and fifties exclusive franchises and banking rights had either been revoked or were no longer sufficient inducement to the promoters, the states, particularly those west of the Mississippi, began to experiment with the disposal of their public lands, money, and credit in their efforts to attract the roads. As the stakes become greater, the bribery and cunning of the preceding generation bloomed in many state capitals into a gaudy carnival of public plunder; accounts of the proceedings commonly list railroad lobbyists as among the more prominent revellers. Thus Miller and Cochran describe as "typical" the scramble for public lands among competing roads in Wisconsin in 1856 where one company

> . . . won the prize of a million acres by distributing about nine hundred thousand dollars in securities to the right people; to 59 members of the Assembly, $355,000 worth; to 13 Senators, $175,000; to Governor Coles Bashford, $50,000; to other state officials, including one judge of the Supreme Court, $50,000; and to the governor's private secretary, $5,000. The rest was distributed among the lobbyists and their assistants who had worked to such good purpose in the legislative halls in Madison. By 1858, the road had gone bankrupt and the bribed got nothing but opprobrium for their greed.[9]

The annals of most of the other western states include episodes dissimilar only with respect to the size and nature of the spoils. Missouri and Minnesota between them used their credit during the early fifties to buy railroad bonds valued at more than $22,000,000, most of which were to turn worthless. Other western legislatures were induced to give away fortunes in timber and agricultural lands. Only Texas appears to have approached its problem with any degree of probity and intelligence.[10]

If the railroads' prewar efforts exceeded any hitherto seen in the republic, they were only a reedy prelude to the immense disorders which followed Appomattox, when as Hurst describes it, "the full tide of economic exploitation swept over institutions totally unprepared to deal with the resulting pressure."[11] No institutions were more unprepared nor more cruelly ravaged than the state legislatures, and it was here that "political degradation reached its lowest depths."[12] The venality which had always flourished more or less quietly in the republic became gross, systematic, and very nearly as open as it was unashamed.

The railroads were by no means the only interest to perceive the opportunities which the legislatures offered for the acquisition of unlimited economic power, but their efforts were by far the most extensive and, for them, rewarding. With their large resources, their larger aspirations, and their curious grip on the public imagination, the roads succeeded in placing a hold on the politics of many states that was to remain unbroken for the balance of the century. In some states, destructive and costly competition was the rule; in others, single lines quickly seized legislative bridgeheads, held them against all challengers, and gradually built upon them more diversified political complexes of virtually unassailable dominance. This process of entrenchment and proliferation was especially, but by no means uniquely, well demonstrated in New Jersey. Railroad power began to assert itself in Trenton soon after the chartering of the Camden and Amboy, later the Pennsylvania, in 1831, and was not seriously threatened until Wilson's accession to the governorship eighty years later.[13] "So absolute was its control of all departments of the state government," writes McKean of the railroad lobby, "that the state itself came to be known derisively among the people of other states as the State of Camden and Amboy."[14] Although the description is not without hyperbole, it does suggest something of the *de facto* fusion of public and private power that took place in New Jersey— and California, and Missouri, and elsewhere.

Lobbyists were often deeply involved in the events by which this fusion was achieved, particularly when the empire-builders were too fastidious to attend to the details themselves. As to the means by which it was achieved, the roads' ultimate technique was simply to buy on a wholesale basis the charters, land grants, loans, or rights of eminent domain they needed. Naked bribery was indiscriminate and broadcast, and the corruption of legislators with the smallest possible investment was, in Paul Reinsch's rather florid reconstruction, "the acme of ambition to the successful lobbyist."[15] The theme of frank and open corruption sounds in most chronicles of the period. Hacker and Kendrick typically assert that:

. . . venality in the state capitals was not even disguised. Not only did the railroads maintain lobbies at all the legislatures, but by favors, threats, and bribes they played a real part in the shaping of legislation. Judges, juries, and state officials were recipients of the largess of the railroads; the pass was the least of the common evils indulged in. In Missouri, for example, it was frankly admitted by all involved that the Missouri Pacific had paid the state legislators several hundred thousands of dollars to release the railroad from the mortgage which the state held.[16]

Postwar periods in the United States have generally been disfigured by perceptible sags in public ethics, but the almost universal shambles of legislative debauchery that marked the railway era was in the nature of a complete collapse, and its origins were more fundamental than mere release from the tensions and constraints of war. Although proof of the point is inherently elusive, the root causes more probably lie tangled in the sheer novelty of large-scale business and finance, in the great wealth and power which political action could make accessible to its practitioners, and in the inviting malleability of the institutional environment. Beyond the ancient common-law restraints on conspiracy and bribery, the legal system placed no outer limits of any force on the competition for privilege. Nor was the deficiency of formal sanctions otherwise supplied. Experience with the grosser irregularities was too fragmentary (as it always is) to have distilled into proscriptive codes of legislative behavior, a politics of protest still lay in the future, and the entrepreneurs, while occasionally grumbling about the costs of doing business, were often able to find positive virtues in oiling the wheels of progress. When Collis Huntington wrote to one of his lobbyists about some Southern Pacific dirty work, "If you have to pay money to have the right thing done, it is only just and fair to do it," he was not, as Hofstadter puts it, being a "sanctimonious hypocrite";

. . . he was merely expressing his passionate American conviction that he had every honest right to come into his own, and it is doubtful that many tycoons of his time would have differed in principle. To imagine that such men did not sleep the sleep of the just would be romantic sentimentalism. In the Gilded Age even the angels sang for them.[17]

While history does not record whether the song was appropriately sweet, it does suggest the enormous costs to the states of the rail-roads' success in having "the right thing done." Conservative esti-mates place state loans for railroad construction at very nearly a quarter of a billion dollars, very little of which was ever returned. The value of state land grants was at least as great; Texas and the Mississippi valley states alone managed to dispose of some 52,000,000 acres. The value of the charters and franchises which the legislatures gave away so easily is, of course, incalculable. Outright money grants for construction have been cautiously pegged at over $700,000,000, from all public sources.[18]

And more than money costs were involved; though difficult to reckon, the imprint left on the political process by a long decade of pillage was both deep and lasting. To say that the railroads bought legislation does not mean that they owned the bodies from which they bought it. To the contrary, the intensity of the competition and the greatness of the stakes, coupled with the roads' mounting dis-regard for costs, inevitably encouraged the professional politicians in some states to protect their own interests by encouraging the roads to bid against each other, as at auction, for the subsidies or protec-tion they required. Thus Vanderbilt and Gould vied in paying larger and larger bribes to the New York Legislature until their contest reached its apogee with Gould's appearance in Albany with a valise stuffed with $500,000 in greenbacks. All of this, notes Josephson quietly, had "the most frenzying and overstimulating effect upon the legislators . . . which it would take many years of disciplined machine leadership to eliminate."[19] The judgment is optimistic only with respect to the permanence of the damage inflicted by this episode and its less extravagant counterparts. No small part of the character and major preoccupations of modern state party organizations derives from their origins and deep involvement in the saturnalia of spoils and plunder that passed for politics after the Civil War.

For willing complicity in their own defloration, the legislatures became the principal target for the current of institutional revision that slowly gathered force in the waning years of the century. Con-stitutional limitations on special legislation and the legislatures' fiscal authority began to appear, as did preliminary essays at "independent" regulation, and, while these were lamentably too late to alter the larger course of events, they served to demonstrate how profligately the legislatures had squandered the central element of their colonial inheritance: their legitimacy in public opinion. It might be difficult to support the proposition that they have yet regained it.[20]

From even this impressionistic account of the railway era, it should be evident that the modes of political influence that began to be subsumed under the rubric of lobbying were mainly of symptomatic importance. The corruption which the term came to imply was common enough, but it had a deeper meaning than could be compressed in the figure of the lobbyist-for-hire, however colorful and/or menacing he might appear. For there would have been—and there were—depredations without lobbyists. Such men were, after all, only the occasional agents of unprecedentedly large-scale economic power seeking to control a political order, both rapidly evolving and newly capable of conferring great and permanent advantages upon those who could direct its evolution; the grosser outrages were typically perpetrated by their ultimate beneficiaries—the railroad builders themselves. The lobbyist was a challenge to the integrity of the political process, but more for what he represented than for himself. Even then, the core problem was the infinitely more difficult one of erecting around the political process defensible boundaries from which economic power could be held at arm's length. It is still the core problem.

Constitutional Regulation

Reaction to the general postwar debasement of political standards was diffuse, tangential, and slow to form. In time, interests bred or disadvantaged by the railroads' political dominance were able to restore a measure of balance and restraint to the conduct of the public business. The means by which this displacement was achieved were political in the strictest sense, and the constitutional limitations on legislative authority that dotted the later decades of the century reflected, rather than brought about, its achievement. For these limitations were in the nature of *post hoc* punishment for bad behavior: belated, incomplete, and ultimately self-defeating.

Legislative corruption had been far-reaching enough during the gilded years to make it inevitable that the more morally sensitive politicians who became the period's residuary legatees should declare themselves against it. The declarations were both practically and juridically superfluous, since bribery of legislators had long been a misdemeanor at common law. Several states had also enacted statutory prohibitions, yet here was bribery on so grand a scale as to demand "the more solemn prohibitions of the organic law."[21] Thus the further proscriptions of bribery written in the 1870's—and there were many—were characteristically engrafted on the state constitutions themselves.[22]

Although their deep involvement may have argued for taking the matter out of the legislatures' hands, these early antibribery provisions essentially duplicated the common-law rule. There were not until 1873 any constitutional or statutory provisions addressed to "lobbying" by means other than simple bribery. When such provisions were enacted, they too were usually attached to the state constitutions. Early constitutions in New Hampshire (1792), Vermont (1793), and Rhode Island (1842) had prohibited legislators from taking fees for the advocacy of, or for acting as counsel in, any cause pending before the legislature.[23] Alabama was actually the first state to take constitutional notice of "lobbying," as it was then understood, and this notice marked only a slight advance over the prevailing antibribery provisions.[24] The label, rather than the underlying approach, was changed when, in 1873, the Alabama Constitution was made to declare:

> The offense of corrupt solicitation of members of the General Assembly, or of public officers of this State, or of any municipal subdivision thereof, and any occupation or practice of solicitation of such members or officers to influence their official action shall be defined by law, and shall be punished by fine and imprisonment.[25]

The statute passed in accordance with this provision in 1874 prescribed punishment for the same "occupation or practice of solicitation" mentioned in the constitutional provision. On the surface, the language would appear to condemn all "solicitation," whether corrupt or not, but since the limiting term "corruptly" is used in the statutory definition of bribery, it can be presumed that a court would supply it in the constitutional provision as well. The presumption is fortified by the terms of a subsequent Alabama statute, currently in force, which specifically prohibits the "corrupt solicitation" or influencing of legislators with respect to the casting of votes, speaking for or against measures, or attending legislative sessions or committee meetings.[26] Although the areas of solicitation are more sharply defined here than they were in 1874, the condemnation of only corrupt solicitation is common to both enactments.

The meaning and targets of the earlier Alabama statute are clear, but they do not at any point employ the term "lobbying." A section of the Georgia Constitution, added in 1877, was the first in which "lobbying" was denominated as such. In this sense, it marks the formal beginning of state regulation in this complex and difficult area. Georgia's pioneer section provided—"succinctly and absurdly," in Robert Luce's view[27]—that "lobbying is declared to be a crime, and the General Assembly shall enforce this provision by suitable penalties."[28]

Although the lessons of history pointed to the relative insensitivity of American legislative bodies to conditions that might threaten their institutional integrity, this provision transferred to the legislature entire responsibility for defining the offense, without any guidance beyond emphatic condemnation. The Georgia Assembly promptly enacted a law which defined (and prohibited) lobbying as "any personal solicitation of a member of the General Assembly during the session thereof, by private interview, or other means not addressed solely to the judgment," to favor or oppose any proposed or pending legislative matter.[29]

This law reflected faithfully the prevailing conception of postbellum lobbying, but the glass was cracked and cloudy. The prohibition of "any personal solicitation" was qualified and limited by a later section which excluded "professional services," themselves undefined, from the reach of the law. The phrase "other means not addressed solely to the judgment" also begged the question of definition, leaving to the courts or subsequent legislatures the task of giving it substance. The inclusion of interviews among such means was doubly arbitrary; even in 1874, personal persuasion on the merits of an issue could not have been unknown. That these difficulties have not been more vexing can only be laid to the laws' total non-enforcement and not to their clarity or superior logic.

California, which by then had abundant opportunity to discover what lobbying meant, became in 1879 the second state to take constitutional action against it. Like the earlier Georgia law, the California provision defined lobbying in order to prohibit it: "Any person who seeks to influence the vote of a member of the Legislature by bribery, promise of reward, or any other dishonest means, shall be guilty of lobbying, which is hereby declared to be a felony."[30]

This definition is more reasonable than that of the Georgia law; personal solicitation uncolored by corrupt methods or intent is, at least, not assumed to be objectionable. But if it is more reasonable, it is no less ambiguous. "Any other dishonest means," like the Georgia catch-all, fails to distinguish lawful from unlawful conduct and leaves with the courts the power "to create crimes after the fashion of the old common law."[31] Ambiguity, furthermore, is here compounded by redundancy; "promise of reward" is basically a species of bribery, and was already punishable under existing law. The accompanying immunity proviso was equally superfluous. Guarantees of the kind were frequent and probably necessary in bribery laws, but their inclusion in a lobbying statute served mainly to demonstrate how elusive was the distinction between the two. The approach and most of the descriptive nomenclature were the same; only the titles were different, and this difference has probably been given more attention than it deserves. For all practical purposes, lobbying and bribery were legally indistinguishable.

Beyond its failure to specify with any precision the persons and practices coming within its purview, there is a more fundamental objection to the California provision, and to those of other states where proscriptions of corrupt lobbying, variously defined, have been written into the constitutions. This is simply that statute law is a more satisfactory vehicle than the state constitution for public action in this area, not because superior definition is more likely in statutes, although their greater flexibility should conduce to this end, but because statutory declarations more firmly express the legislature's determination to exercise control over its own processes and working environment. This view does not dilute the argument that the legislature has usually been too deeply involved to act either freely or wisely, but hopefully assumes that the legislature's practical inability or unwillingness to act will not dissolve its obligation so to do.

The inappropriateness of constitutional regulation is best measured by the fact that since California acted in 1879, only a few states have added comparable matter to their constitutions. Arizona and Montana adopted provisions that closely followed the California statement, and Wyoming provided in 1889 for the punishment of "private solicitation" of members of the legislature.[32] Beyond these, a few other similar constitutional declarations, and the almost universal anti-bribery sections, state regulation of lobbying has taken statutory, rather than constitutional, form.[33] Although a few of the statutes hew closely to the substance of these first constitutional prohibitions, the larger part reflect a vastly different and more positive approach.

The Coming of Disclosure

As the grosser tactics of the railroad era gave rise to the scattered adoption of futile and belated constitutional restraints, so too did statutory regulation of lobbying first develop in response to the efforts of a new generation of entrepreneurs to achieve privileged status. The new challenge came less from the railroads, which by 1890 were either bankrupt, exposed, or glutted, than from a cluster of emergent interests which had not hitherto been important contenders for public largesse. Paul Reinsch has described their entry into the political arena:

> When in certain commonwealths the railways had secured all the franchises, exemptions, and privileges which the legislature could bestow upon them, and when they had given a form to these incidents which could be relied upon as fairly permanent, the railways began to take a somewhat less direct interest in politics, confining their activity to the prevention of unfavorable legislation. Indeed, in some instances they felt able to dispense with the finely wrought and efficient mechanism which they had constructed; this they now hired out to some other 'interest' which had not as yet sufficiently fortified its position. We thus enter upon the public service period of legislative corruption. The 'trolley crowd' and the 'gas combine' became potent factors in legislative life.[34]

Reinsch offers no evidence to support his assertion that the railroads hired out the political mechanism they had constructed, nor does he detail in what respects it was either "finely wrought" or "efficient." Indeed, the dominant characteristic of railroad politics at the flood was an incredible and heedless waste (of which the more perceptive or parsimonious builders were far from unaware). But these cavils are essentially literary; there is little reason to doubt and much to believe that some such general shift in the major sources and foci of legislative interest politics had, by the mid-'eighties, taken place. Changes in lobbying methods were less perceptible, although they had through overuse and exposure doubtless been purged of some of their earlier crudeness. On the legislative side, the blatant auctioneering of votes had generally yielded to more circumspect forms of marketing official boons.

If the tone of state politics was generally firmer, the flurry of lobbying regulation that began in 1890 can best be laid to the incompleteness of the improvement. The newly dominant interests still squeezed more out of the system than a broader political consensus was willing to concede was their fair share, the successive redefinitions of which come close to being the real heart of the democratic mystique. These interests were, moreover, caught with their hands in the till—not very deeply, for the railroads' record in this regard was beyond emulation,[35] but deeply enough to trigger new efforts to reshape the legislative process to widespread expectations that it operate "honestly" and produce "balanced" results. Regulation by disclosure grew, in the end, out of optimistic willingness to experiment with any device that promised to contribute to the reshaping. Actually, only one state engaged in any bold experimentation. Massachusetts passed the first systematic disclosure law in 1890; since then, some twenty-nine states and the federal government have followed suit, but with few embellishments and almost no improvement.

In many respects, Massachusetts was the ideal site for a new approach. Its legislatures, relatively able and sensitive to tradition, had been neither much more nor much less tainted than most others during the gilded years. There had been less jobbery than there had been in New York, but considerably more than there had been in Rhode Island, which in those distant days was regarded as a politically wholesome commonwealth. As early as 1853, for example, a Massachusetts constitutional convention had heard the charge that "there has been a vast amount of outside influence exercised in get-

ting matters through the Legislature."[36] Again in 1869, investigation
of a projected loan by the state to the Boston, Hartford, and Erie
Railroad revealed that the road had spent substantial sums in seeking
to assure favorable legislative action.[37] Another investigation in 1887
uncovered evidence that several interested groups had spent $20,000
in order "to secure influence which would be of weight with members
of the legislature" on a town division bill. After the governor vetoed
the bill, the investigating committee pressed home its findings by
proposing a bill requiring the public registration of hired legislative
representatives. Although the Republican leadership showed little
interest in its passage, their inaction merely postponed the inevitable,
satisfied very few, and provided the Democrats with an issue which
would help to propel their candidate into the statehouse three years
hence.[38]

Matters were brought to a head in 1890 when another legislative
investigating committee found that the Boston street railways, in
promoting a bill that would have authorized them to construct an
elevated line, had maintained a corps of thirty-five lobbyists, and
had made expenditures through them "beyond any legitimate purpose
in securing legislation."[39] The money involved was approximately
$33,000, with half again as much to be paid when and if the bill was
approved.[40] While this was no Chapter of Erie, it was attended by
sufficient publicity to spur the legislature to the action it had earlier
managed to avoid. Attached to the report of the investigating committee was the text of a bill calling for the registration of legislative
counsel or agents, identical to the measure that had failed three years
earlier. This time the bill passed with very little discussion and was
signed by the governor—at the same time, be it noted, as the elevated
railway bill, which, despite the commotion it had caused, had also
passed.[41] Statutory regulation of lobbying, in the modern sense, had
begun.

After seventy years, the principles and provisions of the Massachusetts law no longer seem unique, but in its time it was a distinct
innovation. Essentially permissive in approach, its only prohibition,
that of employment for fees contingent on legislative action, was
incidental to its main design. Unlike any of the constitutional or
statutory provisions that preceded it, it sought not to restrict "lobbying" but to bring it at least partly out of the shadows and into the

light of day. The law required registration with the sergeant-at-arms of the legislature by any person who, as counsel or agent, promoted or opposed the passage of legislation "affecting the pecuniary interests of any individual, association, or private or public corporation as distinct from those of the whole people of the Commonwealth."[42] The registration was to include certain information concerning the terms of the counsel or agent's employment, and was a prerequisite to the performance of any duties covered thereby. Within thirty days after the end of the legislative session, registrants were required to submit a detailed statement of all expenses incurred in connection with their legislative activities. Violations of the law were punishable by fine, imprisonment, or "disbarment" from lobbying for a period of three years. The attorney-general of the commonwealth was charged with responsibility for enforcement.

The law itself was unique, and its sponsors seem to have been genuinely interested in making it operate with maximum effectiveness. But they also recognized that the tool they had fashioned still required honing. Thus Governor Russell, who owed his election in large measure to his vigorous fight for the law, declared in his inaugural address of 1891:

> It is far easier to state the evil than to suggest the remedy. Clearly it is impossible and improper to prevent a constituent or any other person from having the freest access to the legislator. This constitutional right guaranteed to the people gives the opportunity to the lobby to do its work. Prevention by non-intercourse is therefore impossible; and I would suggest . . . making it easier than it now is publicly to investigate the methods used, the money spent on pending legislation . . . by giving power to some proper officer, before a measure finally becomes law, to demand under oath a full and detailed statement as to these matters. The fear of publicity, and through it of defeat, may stop improper practices by making them worse than useless.[43]

Although each generation defines "improper practices" in its own terms, the belief that fear of publicity can limit their value, and hence their use, remains one of the staple premises underlying political disclosure. It still has wide appeal as a vehicle of political reconstruction, as a means by which order, balance, and argument on the merits can be pumped into the system, and the bias of uneven or excessive persuasion pumped out. That this end, even if it could be achieved, may not leave the legislator any freer to make objective choices "in the public interest" is better understood now than it was then.

Governor Russell felt that material good would come from the act of 1890, but that it fell short of being a sufficient remedy: "It makes public the names of all persons employed, but not the acts of the lobbyist. It makes public the expenses incurred, but too late to affect the legislation for which they were incurred."[44] The governor spoke even before the law had become effective, and while subsequent experience in Massachusetts and elsewhere has conformed to his expectations, the problems he foresaw remain unmet. Only three states have acted to require more frequent financial reporting,[45] and Maryland alone has empowered the governor to require special reports of expenditures made in connection with bills coming to his desk for signature.[46] As for making public "the acts of the lobbyist," this has nowhere been achieved.

Governor Russell's main injunctions went unheeded, but other changes were made in the Massachusetts law within a year of its enactment. Originally the law had called for the registration of only those counsel and agents employed in connection with legislation affecting private pecuniary interests as distinct from those of the whole people of the state. In 1891 this distinction was abandoned, and the law made to cover counsel and agents employed in connection with *any* legislation, without further qualification.[47] This amendment considerably extended the law's reach. It had been the intention of the framers of the original bill to draw a sharp line between private and public bills, with the act to apply only to employment in connection with the former, but this soon proved to be a line that even a Massachusetts legislature could not always draw. In the words of Josiah Quincy, author of the 1890 committee report and of the original bill, "Under any definition, there will be room for doubt in particular cases." To this he added a small caveat: "But the attempt to draw any distinction in this respect between private and public acts, or special and general legislation, has now been abandoned; and if any other States ever copy our act, they would do well to follow our example in this respect."[48]

Mr. Quincy's advice has been followed less often than it deserves.

Seven states whose laws otherwise closely adhere to the Massachusetts model continue to use the pecuniary interest formula which Massachusetts so quickly abandoned.[49] In several other states with purely penal laws, failure to disclose "direct interest"[50] or "any interest"[51] in legislation renders personal solicitation illegal. Quincy's objection to pecuniary interest as a measure of the law's fit is still in point: It is a difficult standard to administer, and its language invites evasion.[52] The continuing popularity of this criterion of applicability—it appears, for example, in the new (1958) Illinois law—demonstrates only how deadening the effects can be when statutory borrowing is compounded with legislative inertia. This holds not only for applicability formulae, but for substantive disclosure provisions as well. If the models are good and applicable, there is no necessary objection to the borrowing. But times always change, and in no two states is the texture of the political process even momentarily the same. Although the underlying principle of disclosure is static enough, the specific acts and relationships to which sound public policy should apply it are never only what they once were, or what they have been or are elsewhere.

Wisconsin became in 1899 the second state to enact a disclosure statute, and its law was an almost verbatim copy of the Massachusetts act of 1890.[53] The Massachusetts amendment of 1891 was not included in the Wisconsin law, however, and it thus reached only those persons who acted in behalf of private pecuniary interests. It was many years before this restriction was repealed.

Maryland followed in 1900 with an act drawn along the general lines of the Massachusetts and Wisconsin statutes, but which in one respect appeared to be a significant improvement upon them. While requiring registration and the submission of expense statements within thirty days of the legislature's adjournment, the law also empowered the governor to require sworn statements of expenses incurred in connection with any bill whenever he had reason to believe that "improper expenses" had been paid or incurred in relation thereto.[54] For all of its descriptive infirmities (what expenses are "improper," who decides that they are, on the basis of what evidence, and how conclusively?), the language has obvious and inviting tactical possibilities. That these have not been realized is only one measure of the wide gulf that exists between the theory of disclosure and its practice.

A second rash of disclosure statutes erupted in 1905. Within five years, five legislatures had trumpeted their virtue by adopting registration and reporting laws, and seven others followed suit before the next decade's end.[55] Major responsibility for this flurry of legislation can be laid to two discrete events. The first of these was Governor La Follette's message to the Wisconsin Legislature in May, 1905. La Follette had asked four months earlier for legislation that would make it an offense, "punishable by the heaviest money penalty and by imprisonment as well, for any lobby agent . . . to attempt personally and directly to influence any member of the Legislature to vote for or against any measure affecting the interests represented by such lobbyist."[56] He had asked, in fine, that the legislature put teeth in the distinction that Massachusetts had abandoned as unworkable fourteen years earlier by applying anew the prohibitions against personal solicitation that had proved unworkable thirty years earlier.

The May message went further. After denouncing "the lobby" for having evaded the full intent of the law of 1899, La Follette urged new legislation making it a penal offense for a paid lobbyist "to approach a legislator privately or personally upon *any* matter which is the subject of legislation." Why forbid personal contact? To Governor La Follette, the reasons were overpowering and plain:

> Every legitimate argument which any lobbyist has to offer, and which any legislator ought to hear, can be presented before committees, before the legislators as a body, through the press, from the public platform, and through printed briefs and arguments placed in the hands of all members and accessible to the public.[57]

There have been few clearer statements of the view that it is unwise and unnecessary to permit—and possible to forbid—private discussion between legislators and representatives of private persons, groups, or interests.[58] If it does not sufficiently recognize that legislators sometimes seek the company and advice of other men, or bring their own "legitimate arguments" to bear on their work without outside persuasion, the notion that the legislator should be protected from covert and possibly corrupting influences still has its adherents. That this end can be achieved by statutory means, however, is another matter. Practically speaking, such requirements are unenforceable; theoretically, they raise obvious and substantial questions of personal right. Neither of these considerations deterred the legislature from complying with the governor's wishes, and later in 1905 it amended the original act of 1899 so as to narrow the range of activities in which registered counsel and agents could lawfully engage. Henceforth, personal solicitation was forbidden. The lobbyist was limited to appearances before legislative committees, publications, public addresses, and statements, arguments, or briefs directed to all members of the legislature, twenty-five copies of which were first to be deposited with the secretary of state.

That these provisions did not succeed, as they could not have succeeded, and were eventually repealed does not diminish the importance of the circumstances that produced them. Governor La Follette's message reached a national audience, and it has properly been singled out as one of the landmarks in the development of state regulation of lobbying.[59] If it was a landmark, however, the work of the Armstrong Insurance Investigating Committee in New York was a more imposing monument. Originally concerned with the financing and internal management of insurance companies, the committee eventually unearthed a complex of company political activity which for system and scope was then unprecedented. A number of companies, principally the New York Life, Mutual, and Equitable, were shown to have been organized as:

> . . . an offensive and defensive alliance to procure or to prevent the passage of laws affecting not only insurance, but a great variety of important interests to which, through subsidiary companies or through the connections of their officers, they have become related. Their operations have extended beyond the state, and the country has been divided into districts so that each company might perform conveniently its share of the work. Enormous sums have been expended in a surreptitious manner. Irregular accounts have been kept to conceal the payments for which proper vouchers have not been required. This course of conduct has created a widespread conviction that large portions of this money have been dishonestly used.[60]

More than "enormous" or "surreptitious" expenditures were involved; indeed, the committee's principal concern was with the elaborate arrangements that had been made for their disbursement:

> The large insurance companies systematically attempted to control legislation in this and other states which could affect their interests directly or indirectly. . . . The three companies divided the country, outside of New York and a few other states, so as to avoid a waste of effort, each looking after legislation in its chosen district and bearing its appropriate part of the total expense.[61]

The age of competition had truly yielded to the age of solidarity.

Since most of its findings fell short of demonstrating outright corruption, the committee could only conclude that the existing corrupt-practices statutes, though stringent enough, did not "strike at the root of the evil." The committee darkly hinted that sterner correctives might be needed:

> The pernicious activities of corporate agents in matters of legislation demand that the present freedom of lobbying should be restricted. They have brought suspicion upon important proceedings of the Legislature, and have exposed its members to consequent assault. The Legislature owes it to itself, so far as possible, to stop the practice of the lavish expenditure of moneys ostensibly for services in connection with the support of or opposition to bills, and generally believed to be used for corrupt purposes.[62]

The committee did not deliver on either its threat of restriction or the great promise of its findings; rather, it drew heavily on the Massachusetts and Maryland disclosure statutes and proposed legislation requiring registration of counsel or agents employed on legislative matters. This was familiar enough, but the reporting proposals went beyond the earlier disclosure laws by suggesting that statements be required of "every corporation or association doing business in the state . . . showing in detail all expenses paid or incurred in connection with legislation pending at the last session, including all disbursements paid or payable to counsel or agents."[63] Where under the Massachusetts law the obligation to report rested on the employment of registered counsel or agents, the committee's proposal would have based it on the fact of incorporation or association, with the employment of registered counsel or agents as only one category under which expenditures were to be reported. This relative deemphasis on the hired lobbyist, based as it was on a realistic appraisal of where the power lay, can be counted as the committee's major contribution, if not to the regulatory process, where its full weight has yet to be felt, then at least to an adequate formulation of the problem with which regulation seeks to deal.

When the New York Legislature passed a disclosure law in 1906, it conformed almost exactly to the language of the Armstrong recommendations, their considerable breadth notwithstanding. In fact, the legislature, in its headlong rush for redemption, killed the phrase "doing business in the state" so that the reporting requirement applied to "every person, firm, corporation or association" expending any money in connection with action of the New York Legislature. While it might be inferred from the registration provisions that this language applies only to employers of legislative counsel or agents, the law itself effects no such sweeping exemption. What the law omits, however, administrative practice has supplied, and the limited interpretation has long been the prevailing one.

The New York law differed from the earlier models in prescribing an additional penalty of $100 per day for failure to submit expense reports within sixty days after the final adjournment of the legislature. It also followed the Massachusetts, rather than the Wisconsin, pattern in that it did not seek to restrict the modes of approach to individual legislators. In all other respects, the New York statute conformed closely to its forerunners.

While it was more like its predecessors than the conventional *post hoc* wisdom would argue that it had to be, the New York law was still a factor of major importance in the gradual spread of the disclosure idea to other states. The special circumstances surrounding its enactment commanded widespread attention, and the law itself, more widely publicized than others had been, provided a harmlessly attractive model for other legislatures to adopt whenever local necessities might dictate. It was face-saving, for it put the onus on others; it was soothing balm for public resentment; and it required no more serious reflection than a proclamation of Thanksgiving. The New York law was for most of the legislatures that copied it—and several copied it verbatim—not a starting point but the end of the line.

A few legislatures ground out laws immediately after New York had acted; a few others waited until the press of local circumstance created appropriate occasions. The stream of legislation finally dried up in 1919 (the stream of invention having dried up thirty years earlier), and fifteen states had disclosure laws of the Massachusetts-Wisconsin-New York variety on the books.[64]

The New Regulation

No additional laws were written between 1919 and 1932. Since 1932, however, thirteen state legislatures have enacted disclosure statutes, their efforts being quite evenly spaced over the period.[65] One of the few striking features of these more recent laws is their nearly complete familiarity; their focus and demands are, with few exceptions, identical to those of the laws written fifty, sixty, and seventy years ago. Optimistically, this could be taken as attesting to the vitality of the established approach; realistically, it attests to a persistent legislative reluctance to attack with more than blunted and borrowed ceremonial weapons the deeply-rooted thicket of which legislative lobbying is only a symptomatic surface growth.

The exceptions to the general practice of borrowing verbatim, or nearly so, from the older laws are both few and curious. North Carolina, for example, enacted a conventional registration and reporting law in 1933. In 1947, the legislature sought to dampen the promotional activities of several organizations of uncertain origins and anonymous backing by passing a second law requiring additional registration and reporting by all those persons and groups "engaged in the business of influencing public opinion."[66] Apart from its specific targets and differing applicability, the second law was derived wholly from the first.[67] California also diverged somewhat from the usual pattern when it passed a disclosure law in 1949. Instead of taking its law from the Massachusetts, Wisconsin, or New York statutes, the legislature used the Federal Regulation of Lobbying Act as its model. Prototype and copy were relatively superior, but the process was no less imitative. Except for California, as always *sui generis*, the most substantial changes on the original Massachusetts format have been rung in states like Wisconsin which enacted their laws quite early. Most of the newer statutes have been less critically constructed and considered than the small handful of older ones that have been selectively revised. Imitation has not meant flattery, but only imitation.

This conceptual similarity can be partly ascribed to the fact that many of the newer laws have emerged from circumstances at least roughly similar to those that first prompted the Massachusetts General Court to act in 1890. The motive force has usually been supplied not by corruption in a literal sense but by evidence or allegations of "excessive" legislative activity by particular interests. To this proposition there have been the usual exceptions; the Michigan act of 1947, for example, was part of the wash of a scandal which three years earlier had seen a score of legislators implicated (and a number imprisoned) for trafficking in favors with several small-loan companies. More often, however, the impulse has come from something other than charges or proof that legislative votes had been purchased outright. Typically, the laws have been hastily assembled in response to widely aired assertions, substantial or otherwise, that some interest has sought to get more from the legislature than the strength of its cause, or abstract equity, or the requirements of "honest" or "visible" politics (as these things are locally defined) might seem to warrant.

Newspapers have in a few instances been the catalysts for definition. The North Carolina law, for example, was passed in 1933 largely to quiet the insistent voice of the *Raleigh News and Observer*. The origins of the 1938 Virginia law were somewhat similar. "Annoyed" at being unable to identify witnesses before committees, several state senators introduced a registration and reporting bill (a close copy of the North Carolina law), and heavy support from both Richmond papers contributed tellingly to its passage.[68] In Wisconsin, the *Madison Capital-Times* has been a leading protagonist for most of the useful revisions that have been made in that state's law. More generally, however, the recent laws, like the earlier ones, have been in the nature of reflexive legislative reactions to charges of undue influence, often by means purported to be questionable, or with the former advanced as presumptive evidence of the latter. While the press is typically prominent in the airing of the charges, the key roles in forming the reaction have usually been played by the governor and the more institutionally sensitive members of the legislature itself.

California's experience in 1949-1950 provides an arresting case in point, not only of the characteristic origins and content of state disclosure laws, but of the wondrous ways by which legislatures can back into their enactment. This sunny *opera bouffe* began with the appearance in midsummer of 1949 of two articles in *Collier's* magazine.[69] Written by Lester Velie and entitled "The Secret Boss of California," these vivid essays explored the life and not-so-hard times of Arthur H. Samish, who had hitherto enjoyed a merely local reputation as Sacramento representative of the California State Brewers' Association. Samish was portrayed as a powerful master-fixer who made his way via campaign money and legal business for legislators, and good drinking whiskey for everyone. Velie quoted Governor Warren as saying ruefully, "On matters that affect his clients, Artie unquestionably has more power than the Governor." Samish modestly dismissed the articles as "clowning and nonsense," and admitted only that he directed policy and acted as "lobbyist" for the Brewers' Association, which he described as an organization of "terrific strength."[70]

Two months after the Velie stories first appeared, a committee of the legislature held a one-day investigation, for which "inconclusive" would probably be a suitably generous description.[71] But Governor Warren, less involved and more persistent, called a special session of the legislature for the specific purpose of enacting lobbying legislation, observing in his summons that the Samish revelations involved "the Honor of our State," which they more or less did.[72] When the legislature assembled, Warren presented it with a disclosure bill largely culled from other state laws, but with an additional provision which would have barred lawyer-legislators from practicing before state agencies.[73] Although this struck close to the heart of "Samishism," it was apparently too large a pill for the legislature to swallow, and both houses passed the governor's bill without it. The Assembly went even further, tacking on an amendment "which in effect made the bill apply to no one."[74] The bill went to conference but died there when the Assembly adjourned without waiting for the conference report,[75] although it had earlier taken the precaution of passing a Senate-approved resolution which banned Samish "forever" from appearances before the legislature or its committees. Since he had not done so for years, this resounding declaration was generally recognized for what it was: "dust in the public eye."[76]

While the Senate had gagged on the lawyer-legislator provision, it was otherwise disposed to act, and its passage of the governor's bill in fairly stringent form stung the Assembly into approving before its adjournment not one but three nearly-verbatim copies of the Federal Regulation of Lobbying Act. The Senate concurred in all of them, and Governor Warren was confronted with disclosure in triplicate.[77] He signed one of the bills but criticized it as "half a loaf" and called another special session in 1950, largely to improve upon the act which had just been passed.

The legislature, meanwhile, had created a Joint Interim Committee on Lobby Regulations which, in March, came up with a new bill (the Erwin Bill). This proposal was silent on the lawyer-legislator question because, in the committee's words, "only confusion can result from an attempt to cover, in a measure designed to regulate the activities of professional lobbyists, the subject of corrupt practices by some members of the electorate, and the subject of what activities a Member of the Legislature may properly engage in." Further, "an attempt to cover so broad a field in one bill would be the surest way to insure its defeat by those who want no regulation of lobbyists."[78] It is profitless to argue that this self-denying realism was unnecessary. The course of events suggests that the committee was probably "right," if only within the limited context of choice that it helped to provide. That other choices existed and that the circumstances favored a more heroic effort to drive them home is, like most retrospective wisdom, suggestive but irrelevant.

While the committee bill skirted the key question of group-legislator financial involvement, it otherwise expanded and clarified the act of 1949, straightening out its applicability and adding four new substantive provisions. One of these required disclosure of the employment of legislators by lobbyists or their employers; the second prohibited the contingent employment of "legislative advocates" (the California euphemism for lobbyists); the third set up a list of "obligations" for hired lobbyists, violations of which would constitute cause for the revocation of their licenses; the fourth proposed the establishment of a permanent joint legislative board to serve as an agency for investigation and enforcement.

Although Governor Warren was still not entirely satisfied, the Senate overrode his objections and rewrote the Erwin Bill in the form of an amendment to the 1949 law. The Senate draft was diluted in the Assembly and further reworked but eventually approved in conference. The end result of this process was a much-amended Erwin Bill and several strengthening amendments (principally in the enforcement sections) to the act of 1949. With some reluctance, the governor signed the measure. Disclosure had come to California.[79]

This tangled and dispiriting performance may help to suggest the legislator's generic antipathy to applications of the disclosure principle which he perceives as threatening his own political lifelines, group memberships, or financial interests. In California as elsewhere, essentially toothless statutes have been used by their generally reluctant sponsors mainly as exercises in legislative public relations. They have typically been enacted *in extremis*, under the pressure of widespread suspicion that the legislature has been unduly responsive to narrowly defined interests. As David Truman puts it, disclosure laws "have usually emerged from publicized allegations of privileged access or from charges of attempts to achieve such a position through covert means."[80] While "privileged access" is, in Truman's typology, the general end of group tactics, its real meaning lies in the nurturing and quiet exploitation of those group-legislator identities of interest by which it is most often achieved. Except in the dream world of his public discourse, the legislator is not so much *against* the pressure system as he is *of* it. Under these circumstances, it should not be surprising that legislators seldom see disclosure as a means of protecting themselves (for they see nothing against which they need protection), or as a technique to promote legislation in the "public interest." The amount of meaningful disclosure that they are willing to stomach is invariably less than other parties are ready to prescribe.

California's experience was in some respects atypical of recent lawmaking in other states. The Samish episode erupted nationally, and it put the legislature on the spot. Further, Governor Warren presented the legislature with limited and unattractive choices: It could cut the heart from the governor's proposal, but only at the cost of conceding most of the other provisions. The end result was a law that was a distinct (if, in practice, mainly literal) advance over the disclosure statutes of other states. The combination of national publicity and executive determination foreclosed at least some of the easy face-saving that has obscured recent legislative action elsewhere.

The trickle of legislation still continues to flow. Texas and Illinois enacted disclosure statutes in 1958 (that of Texas replacing a system of registration by legislative rule), but neither their provisions nor the circumstances surrounding their enactment departed substantially from patterns by then well established. The Montana act of 1959 was a nearly verbatim copy of the then-current version of Wisconsin's much amended law.[81] With the major exception of California, the states that have passed disclosure laws since 1932 might well have passed them sixty years ago. While there may be chilly comfort in the imputation, neither styles nor systems of politics, nor our knowledge of the inefficiency of statute law as a means of altering them, are as changeless as all that.

The infirmities of state disclosure laws go beyond the merely textual, although these abound. The more fundamental difficulty is that these laws have not been little Sherman Acts, given second and third lives by periodic readjustments in administrative or judicial construction. There is more than enough to construe, but no compelling interest in the task. It should be unnecessary to observe that the most palpable of statutory inadequacies will not correct themselves.

The postenactment torpor that quickly fastens on most state disclosure laws is demonstrated by the infrequency with which they have been amended. Of those enacted since 1932, only the California and Virginia laws have been altered, and in neither case were the changes basic.[82] Among the older statutes, only those of Nebraska and Wisconsin have been seriously amended in recent years.[83] The Massachusetts law, revised five times in its first twenty years, has had no major amendments since 1911. Most legislatures have been reluctant to make even technical corrections, which would in no way alter or extend the laws' reach.[84]

If minor changes are difficult, major ones are practically impossible. Support for the point can be adduced from the backing and filling that has attended recent revisions of the Wisconsin law, generally regarded as one of the superior statutes of its type. A revision jointly drafted in 1947 by the chief of the legislative library, the assistant attorney-general, and a representative of the secretary of state, called for the establishment of a joint standing committee of the legislature, to consist of three senators and three assemblymen and to be known as the Committee on Lobbying. This committee was to have power "to issue, suspend, and revoke [lobbyists'] licenses, to establish rules and regulations defining and prohibiting unfair or unethical lobbying practices, . . . and all other powers necessary and proper to carry out the provisions of [the law]."[85] For all its apparent merit, the proposal was unacceptable to the Republican leadership, and that was the end of it.

The Wisconsin Republicans had no corner on this kind of enterprise, however; two years later it took nine Democratic votes to defeat a bill requiring registered lobbyists to name the legislators for whom they reported entertainment expenses.[86] In 1957, the legislature, with appropriate solemnity, finally prohibited furnishing to any legislator or other employee of the state "any food, meal, lodging, beverage, or transportation," but mainly because Governor Nelson made enactment of the prohibition a precondition to his approval of increases in legislative salaries and expenses.[87] More than immediate self-interest may have been at work; plainly, the earlier proposals could have had more disruptive consequences than those which the legislature eventually was compelled to accept. Most state legislators see more menace in disclosure than foreclosure (particularly when the latter is apt to be unenforced), and they are rarely in need of partisan spectacles to observe the distinction.

Legislatures occasionally pass resolutions requesting that the secretary of state or other responsible registration officer provide members with weekly or biweekly lists of registered lobbyists and their employers, but even this sort of action, which changes neither the substance of the law nor the surrounding context of relationships with which it purports to deal, is infrequent.[88] In the great majority of states, a disclosure law, once passed, lies dormant. The first gesture is usually the last.[89]

There is, of course, no intrinsic reason why a law should require periodic rebuilding if it was properly put together to begin with, and if the phenomena it seeks to order stand reasonably still for it. Although it does not deserve high marks for its prevision, the Massachusetts General Court attacked its problem with honesty and intelligence in 1890. Most other legislatures have been content to enact their laws without any of the conscientious searching that distinguished Massachusetts' early experience. It is difficult to withhold the conclusion that for these sovereign assemblies, disclosure laws have been conceived and adopted largely as defensive tactics, acts of tardy, incomplete, and one-sided self-purification. That these laws might serve larger purposes does not alter the fact that the generality of them were not so meant.

As for the test of stability, it should be sufficient to say that during the seventy years that the states have been copying each other's borrowed laws, the configurations of the process that they seek to capture have profoundly changed. The most prominent of these changes relate to the formation, growth, and characteristics of political interest groups—associations of like-minded men who confront government collectively rather than competitively. These groups are politically active through the medium of skilled group bureaucracies as well as lobbyists of the traditional variety, before administrative agencies as well as legislative committees, by political action at the grass roots as well as personal persuasion under the capitol dome. They are active in a political process where involvement explains more than external pressure, and which has become complicated beyond the ability of the ordinary citizen fully to comprehend, or of circumscribed disclosure to reflect. In both content and effect, state disclosure laws have been unable to escape their nineteenth-century origins.

Chapter 3

THE STATUTORY BASIS OF STATE REGULATION

State lobbying laws, like skim milk, have not much thickened in the churn of time. The newer statutes, like the older ones, reflect individual but similar blends of embarrassment, outrage, optimism, and patent face-saving, the dominance of one or the other of the strains depending largely on local circumstances. Although the setting in which they operate has changed profoundly in the past seventy years, the laws' content and formal rationale remain essentially what they were in the beginning. The rationale is still, "Let the facts be known," with the implicit corollary that democratic politics will provide the vehicle for whatever remedial action they may appear to the *polis* to require. We are here concerned with how these laws define the facts, provide for their collection, and make them known.

Lobbying Defined, and Defined, and Defined

A meaningful definition of terms is useful in any human enterprise, and indispensable in one that seeks to impose penalties on those who do not or will not conform to prescribed standards of conduct. This is a hallmark of good legislation. It is also one of those *ex cathedra* truisms that are considerably easier to assert than to practice. Writers in the field have long agreed that any public action concerning "lobbying"—whatever it is—should proceed from a careful delineation of the persons and practices to be acted upon.[1] Beyond a general and appropriate consensus that the present statutory definitions are "woefully inadequate," "vague," or "ambiguous," however, they have found no common ground as to how precisely such a statement should be framed. There have been definitions enough, but none that can meet every need or survive every objection. On the one hand "lobbying" has been defined as "corrupt solicitation of legislators"; on the other, as "any direct or indirect attempt" to influence legislative action. In either case, the language is such that reasonable men can find divergent meanings in it. For all of its palpable deficiencies, however, nobody has yet proposed any radical or striking improvements. That some of these definitions have been in operation for nearly a century may mean that our legislators have for this long been wanting in perception, inventiveness, or both. It may also mean that the problem of definition is neither urgent nor soluble, or that there is nothing to be gained from its imperfect solution.

LOBBYING AS CORRUPT SOLICITATION

If the existing constitutional and statutory definitions of lobbying variously fall short of the ideal, they do at least have the modest virtue of being relatively easy to classify. Five general (if somewhat overlapping) categories can be distinguished. In the first belong those early and, in most cases, still extant expressions of belated self-righteousness that were written in the wake of the legislative debauchery of the 1860's and 1870's. The recurring theme of these definitions is corrupt solicitation of the individual legislator, and the California constitutional provision is typical of them in both language and spirit:

> Any person who seeks to influence the vote of a member of the legislature by bribery, promise of reward, intimidation, or any other dishonest means, shall be deemed guilty of lobbying, which is hereby declared a felony.[2]

As in several other states, this provision is allowed to coexist with a more or less advanced registration law. On the one hand, we declare "lobbying" to be a felony; on the other, we go to considerable length to license its practitioners.

In a similar vein, the Alabama statute makes "lobbying with [a] legislator a felony," describing the offense as follows:

> Any person who, for or without reward of any kind, gift, gratuity, or other thing of value, or the promise or hope thereof, corruptly solicits, persuades or influences, or attempts to influence any senator or representative to cast his vote . . . is guilty of a felony.[3]

Provisions of this kind were doubtless well intentioned at the time of their enactment, and if they had little value as law they had some significance as moral purgatives. Then as now, however, they not only duplicated the almost universal bribery laws,[4] but also expanded the common-law offense of bribery to include the use of deceit, intimidation, menace, force, or such other means of personal persuasion as a court might hold to be corrupt, corrupting, or dishonest.[5] If such language was vague and redundant in the 1870's and ceded to the courts a peculiarly legislative responsibility, it was at least rooted in the needs and life of the time. It suffers today from the more conclusive defect of irrelevance; corruption in the politics of interest has become less a juridical problem than a moral one, and of such dimensions as to be beyond the reach of simple proscriptions of largely abandoned tactics. While these definitions still support occasional prosecutions of old-fashioned miscreants, they are mainly of retrospective interest.

LOBBYING AS CLAIMED INFLUENCE

A second group of definitions, related to the first yet distinguishable from it, defines lobbying as the claim or representation of improper influence. Typical of this group is the Utah law which provides:

> *Lobbying for Hire.* Every person who obtains or seeks to obtain money or other thing of value from another person upon a pretense, claim, or representation that he can or will improperly influence in any manner the action of any member of any legislative body in regard to any vote or legislative matter is guilty of a felony.[6]

Comparable provisions are still in effect in California,[7] Arizona,[8] and Montana.[9] The Washington and Nevada laws similarly make the solicitation of money on the claim of being able to secure governmental action a gross misdemeanor "unless it be clearly understood and agreed in good faith . . . that no means or influence shall be employed except explanation and argument upon the merits."[10] Here the emphasis is not on acts of corruption *per se* but on claims or promises that such acts can or will be performed. In most cases, these provisions are accompanied by others which specifically proscribe corrupt acts; still, it is the claim of improper influence rather than the act itself that is called "lobbying."

There is the same redundancy here as there is in the related corrupt solicitation definitions. There is also the same opacity of language; such terms as "improperly influence," "in any manner," "explanation and argument upon the merits," etc., are something less than models of clarity. And there is, finally, the same irrelevance to political actuality. To be sure, every state capital has its quota of harpies and vultures who hint darkly and with an open hand of intimate connections with the right people. But the claim seldom mirrors the fact, and there are hardly enough credulous citizens to go around. The real power more often belongs to those who have no need to vend it.

LOBBYING AS APPEALS TO UNREASON

A third group of provisions defines lobbying as personal solicitation of the legislator by means other than appeals to reason. The identical Georgia and Tennessee statutes provide:

> Lobbying is any personal solicitation of a member of the General Assembly during the session thereof, by private interview, or letter, or message, or other means not addressed solely to the judgment . . . by any person who misrepresents the nature of his interest in the matter to such member, or who is employed for a consideration by a person or corporation interested in the passage or defeat of such bill . . . for the purpose of securing the passage or defeat thereof. But this shall not include such service as drafting petitions, bills, or resolutions, attending to the taking of testimony, collating facts, preparing orally, or in writing, to a committee or member of the General Assembly, and other services of like character intended to reach the reason of legislators.[11]

Just what this means is anybody's guess. For Lincoln Steffens' classic state legislator—and there are still a few around—who "came from the country, and came to be bought," judgment is no less judgment because it is execrable, or because its consequences are illegal. If this objection is perhaps speciously literal, one could also point to the inclusion of interviews, letters, and messages among the "other means not addressed solely to the judgment." Obviously, these approaches not only can be, but usually are, addressed to the judgment; few courts would be willing to support the proposition that they were, *per se*, improper, without accompanying evidence that they were integral parts of a plan or intent to corrupt. Nor does it help the situation to allow other means, such as "drafting petitions," and so on. While this statement of exemption was manifestly intended to clear such professional services as might be rendered by a lawyer, it does so by prohibiting other equally neutral services which he might no less often render.

Note, too, that two quite different criteria of "lobbyist" are used here. On the one hand, he is a person who "misrepresents the nature of his interest" in a legislative matter; on the other, he is a person who is "employed for a consideration" by a corporation or by another person. This type of misrepresentation falls within the common-law meaning of fraud; the simple fact of employment by interested parties does not. That this employment may involve evils against which the state can protect itself is patent; that it must involve such evils is no more than arbitrary presumption.

The early Texas law deemed guilty of "lobbying" any person having a "direct interest" in a measure pending before the legislature who "in any manner, except by appealing to his reason, privately attempts to influence the action of any member of such legislature during his term of office, concerning such measure."[12] The Louisiana law similarly sought to limit private address by providing that any paid agent, representative, or attorney who attempts to "privately or secretly solicit the vote, or privately endeavor[s] to exercise any influence, by threat or by promises, or by offering anything of value, or any other inducements whatever" concerning pending measures was also guilty of "lobbying."[13] "Anything of value" is a term of art with which the courts have grappled long enough to have established for it at least a general residuum of meaning. "Any other inducements whatever" and "in any manner" remain empty vessels, however, and both phrases reach so far into the area of legitimate personal contact as to be beyond either refinement or enforcement.

A number of states also forbid attempts personally, directly, or privately to influence the vote of a legislator except through committee appearances, newspaper publications, public addresses, and written or printed statements, arguments, or briefs.[14] Although these limiting provisions are somewhat more descriptive than their obverse ("means not addressed solely to the judgment"), they plainly do not exhaust nonpersonal, nonprivate, or nonsecret solicitation. They place beyond the pale any means not specified, yet this is peculiarly an area in which no restrictive enumeration of means ever was, or long will be, sufficient. The law is no better than its initial logic and capacity for growth, and both are wanting here.

It is equally unprofitable to require, as do the Washington and Nevada laws, that securing money for lobbying is illegal "unless it be clearly understood and agreed in good faith between the parties thereto, on both sides, that no influence shall be employed except explanation and argument upon the merits."[15] "Argument upon the merits" is essentially synonymous with "addressed solely to the judgment." And what does a clear understanding "in good faith" require? A written instrument that a court could enforce? Would its absence imply the mutual expectation of unlawful acts? So the language would seem to suggest.

When all the word play is done, the crucial flaws in these definitions are more in their focus and underlying assumptions than in their language. They use corrupt or private solicitation as the criterion of lobbying, and private solicitation—corrupt or otherwise—is no longer the dominant means by which men and groups of men seek to influence what legislatures do. Their history suggests that these definitions were intended to preserve what was once regarded as "honest" or "useful" lobbying.[16] If we still formally view a wide range of *ex parte* relationships as tainted with at least the possibility of mischief, we are also far less inclined to tolerate explicit restrictions upon them. These definitions go unobserved because it is inconceivable that a modern constitutional court would allow their literal application. Their main value from the outset has been in the defense of civil actions for the recovery of compensation under contracts to perform lobbying services.[17]

LOBBYING AS PRIVATE INTEREST

In the fourth category, definitions of lobbying hinge on the pursuit of private pecuniary interests as opposed to the interests of the whole people of the state. The Kentucky law typically declares:

> . . . lobbyist means any person employed as legislative agent or counsel to promote, oppose, or act with reference to any legislation which affects or may affect private pecuniary interests, as distinct from those of the whole people.[18]

This definition, counterparts of which can be found in the registration laws of nine other states,[19] has the virtue of recognizing that private gain is what government and politics and lobbying are mostly about. As a standard for statutory application, however, it suffers from the concession it implies, i.e., that one's interests are not identical with those of "the whole people."[20] Although the reasons that impelled Massachusetts to abandon this distinction in 1891—the difficulty of distinguishing between public and private bills—are still persuasive, the major objection to this kind of provision remains the practical difficulty of prodding some groups to acknowledge the privateness of their interests when they might find themselves flayed as "selfish" for their candor.

The Oregon law treats the question of interest somewhat differently, but with no greater realism. It provides that if any person or his agent, having "any interest" in a measure before the legislature

> . . . shall converse with, explain to, or in any manner attempt to influence any member of such assembly in relation to such measure without first truly and completely disclosing to such member his interest therein . . . such person, upon conviction thereof, shall be punishment by imprisonment . . .[21]

"Any interest" is no clearer than the "private pecuniary interest" of the Kentucky law, and this objection is no less applicable to the requirement that this interest be "truly and completely" disclosed. It need hardly be said that this kind of language can be variously read, or that when criminal statutes either forbid or demand the performance of an act in terms so vague that the ordinary citizen must guess at their meaning or differ as to their application, courts have frequently held them in violation of the basic requisites of due process.[22] The rule of invalidation for ambiguity is, of course, far from inflexible, and it is not necessary to conclude that the Oregon act and others like it are void. While none of these laws has been upset, however, the same imprecision that discourages their application exposes their flanks to constitutional attack.

LOBBYING AS ALMOST ANYTHING

A fifth type of definition, common in disclosure laws, includes virtually any influence situation in which legislators and other parties are involved. The Wisconsin act, specific in most respects, typically declares that lobbying is "the practice of promoting or opposing the introduction or enactment of legislation before the legislature, or the legislative committees, or the members thereof."[23] While other statutes in this group do not always define "lobbying" or "lobbyists" in quite these terms, their applicability is essentially the same. Thus Virginia does not define lobbying, but it defines "legislative counsel and agent" as "any person employed to promote or oppose in any manner the passage by the General Assembly of any legislation."[24] The distinction between this language and the Wisconsin definition is only the distinction between agent and process; the area covered— the promotion of or opposition to legislation—is identical.

Other states play variations on the general theme of lobbying "in any manner." Florida uses "in any wise,"[25] while Connecticut, Maine, Nebraska, New Hampshire, New York, and Vermont reach the same result with "directly or indirectly."[26] Maryland double-locks the ambiguity by using both "in any manner" and "directly and indirectly."[27] Still other states, of which Massachusetts is the oldest example, achieve a similar end by distinguishing between legislative counsel and agents. Counsel are ordinarily defined as attorneys whose lobbying services are restricted to appearances before legislative committees; agents are those performing "any [lobbying] act . . . except to appear at a public hearing."[28]

The relatively new (1947) Michigan law defines "legislative agent" as any person employed "to engage in promoting, advocating, or opposing" any matter pending or likely to come before the legislature. "Advocating," "promoting," and "opposing" are then defined as "any act or acts, performed directly with a member of the legislature, for the purpose of influencing him to vote or to use his influence for or against any matter pending before either house of the legislature or any committee thereof."[29] The law extends only to activities "performed directly" with legislators, leaving untouched all the indirect promotional activities that have become so prominent a part of modern group tactics. This law might well have been written by a conscientious legislature of the 1890's; it was a lackluster performance from a body which should have been two generations wiser in the ways of the world.[30]

Of the state provisions that define lobbying broadly, or that give broad scope to a registration law, the California provision is the most unusual. While it is not an express definition, it is an operating one since it partially sets the law's applicability. Derived practically verbatim from the Federal Regulation of Lobbying Act, section 9903 of the California law applies its requirements to "every person receiving any contributions or expending any money" for the purpose of influencing legislation.[31] This kind of language is unique in state disclosure laws. It achieves a broad reach by using as its criteria the receipt and expenditure of money for stated (if general) purposes, as against the usual definition in terms of persons or practices. There are obvious difficulties in this more or less fiscal approach to definition, yet it has the virtue of being incomparably hard-headed. Money makes the system go. Interest groups are interesting socio-political phenomena, but they do not run on air.

In this fifth group, then, "lobbying" can be compositely defined as the receipt and/or expenditure of money to promote or oppose the passage of legislation, in any manner, directly or indirectly. There is some value in each component of this broad definition, but it is hardly clarity of language. As a result, the courts are again left with the ultimate responsibility for defining the laws' reach, case by case.

That this is probably a generic difficulty has not stayed criticism of the present statutory definitions; nor should it, for criticism is both healthy and generally deserved. It is deserved, however, less for the content of the definitions—although this is frequently archaic or narrow—than for the intemperate haste and thoughtfulness with which most of them were framed. Professor Zeller, for example, writes that "the existing statutes either make no attempt at definition or . . . dispose of the question in such vague and meaningless phrases as to make them difficult, if not impossible, to interpret and enforce."[32] One can concede the difficulty (if not quite the impossibility) of interpreting the present definitions; but to argue that their vagueness has much affected enforcement is another matter. Wisconsin has a definition which is "vague" by any standard—"the practice of promoting or opposing the introduction of legislation before the legislature, or the legislative committees, or the members thereof"—yet its law is relatively well enforced, and to all appearances, relatively well observed.

That most state disclosure laws have not been equally effective is better laid to administrative indifference and legislative hostility than to imperfect statutory language.

Another observer has belabored the definitions with even more zest, and even less accuracy: "Of the thirty-five states that have lobby regulating laws, not one contains a clear and specific definition of lobbying. Most of the acts are deliberately vague and meaningless. They are patent shams. Some are outright farces."[33] If one starts with the assumption, as this observer does, that "the legislatures are the bawdy houses of state government,"[34] the conclusion that state lobbying laws were made "deliberately vague and meaningless" has a certain remorseless logic to it. But most of the history of state regulation argues against him; as often as not, these statutes have been the handiwork of the "better element" in the legislatures—honest men still capable of anger, but often rendered impotent by it. Their real offense was not that they sought refuge in ambiguity, but the more deadly one of not perceiving fully what they were about. As one writer has remarked, "The failure is not merely in the adequacy of the statutory language but in the more basic fault of which lack of precise definition is a manifestation: the inability of state legislatures to see pressure group regulation in its relation to the whole decision-making process."[35] The observation might be even more trenchant if "activity" were added to "regulation."

It has been said that disclosure laws should define lobbying "specifically," and that a proper definition would detail "the practices that are permissible and those that are not."[36] But neither reason nor experience support the view that any such enumeration would be either presently or permanently complete, or that a catalogue of the permissible would not quickly become a blueprint for evasion and thereby further complicate an already difficult problem. Certainly the laws which confine the lobbyist to committee appearances, circular statements, and the like, have not in any sense been more effective—and have probably been considerably less so—than those that define vaguely and without limiting specificity. Long experience with these restrictions, which obviously fall far short of exhausting the activities that modern practice would either sanction or demand, suggests the dubious values of definition purporting to be precise.

There is more appeal to the argument that only broad definition can keep disclosure laws apace of the realities they should reflect. The best of statutes can capture only momentary images of a world that keeps on changing. For the ultimate purposes of disclosure, the world is not much less than the total political system. If it is, as it has always been, a world too wide to comprehend, we do not shrink it by assuming it to be no wider than our view. Until we have begun to ask the really hard questions about the place of private interest in the policy-making process, and about the utility of disclosure requirements as a means of either promoting or reflecting a well-ordered relationship between the two, no statutory definition of lobbying can alone much advance a solution to the deeper problems of which "pressure" on the legislature is only a partial, if absorbing, symptom.

Registration

Beyond whatever interest they may have as semantic exercises, definitions of "lobbying" and/or "lobbyists" serve two main purposes: In those states that regulate lobbying by means other than registration and reporting, the definitions determine the application of criminal prohibitions of bribery, corrupt solicitation, or other forms of illicit personal contact. In those states that require registration, the definitions generally stake out the coverage of the registration requirements. The latter provisions concern us here.

Beginning with Massachusetts in 1890, a total of twenty-seven states have enacted legislation setting up formal registration systems.[37] In addition, Florida, Minnesota, and Oklahoma have laws requiring *ad hoc* lobbyist registration with legislative committees. Colorado, Florida, Minnesota, Washington, and Iowa also require registration, but by legislative rule rather than by statute.

While definitions vary somewhat, the registration provisions of the twenty-seven comparable state laws are sufficiently alike that almost any one of them could serve as an analytical model. Since Ohio's statute is in most respects typical of the group, it can be used as a standard against which the few unusual features of other laws can be discussed. There are "better" laws, and there are "worse," but like so many other things Ohioan, its disclosure law is probably located quite close to the center of American experience. Who registers as a lobbyist in Ohio? The law provides:

Any person, firm, corporation or association, or any officer of a corporation or association, who or which directly or indirectly employs any person or persons, firm, corporation, or association to promote, advocate, amend or oppose in any manner any matter pending or that might legally come before the General Assembly or either house thereof, or of a committee of the General Assembly or either house thereof, shall within one week from the date of such employment furnish in a signed statement to the Secretary of State [certain information].[38]

This statement in lieu of definition puts the Ohio law in the "lobbying-as-almost-anything" category, and with few exceptions the twenty-seven registration laws lay out a comparably broad coverage for their registration requirements. Even Georgia, whose constitution declares lobbying to be a crime and whose early but still extant law defines it in the narrowest terms of illicit address, requires every person employed "to aid or oppose, directly or indirectly" the passage of legislation to register as a lobbyist—and charges him $250 for the privilege.[39]

Broad coverage is usually obtained by extending the law to *any* person employed for the purpose of directly or indirectly influencing legislation. Eight states, however, distinguish between "legislative counsel" and "legislative agents."[40] The Vermont law of 1939 characteristically defines the former as "any person who for compensation appears at any public hearing before committees of the legislature in regard to proposed legislation." "Legislative agents" are then defined as any person, firm, association, or corporation?

. . . that for reward or hire does any act to promote or oppose proposed legislation except to appear at public hearing and shall include all persons who for compensation shall approach individual members of the legislature or members-elect thereof with the intent in any manner, directly or indirectly, to influence their action upon proposed legislation.[41]

Since this leaves to legislative agents the remaining range of permissible activity, the total coverage of the registration requirement is broad. Since, too, the rest of the law applies equally to agents and counsel, the only practical effect of the distinction has been to add somewhat to the burden of administration, as separate registration dockets for agents and counsel are specifically required by all those laws making the distinction.

Broad coverage is thus the rule, but there are the usual exceptions. The Mississippi law, for example, begins by requiring registration of any legal person who directly or indirectly employs any other legal person to "attempt at any time to influence in any manner" the act or vote of a member of the legislature. Then come the statutory "but's": the law is not applicable to municipalities, counties, levee boards and their officers, representatives, or attorneys; to those appearing before the legislature or its committees by invitation; to representatives of "any of the institutions owned, fostered, or maintained or controlled by the state"; to those performing purely "professional services" in connection with legislation; nor to anyone who attempts to influence only by "arguments, briefs, or written statements."[42]

Although few other laws have quite so many exemptions—the concern with levee boards is unique—most have one or two. The Ohio statute, in this case untypically, and the Kansas and Michigan laws follow Mississippi in relieving those who appear by invitation before the legislature and its committees of any liability to register. In addition, the Wisconsin, Montana, Michigan, and California laws are not applicable at all to persons whose legislative effort consists solely of committee appearances, whether by invitation or not.

Exemptions of persons rendering professional services, such as bill or petition drafting or analysis, appear in the laws of Mississippi, Ohio, and four other states. The usual form of these waivers of applicability follows that of the Ohio law, which reads:

> The provisions of this act shall not be construed as affecting professional services in drafting bills, preparing arguments thereon, or in advising clients and rendering opinions as to the construction and effect of proposed or pending legislation where such professional services are not otherwise connected with legislative action.[43]

These provisions help to mitigate one of the difficulties inherent in broad definition, but they make explicit what any court would probably imply. Advising clients is not influencing legislation, except by a tortured construction of the meaning of indirect influence. In principle, however, it is desirable to make either prohibitions or exemptions express rather than subject to judicial determination.

Somewhat similar in purpose and effect are those provisions that exempt persons whose legislative activities consist solely of newspaper publications, public addresses to persons other than legislators, and arguments or briefs delivered to each member of the legislature. Wisconsin extends exemption to all of these practices; Mississippi, to arguments, briefs, or written statements only; and Michigan exempts persons who confine their activities to "written communications or formal appearances" to or before legislative committees.[44]

The Ohio, Mississippi, and Virginia laws also declare that their provisions do not reach "the furnishing of information or news to any bona fide newspaper, journal, or magazine for publication, or to any news bureau or association which in turn furnishes the said information or news only to bona fide newspapers, journals, or magazines."[45] The California law follows the language of the Federal Regulation of Lobbying Act in exempting newspapers, periodicals, their publishers and employees from the registration and reporting provisions of its law, provided that their activities in behalf of pending legislation are limited to the publication of news items, editorial or other comment, paid advertisements relating to legislation, or committee appearances in connection with such legislation. It goes beyond the federal law by extending the exemption to radio and television stations and their employees. The Illinois language is even broader, exempting members of "the working press, radio, television, magazine, or other mass media of news."[46] Again, the value of these exemptions is greater than their necessity, since they make express what most courts would almost certainly imply. From a functional standpoint, of course, mass media editorials that relate to pending legislation meet the central criteria of intent and expenditure; in this sense, they are "lobbying," but the First Amendment is not without sense of its own, and it is unquestionably wise to invoke it as a limitation here, irrespective of the minimal regulation involved.[47]

The California law has another unique exemption: Persons representing a church to protect its right to practice its doctrine are not liable to the registration requirement.[48] Here again, the deeper meaning of the First Amendment intrudes upon rational definitions.

Finally, some seventeen states exempt public corporations and/or officials and employees from their acts' requirements, although in varying degrees.[49] South Dakota, for example, exempts "public corporations" but requires that no official or employee of the state or of the United States shall lobby "except in the manner authorized herein in the case of legislative counsel and legislative agents."[50] The majority of exemptions are more comparable to those of the Kansas act, which provide: "This act shall not apply to any municipal or other public corporation or its accredited attorneys, agents, or representatives while acting for such municipal or other public corporation."[51] Only California limits the exemption to state and elected officials, the qualification having been added in 1961 following unregistered appearances by representatives of several state institutions and special districts.[52]

On the federal level, this kind of waiver is coupled with a stringent prohibition against the use of appropriated monies for lobbying services.[53] In most states, however, the exemption stands alone— a questionable arrangement. Legislative activities by state administrative officers ideally require separate treatment, whether in the form of prohibition or disclosure. In the absence of such treatment, the general law might well apply.

All of the foregoing are express exemptions. Of even greater effect are those which can be (and often are) implied from imperfect statutory language. The "pecuniary interest" definition, for example, serves as a practical exemption to an otherwise broad registration section. The usual procedure is to define "Lobbyist" or "legislative agent" as a legal person representing private pecuniary interests as against those of the whole people of the state, and then to require that all such persons register. Provisions of this general kind appear in the laws of nine states.[54] While self-serving claims of disinterest should obviously be treated with suspicion, "private pecuniary interest" is generally a term more polemical than juridical, and more easily asserted than established. Wherever doubt exists, sound public policy should call for compliance, but this is more a demand of good conscience than of the law.

A more significant implied exemption springs from the universal application of registration laws to only those persons *employed* or employing others for the purpose of influencing legislation, regardless of whether or not they or their employer have a private pecuniary interest therein. The common criterion of "lobbyist," or "legislative counsel," or "legislative agent" is their employment for compensation to influence legislation. Employment to influence legislation as a condition precedent to compliance can and does restrict the coverage of registration provisions. Self-employed persons, for example,—most typically unincorporated proprietors—can seek to influence legislation without any obligation to register, as can volunteer or otherwise uncompensated lobbyists (and there are a few). The Illinois law in terms exempts those seeking to influence legislation in their own behalf; in other states, the exemption is sanctioned by longstanding administrative practice.[55]

Most important of all, persons who can claim that their employment or professional service is not specifically for the purpose of lobbying, or that they are not compensated specifically or at all for lobbying services, or that their employment is multipurpose and includes both lobbying and other activities without corresponding allocation of time or remuneration, can avoid registration with general impunity.[56] What appears to be a narrow legalism becomes a broad exit-gate for such assorted parties as corporate or other attorneys on annual retainer; for virtually all public relations personnel; and for executives or professional employees of labor unions, corporations, trade and other associations—all of whom may have an obvious and immediate interest in legislation.

This tacit exemption, which has its ultimate roots in the persisting notion that "lobbying" describes only the face-to-face relationships between legislators and hired lobbyists, could clearly become an almost unlimited one. How is it, then, that people in any of these categories register at all? Many simply do not. For those who do, the motivation is less likely to be high-minded devotion to the spirit of the law than it is abundant caution, coupled with the recognition that registration is not only harmless but can often be turned to good public relations advantage.

Since many laws extend to employment to influence legislation "directly or indirectly," the latter part of this description would appear to be broad enough to reach the persons in question. But it can as reasonably be argued that applicability hinges on the purpose of the employment and not on the character of the means by which it is pursued. While sound public policy should call for the widest disclosure, these are, after all, statutes and not codes of citizenship. So long as such free-wheeling interpretive options exist—and to a greater or lesser extent they exist everywhere—the laws' reach will continue to exceed their grasp.

TIME AND PLACE

The requirement that registration be executed within one week of employment is usual, although not invariable. Maine and Vermont require that no more than forty-eight hours elapse between commencement of employment and registration.[57] Mississippi allows five days, while California, Connecticut, and Georgia require that a counsel or agent register before acting as such. Nebraska and New York require registration as a precondition to lobbying "in each and every year" that a person may be so engaged. Wisconsin and Montana license lobbyists for a period that expires December 31 of every even-numbered year (as does California for each even biennium), but they also require registration by licensed lobbyists within one week after the beginning of any specific employment.

Registration in most states is with the secretary of state. Among the generally comparable laws, only those of Kentucky, Alaska, Massachusetts, Texas, and California specify that it be with some other officer. The attorney-general receives registrations in Kentucky, as does the Department of Administration in Alaska. Registration is with legislative officers in the other three states: the sergeant-at-arms in Massachusetts, the chief clerk of the Assembly in Texas, and both the clerk of the Assembly and the secretary of the Senate in California.

Of these several arrangements, some form of legislative registration is probably the most appropriate. The other responsibilities commonly assigned to the secretary of state are not such as to suggest that his office is properly equipped to meet the special needs of disclosure administration. Although he is responsible for the law's enforcement, registration with the attorney-general implies undue concern with the penal aspects of the law. Disclosure laws are, after all, concerned with efforts to influence legislative action. As it should be one of the principal beneficiaries of an effective disclosure statute, so too should the legislature assign itself principal responsibility for the law's administration. The logic of this arrangement has not prevailed over tradition, however. The first Massachusetts law, since amended in this respect, specified registration with the secretary of state, for reasons now impossible to discover. Subsequent enactments in other states have characteristically followed the early model without inquiry into the good reasons which prompted its revision.

WHO TELLS WHAT?

There is no common requirement as to whether registrations should be submitted by agent or employer. Eight states require that the counsel or agent alone register,[58] while three states make registration for the agent the employer's responsibility.[59] In Maine, Vermont, and Nebraska, it is the responsibility of the agent or counsel to register and, secondarily, of the employer to "cause their names to be entered upon the docket." In the remaining states, it is the employer's responsibility to cause the agent's registration, with the same responsibility falling secondarily upon the agent.

It should be desirable to require some form of joint registration, as ten states do, since this could provide at least a rough check on the accuracy of the information filed by one or the other of the parties. In practice, this putative virtue is seldom realized, either because the two registrations were obviously prepared by the same hand, or because one of the parties—usually the employer—fails to comply at all.

In all events, the information required on registration of the agent, employer, or both, hews to a common pattern in all of the twenty-eight states. Ohio, for example, requires that the employer submit:

1. If an individual, his full name, place of residence and place of business.
2. If a firm, its correct firm name, place of business, and the full name and place of residence of each partner.
3. If a corporation or association, its full name, the location of its principal place of business, whether a corporation or voluntary association, whether a domestic or foreign corporation, and the names and the places of residence of each of its officers.
4. The nature and kind of his, their, or its business, occupation or employment.
5. The full name, place of residence, and occupation of each

person, firm, corporation or association so employed, together with the full period of employment.

6. The exact subject-matter pending or that might legally come before the general assembly or either house thereof or before any committee thereof with respect to which such person, firm, corporation or association is so employed.

7. When any change, modification or addition to such employment or the subject-matter of the employment is made, the employer shall within one week of such change, modification or addition furnish in writing full information regarding the same to the secretary of state.[60]

No other state requires such detail on registering corporations as does Ohio in subsection (3); otherwise, the section is fairly representative of comparable provisions, of which the basic requirements are generally the same: identification of agent and employer, disclosure of legislative interest, and notification of changes in terms of employment or legislative interest.

The Michigan law requires that the registration state the name of the custodian of whatever funds are used for lobbying purposes, but the main substantive addition to the Ohio requirements has been made in the California statute. Here, the individual registrant must also indicate "how much he is paid and to receive, by whom he is paid or is to be paid, how much he is to be paid for expenses, and what expenses are to be included."[61] Experience under the federal law, from which this provision was taken verbatim, suggested that there was little to be gained from it, since the information required can often be supplied only in the most general terms at the time of registration, and since comparable but more exact information must be submitted in the periodic financial reports. In practice, the data filed in the registrations have been more valuable than might have been expected, since it is to these rather than to the subsequent reports that the press has given most attention.

Two unique registration requirements of the Indiana law should also be noted. One provides:

Every person not residing within the state and every foreign corporation, firm, or association employing legislative counsel, or legislative agents in relation to any legislation pending or proposed in the general assembly of the State of Indiana, shall be required, as a condition precedent to filing the statements required by this act, to file with the secretary of state within one week after the date of such employment . . . a bond of a surety company, or a bond with sufficient personal security, approved by the secretary of state in the penal sum of one thousand dollars, payable to the State of Indiana.[62]

The bond is conditioned on the filing of "correct reports" under the law, and actions of forfeiture may be brought by the state attorney-general. This provision is aimed primarily at securing full compliance with the later financial reporting sections of the act, but the phrase "as a condition precedent to filing the statements required by this act" should comprehend accurate compliance with the registration requirements as well.

Indiana has more recently (1955) added an even more unusual requirement to its registration provisions: a noncommunist affidavit. Both lobbyists and their employers—including all of the principal officers if the latter is a corporation—must depose that they are not, and never have been, members of the Communist Party; that they do not belong to any organizations on the United States Attorney-General's subversive list; and that they have "never failed or refused to answer any question propounded to him by any committee or sub-committee of the Congress of the United States of America concerning affiliation with the Communist Party." The provision emulated an Alaska territorial statute of 1951, which required all registered lobbyists to take the same noncommunist oath required of territorial employees, and made it unlawful for members of communist, fascist, or other "subversive organizations," as listed by the United States Attorney-General, to attempt to influence legislation.[63] No other states have sought to use disclosure laws as weapons in the Cold War.

Most state disclosure laws avoid referring to those subject to their requirements in terms other than those used in the law itself, i.e., "person," "firm," "corporation," "association," or "employee." In line with their generally realistic approach, the Wisconsin law and the Montana statute derived from it frankly call their clientele "lobbyists," indicating as they do that no opprobrium is attached to the term. The avowed purpose of both acts is "to promote a high standard of ethics in the practice of lobbying, to prevent unfair lobbying practices," and only incidentally "to provide for the licensing of lobbyists and the suspension or revocation of such licenses."[64] Given the premises and targets of the laws, their rejection of the more florid euphemisms has much to recommend it.

The California law fuses both approaches. The substantive requirements of the act operate on "persons" doing certain things, the registration section of the law is subtitled "Registration by Lobbyists," and the final two sections outline the obligations of "legislative advocates" and the means by which their credentials as such are to be approved or withheld. This latter description has been accepted—without great enthusiasm, one suspects—by most of those to whom it might fairly apply, but news stories about lobbyists in Sacramento generally do not shrink from using the word "lobbyist" to describe them.

If terms like "legislative representative" or "legislative counsel" or "legislative agent" have a neutral color (and are doubtless often used because they do), at least the last two of them have been borrowed from, and reinforced by, the language of the law. As indicated earlier, eight registration statutes distinguish between "counsel" and "agent," and by implication restrict each to separate areas of activity. Both counsel and agents are required to register, and their registrations must state in what capacity they are employed. The responsible officer is charged with maintaining separate dockets for the two categories of registrants—an obligation that is, incidentally, as generally ignored as it deserves to be, since the registrations and financial reports required of each are otherwise identical.

REGISTRATION AND PUBLICITY

Disclosure statutes are often described as "publicity laws," and this description fairly expresses much of their underlying spirit. But what kind of publicity? How is it to be obtained, by whom, and for what ends? Do these laws rest on the hope that, in the words of a California legislative committee, "undesirable activities can best be controlled by publicity," or is publicity sought for itself without more than tacit regard for its consequences?[65] The distinction is important, and it involves very much more than a legislature's reluctance to say exactly what it wants.

Despite their common origins in evidence or allegations of excessive influence by particular interests, or undue responsiveness to such influence by the legislature, the laws themselves are silent as to the nature and ultimate uses of whatever "publicity" they may provide. They speak to the question of means, not of ends, and the means are minimal. The Ohio statute accurately reflects most of them when it charges the secretary of state with maintaining a separate book for lobbyist registrations, "which book at all times shall be open to public inspection."[66] Here "publicity" begins, and ends.

What this means, then—and there is a comparable provision in every state disclosure law—is that "publicity" consists of the availability of information to interested persons. This is a passive conception of so volatile a term, but few laws establish any procedure for giving it a more active meaning. The North Dakota law provides that if the legislature is in session at the time of any registration, copies of this registration shall be given to the clerk of the House of Representatives and the secretary of the Senate, presumably so that they may inform their respective houses, although this is not spelled out in the law.[67] Wisconsin and Montana go slightly further by requiring that such reports be delivered to both houses by the secretary of state on the third Tuesday of every regular or special session, and on every Tuesday thereafter. The Wisconsin law also requires that these reports on registration be formally read into the journal of each house.[68] The Michigan law is substantially similar, except that it charges the secretary of state with furnishing copies of registrations to all members of the legislature rather than to the legislative bureaucracy.[69] The Illinois statute similarly commands the secretary of state to publish in bulletin form the name, address, employer, photograph, and such other information about registrants as the secretary deems pertinent. Such bulletins are to be published as soon as possible after the General Assembly initially convenes, and subsequently at two-week intervals, if necessary. Copies are to be distributed to each member of the General Assembly, all elected state officials, and "those members of the press assigned to cover activities of the General Assembly." Copies will be given to "others" only upon request and upon payment of $10.00 for each bulletin, an arrangement hardly calculated to stimulate public curiosity.[70]

In this respect as in others, the California provisions are advanced. The law requires that "all information . . . filed"—registrations *and* financial reports—be compiled and printed in the Assembly Journal "as soon as practicable" after the month of filing, or preceding the final adjournment of the legislature. Although the law is silent as to the form or distribution of such publication, both have been generously construed and there has been regularly available to legislators, officials, lobbyists, press, and interested citizens a broader flow of information than anywhere else in the country. If it is not yet "publicity," it is "availability" in the best sense.[71]

Beyond the fact that there are so few of them, the most obvious feature of these statutory efforts to give publicity a more positive dimension is that they are largely confined to informing the legislature. Although this in itself is worth doing, the laws are silent with respect to the need or means of informing a larger public. From place to place and from time to time this happens, but it happens less because the laws say that it must than because working newsmen think that it should. It does not happen more often than it does because responsible officials do not commonly read their statutory responsibility as including a missionary zeal for the disclosure idea, and most newsmen do not read theirs as requiring that they supply the deficiency. This is not the result of a conspiracy of silence between "the interests" and the "lords of the press," but a function of the kind of data that the typical law provides and the form and setting in which it provides them. For the data are often surpassingly trivial and dull, and they are almost always available only in raw, unprocessed bulk. That it need not be this way is a matter more appropriately discussed below; it is enough to say now that the statutory framework for publicity is skeletal, and that this is perhaps the largest textual gap in state disclosure law.

REGISTRATION: MISCELLANEOUS

Several other provisions relating to registration deserve mention. A number of states have duplicated the Ohio provision requiring the issuance of a certificate upon registration, such certificate to serve as *prima facie* evidence of both the lobbyist's employment and his compliance with the law. Ohio also forbids a lobbyist to appear before a legislative committee without having first obtained this certificate.[72] Designated committees of the California legislature are charged with issuing certificates to properly qualified "legislative advocates" applying for them, but issuance has been held *not* to be a condition precedent to applicants engaging in legislative activities.[73] Illinois, Indiana, Ohio, Mississippi, Montana, and Wisconsin issue certificates only after the payment of a fee—$1.00 in Mississippi, $2.00 in Indiana, $3.00 in Ohio, $5.00 in Illinois, and $10.00 in Montana and Wisconsin. Alaska, Connecticut, Michigan, North Dakota, and Georgia also exact fees upon registration but do not issue certificates in return. The Connecticut and Michigan fees are $5.00, North Dakota charges $20.00 for each employer represented, and Alaska's fees range from $10.00 to $100, depending on the residency of agent and employer. In Georgia, the registration "tax"—and it is called that in the law—has been set at $250 since its enactment in 1927. It should not be surprising that no one has paid it since 1941.[74]

Finally, eleven other states have provisions requiring each registered lobbyist to file, usually within ten days of registration, a written statement signed by his employer authorizing him to act as lobbyist.[75] These provisions were originally aimed at the "strike," or "regulator," a blackmail operation where a lobbyist (or a legislator) secures, or alleges that he has secured, the introduction of a regulatory measure so that he can offer his services to those who might suffer from it. These things still happen,[76] but the requirement of a signed authorization is not likely by itself to deter them. When authorization provisions are joined with less circuitous approaches, the results are somewhat better. In the latest revision of its law, Wisconsin deemed guilty of "unprofessional conduct" any registered lobbyist who, among other things, instigated "the introduction of legislation for the purpose of obtaining employment in opposition thereto."[77] The punch to this is that a charge of "unprofessional conduct" makes the lobbyist liable to civil action for the revocation of his license, no small matter in a state that has taken its registration law quite seriously.

The more practical advantage of an authorization provision is that it erects a legal defense against persons putting the name of an individual or group to unauthorized and self-serving use, such as posing as agent for one client in an effort to secure others. The provision can thus afford some minimal protection both to reputable groups and credulous clients. Needless to say, it can never protect the latter from themselves.

AD HOC REGISTRATION

These are, in outline, the registration provisions of the twenty-eight comparable state laws. As indicated earlier, two other states provide for registration on an *ad hoc* basis. A Florida law requires that whenever any person appears before a legislative committee, any of its members may demand that this person declare in writing and under oath whether he appears in his own interest or whether he is paid for so appearing. In the latter case, however, he need not state how much he is paid. Whenever such a written oath is made, it must be "spread upon the journal of each house for the information of the members of the legislature." Misstatements of fact in the oath are deemed "false swearing" and are punishable by imprisonment up to twenty years. This permissive arrangement, especially when coupled with the ridiculously stringent penalties, has little to recommend it, and long-standing legislative practice "seldom requires a lobbyist to take the oath."[78]

In Oklahoma, before a paid "legislative counsel" or "legislative agent" appears before a legislative committee, he must apply for a permit to the presiding officer of the house concerned. Upon a majority vote of the house, usually automatic, the application is approved and the applicant is permitted to go before the committee to deliver testimony, arguments, or briefs. Either house, however, has the power at any time to revoke any permit issued by either itself or the other house, and this revocation cancels official recognition as counsel or agent.[79]

As to publicity, the law provides only that twenty copies of any statements, arguments, or briefs delivered by counsel or agents before committees shall first be deposited with the chief clerk of the house before which they appear, and these are open to the usual "public inspection." No other provision is made for general dissemination of any of the information submitted in applications for permits (name, employer, fee paid, and legislative interests). The law is thus a "publicity law" in the same minimal sense as most other registration laws. It is an inferior one only in the sense that its operation is relatively cumbersome.

This brings to thirty the number of states that, by statute, require some form of registration. The Idaho law has been said to require registration but seems misclassified.[80] It merely states that paid lobbyists can seek to influence legislation only by committee appearances, newspaper publications, public addresses, or written or printed statements, arguments or briefs, two copies of which must first be deposited with the secretary of state. This is not registration, however, since none of the data required under the conventional registration law need be filed.

REGISTRATION BY RULE

In addition to these statutory requirements, both houses in Colorado, the Minnesota Senate, the lower houses in Florida, Iowa, and Washington, have rules requiring that lobbyists wishing to be heard by legislative committees must first register with the chief clerk, secretary, or speaker of the house concerned, indicating their employers and their legislative interests.[81]

The rule of the Texas House, only recently superceded by a disclosure statute, was somewhat more ambitious. It established a five-man standing Committee on Representation Before the Legislature, appointed by the speaker. This body prescribed the form of statements which lobbyists were required to file with the chairmen of any other legislative committees before which they appeared. These statements, which included only the name of the agent and the name and occupation or business of the employer, were delivered by the committee chairmen to the Committee on Representation, of whose records they then became a permanent part.[82] If the substantive demands of the rule were not exacting, the provision for continuous legislative oversight was in line with the best practice elsewhere.

Prohibitory Provisions

The purpose of state regulation of lobbying is essentially non-restrictive, apart, of course, from the nearly universal antibribery provisions, which forbid certain acts that centuries of experience have shown to be destructive of free government. Notwithstanding their generally permissive and remedial character, however, state lobbying laws frequently include several types of prohibitory provisions. Some of these are unquestionably valuable; others raise exceedingly delicate questions of legal right and sound policy, some of which have not yet been satisfactorily resolved.

The most common prohibition condemns lobbying contracts calling for compensation contingent on the action of the legislature. Among the states with registration systems, only New Hampshire does not specifically forbid contingent fees, although the skeletal Florida and Oklahoma laws are also silent on the matter. The Ohio act typically provides:

> No person, firm, or corporation or association shall be employed with respect to any matter pending or that might legally come before the general assembly or either house thereof, or before a committee of the general assembly or either house thereof for a compensation dependent in any manner upon the passage, defeat, or amendment of any such matter, or upon any other contingency whatever in connection therewith.[83]

The prohibitions are not always this well designed. Several refer specifically only to those contracts in which the contingency is action by the whole legislature.[84] This overlooks committee action, which may, of course, be decisive.

A contingency prohibition appeared in the Massachusetts act of 1890, where it represented the first legislative recognition of a principle that had been frequently asserted earlier by both state and federal courts and which is still being asserted today, although with much less vigor and many more qualifications. Originally, contingent employment and covert or corrupt solicitation were assumed to go together. While recent decisional law has tended to dissociate the two, the continued condemnation of contingent contracts to influence legislation as against sound public policy is probably unexceptionable, if only in terms of putative effect.[85]

A second group of provisions denies paid lobbyists access to the floor of either house of the legislature while it is in session, except by "invitation of such house extended by a vote thereof."[86] Eight states with registration systems have provisions of this kind, as do four others.[87] Several other states which do not by law bar paid lobbyists from the floor have legislative rules to the same effect.

There is little reason to question the propriety of this kind of regulation, or of the competence of the legislature to adopt it, either by law or internal rule.[88] The formal exclusion of all registered lobbyists from the floor is, of course, diluted by the common legislative practice of extending the privileges of the floor to ex-members, some of whom will almost certainly be registered. There have, in all events, been no reported cases of ex-legislators having been ejected from the floor, and few enough involving the ejection of other persons.

The questionable prohibitions are those that specify the range of activities in which registered lobbyists may lawfully engage. There are, for example, the restrictions specified in the distinction between "legislative counsel" and "legislative agents" made in the laws of eight states. This distinction first appeared in the pioneer Massachusetts law, where it was defended as the only feasible means of distinguishing between the counsel "who presented his case publicly to a committee and the agent who buttonholed members in private."[89] Presuming the logic of distinguishing between the two at all, such a distinction could practically be based only on the character of the services performed by each, and the drafters of the act felt that it wisely left undefined the services that might properly be performed by legislative agents.

The distinction is perhaps better treated as an effort to define—in part, by nondefinition—than as an effort to restrict. It has not been enforced as a restrictive requirement; in fact, it is rarely enforced at all. Yet much depends on how it is construed. If it is read as merely instructing registrants as to the form of their compliance, it is patently innocuous. If, however, it is read as permitting a registrant to perform only one series of separately lawful acts or another, then it would appear to be vulnerable on obvious constitutional grounds. One author tacitly accepts the latter sense when he argues that counsel, "restricted" to committee appearances and legal work incident thereto, are probably afforded less opportunity for "undesirable conduct" than are agents, whose activities are not equally confined.[90] This proposition might hold if the distinction were enforced, as the author apparently assumes it to be. But it is not. This does not mean that "undesirable conduct" has resulted from nonenforcement. And it surely does not mean that nonenforcement washes away the possibility of restriction; administrative neglect is an unreliable remedy for bad law. It means only that the agent-counsel distinction has not yet been used restrictively, nor has it been of much value as a guide to registration compliance, since the other sections of the eight laws apply to counsel and agents with equal force.[91]

Less inferential problems of interpretation have been raised by those laws that in terms seek to restrict registered lobbyists to a limited range of activity. Wisconsin first enacted such limitations in 1905 following Governor La Follette's demand for a law prohibiting private solicitation of members of the legislature. Five other states with registration systems have since enacted similar restrictions,[92] while several others without registration laws have also sought to describe and limit permissible practices, usually by stating that they do not fall within a criminal definition of lobbying.[93]

These laws have commonly specified the same activities permitted under the Wisconsin revision: committee appearances; newspaper publications; public addresses; and written or printed statements, arguments, or briefs directed to all members of the legislature. Some statutes are even more narrowly focused, however. The Kentucky provision, for example, states that "no person shall render any service as a lobbyist other than appearing before committees and doing work properly incident thereto."[94] It requires tolerant construction to enlarge "work properly incident thereto" to include personal confrontation of individual members of the legislature.

The manifest purpose of these provisions was to curb the evils which were presumed to be associated with *any* private contact between lobbyists and legislators, even at the cost of sacrificing what one writer has generously described as its "few legitimate advantages."[95] But these advantages are neither few nor unimportant, and it is highly questionable that they can easily—or legitimately—be sacrificed to whatever fugitive impulse may prompt the legislature to try. When personal solicitation is unaccompanied by other acts that the state has a right or duty to forbid, its presumptive tendencies are not enough to justify palpable intrusions on the exercise of the right of petition, around which the courts have in recent years erected a formidable protective barrier. There has been no determined constitutional attack on these restrictions in any of the states where they still exist, but only because no one has been aggrieved by them. Like so many other facets of state disclosure law, they have simply been ignored.

If these prohibitions are neither enforceable nor realistic, there is no persuasive reason why they should not be abandoned or relaxed. Nebraska took the former course in 1945.[96] In its 1947 revision, Wisconsin retained its original list of permissible activities but changed their application so that it became unlawful for anyone *other* than registered lobbyists to attempt personally and directly to influence a legislator except by committee appearances, briefs, and so on.[97] The solution is an imperfect one, particularly for those not otherwise liable to the requirements of the law. Restrictions objectionable in themselves are not much diluted by incorporation into a system of professional licensing, whatever its other values.

These exhaust the common prohibitory provisions of the various registration laws, but there are also a few uncommon ones, some of which are uniquely interesting and constructive. The Massachusetts law was amended in 1911 to provide that "no member of a state or district political committee shall act as a legislative agent."[98] Indiana similarly debars from acting as legislative counsel or agent any representative of any newspaper or press association, or any "other person" having the privilege of the floor of the legislature.[99] Although there is no evidence as to precisely what the Indiana Legislature intended, the phrase "other person" could obviously be (but as obviously has not been) applied to former members. Both of these provisions can be taken as demonstrations of the occasional ability of state legislatures to realize what "lobbying" is about: It is not separable from politics in the narrow sense, nor public opinion in a broader one. At bottom, what we mean by "lobbying" comes close to being what we mean by the political process itself—a continuous and endlessly complex process of influence.

The Wisconsin law also contains two perceptive and realistic sections which appear otherwise inconsistent with their context. The first, labelled "logrolling prohibited," does precisely that, making it a felony for a member of the legislature to give his vote or influence on a measure on condition that another member give his in return. The companion section prohibits legislators from trading votes for gubernatorial support or disapproval of other measures, or promises of appointment to, or removal from, state office.[100] Again, the law relates less to what lobbying is supposed to be about than to what politics really is about. That these provisions are "impractical" or "unenforceable" should not detract from their significance as guideposts to the way the system really works. And this is the system that disclosure must comprehend if it is ever to prove worth its salt.

Financial Reporting

As registration is designed to illumine the "who" of interest politics, periodic financial reporting speaks to the inevitable corollary: "how much." The presumption—and it is a good one—is that efforts to influence what the legislature does are a peculiarly public matter. The question of "who" reflects a proper curiosity; the question of "how much" reflects nothing so much as our unique respect for the power of the dollar. These are questions well worth asking; they are also questions that state disclosure laws do less than they might to answer.

Only seven states with registration laws do not require financial reports by lobbyists, their employers, or both.[101] The New York law states the obligation in these terms:

> It shall be the duty of every person, firm, corporation or association within two months after the adjournment of the legislature to file in the office of the secretary of state an itemized statement verified by the oath of such person, or in case of a firm a member thereof, or in case of a domestic corporation or association of an officer thereof, or in case of a foreign corporation or association of an officer or an agent thereof, showing in detail all expenses paid, incurred or promised directly or indirectly in connection with legislation pending at the last previous session, with the names of the payees and the amount paid to each, including all disbursements paid, incurred or promised to counsel or agents, and also specifying the nature of said legislation and the interest of the person, firm, corporation or association therein.[102]

This is a standard statement of the expenses to be reported: basically, all those directly or indirectly connected with legislation, including payments to counsel or agents. There are two main deviations from this format. The Indiana law confines the report (filed by the employer) to "all expenses paid or incurred . . . in connection with the employment of legislative counsel or agents."[103] Other direct or indirect expenditures in connection with legislation need not be reported, as they must be under the more typical New York law.

In the Kentucky, Maryland, Massachusetts, South Dakota, and Wisconsin laws, the employer's expense report must include "all expenses paid or incurred by the maker of the statement . . . in connection with the employment of lobbyists or the promoting or opposing of legislation."[104] The language seems like that of the Indiana law, but the "or" extends it to require detailed reports of all legislative expenses without qualification, except that the costs of maintaining lobbyists must be included. The Indiana provision is thus the only true exception to the rule of nominally broad reporting requirements. Employment of legislative counsel or agents is the usual criterion of these requirements' applicability, but the substantive content of the reports is not limited to this kind of expenditure.

There is no single pattern as to who should file reports. The California, Mississippi, Nebraska, Ohio, and Wisconsin laws literally require separate reports by both agent and employer, but only in California and Mississippi should the two reports contain basically different information. The other sixteen laws require the filing of reports by either the lobbyist or the employer, often in terms so ambiguous as to make it difficult to determine upon whom the obligation falls.[105]

Dual reporting, like dual registration, is the preferable arrangement. Since the information required of agent and employer usually overlaps considerably, the two reports should serve as a check on the accuracy of the agent's reporting of his receipts and the employer's reporting of his expenditures. As noted earlier, however, both sets of reports are usually prepared by the same person wherever the requirement is still observed. In Ohio, in fact, the explicit requirement that employers report has been allowed to lapse, and a single statement of receipts and expenditures by the agent is now accepted as full compliance.

There is a real paucity of unique provisions among the various reporting requirements. Fourteen states require that the reports be rendered within thirty days of the final adjournment of the legislature.[106] Three states require reports within two months of final adjournment.[107] Only Texas, Nebraska, Wisconsin, and California require that several reports be filed at stated intervals during the legislative session. In Nebraska, both agent and employer must file reports with the secretary of state during each month of the legislative session, and also upon the legislature's adjournment. The information required in these reports, however, is substantially the same as that required elsewhere. In Texas, monthly reports during the legislative session are required only of the agent.

The Wisconsin law also prescribes monthly financial reports of all "expenses made and obligations incurred" by registered lobbyists. These reports are forwarded weekly by the secretary of state to the legislature, as are the names, employers, and legislative interests of new registrants. They may be entered in the journal of either house, but only on specific order. The law further states that the lobbyist need not list "his own personal or travelling expenses," although "any expenditure made or obligations incurred by any lobbyist in behalf of or for the entertainment of any state official or employee concerning pending or proposed legislative matters" must be reported. Employers, or "principals," are required to file but a single report, this to be delivered to the secretary of state within the usual thirty days of the end of the legislative session. The information required in this report is conventional: "a complete and detailed statement of all expenses paid or incurred by such principal in connection with the employment of lobbyists, or in connection with promoting or opposing in any manner the passage . . . of any legislation affecting the pecuniary interest of such principal."[108] The names and addresses of payees and payers, and the amounts paid to, and received from, each, are not required, but these are seldom reported even where they are required.

California's reporting requirements, like those of the parent federal statute, are the heart of its law. The California act has a distinct reporting provision applicable to paid lobbyists, but it also requires reports from any "person" receiving contributions or expending money for the purposes specified; i.e., influencing legislation. "Person" means individuals and groups employing registered lobbyists, but it can also mean individuals and groups that do not employ registered lobbyists but are nonetheless significantly engaged in efforts to influence legislation. In sum, the criteria of applicability are entirely functional: the receipt and expenditure of money for the purpose of influencing legislation.[109] Elsewhere, the usual test is the employment of persons who qualify as lobbyists—a relevant test, but a limited one. There are many statewide or national groups active in legislative affairs that, either by choice or accident, do not employ persons who can reasonably be classed as lobbyists, or at least who will register as such. The whole of these groups is, in a sense, greater than the sum of their parts. Only in California and on the national level can such groups come within the purview of the reporting provisions.

The California law does not make unusual demands of the individual lobbyist. He must in his initial registration indicate how much he is to be paid, by whom, and the amount and character of his reimbursed expenses. He must also file monthly "a detailed report of all money received . . . in carrying on his work," and of each expenditure of more than $25.00. He must also report the names of any publications in which he caused matter to be printed, and the particular legislation he is employed to support or oppose.[110] With the exception of the last two items and the $25.00 floor on reportable disbursements, the information required is essentially that required by the typical law.

The unique provisions of the California act are those requiring "persons"— defined to include committees, associations, corporations, and any other organization or group of persons—who receive any contributions or expend any money to accomplish the "passage or defeat of any legislation by the Legislature of the State of California or the approval or veto of any legislation by the Governor of California," to file monthly statements with the clerk of the Assembly and the secretary of the Senate. These statements must show the total of all contributions and expenditures; the total of all contributions received, along with the names and addresses of contributors of more than $100; and the amount, purpose, and name and address of the payee of each expenditure of more than $25.00. The statements must be cumulative for the calendar year and are renderable so long as the legislature remains in session.[111]

The plain meaning and potential impact of these provisions have been systematically diluted by administrative construction, particularly since the United States Supreme Court's decision in *U.S.* v *Harriss* in 1954.[112] The Court, speaking through Chief Justice Warren who, ironically, had earlier been largely responsible for the enactment of the California law, held that the parallel provisions of the Federal Regulation of Lobbying Act applied only to persons whose principal (i.e., nonincidental) purpose was to influence legislation, and whose intended method of accomplishing this purpose was through direct communication with members of Congress. This saved the Act at the cost of gutting its most important section, and it has had much the same effect in California.

For all that it might have been and isn't, the California law is considerably more demanding than other state laws, as those subject to its terms have long been uncomfortably aware. As early as 1950, the Joint Interim Committee on Lobby Regulations reported that registrants "who appeared and testified before the Committee were unanimous in their criticism of the legislation. . . . They objected to the complete disclosures required of their private financial affairs."[113] The answer might have been that lobbyists' "financial affairs" always lose some of their private character under a disclosure law. For reasons of its own, the committee did not choose so to reply.

Several of Indiana's old (1915) reporting provisions are literally as searching as the newer California requirements. It is illegal in Indiana for any unincorporated association or "combination of two or more persons to collect, receive, keep, or expend any money for the purpose of promoting or opposing legislation" until it has appointed a treasurer to superintend its finances. Within one week of his appointment, this treasurer must submit to the secretary of state a statement showing the group's officers, its legislative interests, and the identity of any persons employed by it as legislative counsel or agent. In addition to this preliminary statement (which is essentially a lobbyist's authorization to act, in reverse), the treasurer must also submit within thirty days following the end of the legislative session "a complete and detailed report" showing "the itemized list of all money received, from whom received, all money disbursed, to whom paid, and for what purpose."[114]

The major point of comparison with the California law is the phrase that requires the listing of "all money received," and "from whom received." The language is, in fact, broader than the corresponding California provision which specifies the detailed reporting of only those contributions which are: a) larger than $100, and b) received for the purpose of influencing legislation. This last can, in turn, be construed to mean only those contributions that are specifically earmarked for legislative purposes.

There are no such limitations in the Indiana language; it literally covers all interest group receipts, regardless of size or purpose. If this construction seems to be excessively demanding, it has, in all events, long been inoperative, apparently by the mutual consent of all concerned. The writer has examined hundreds of Indiana reports without finding one that began to comply with this part of the law. This is partly due to the language of a previous section which requires that the employer need report only those expenses paid in connection with the employment of legislative counsel or agents.[115] But deliberate noncompliance is also involved. Compliant organizations simply do not disclose their sources of financial support, and they so act with impunity. Experience with the California law supports much the same conclusion: The group reporting requirements are unmistakably clear, but generally unobserved.[116]

These two laws, whether they work well or badly, are the only ones that approach reporting in an unconventional way. In only a few other states do any of the reporting requirements diverge materially from the usual pattern. Massachusetts attempts to reach multifunctional registrants by providing that when payment for lobbying services is included in an annual salary or retainer, "the statement shall specify the amount of the salary or retainer apportioned therefor." If the salary or retainer is not apportioned into legislative and nonlegislative categories, "then the total salary or retainer which includes such lobbying services shall be stated."[117] This provision is a good start toward more complete and useful reporting. One of the common compliance problems in other states has been the general reluctance of attorneys and corporation or association officials to state their fees, retainers, or salaries when their whole time or effort is not given over to what they deem to be "lobbying" (and occasionally when it is). The Massachusetts provision does not specify a standard basis for apportionment—time, for example—and it would be more valuable if it did. Even as it stands, however, it lays the basis for fuller disclosure of legal fees and other services than is possible under other state laws.

Although some states—notably California—have sought to require apportionment by administrative direction, the only other *laws* which approach the problem at all do so only by implication and within narrow limits. The North and South Carolina statutes are expressly applicable to the officers of all corporations (and in South Carolina to

"any member of their legal staff") who "undertake in such capacity
to perform services as legislative counsel or agent for such corporation, regardless of whether they receive additional compensation for
such services."[118] This language clearly requires that multifunctional
corporate officials register. It can also be construed to require an
apportionment of salary or retainer, or disclosure of the entire figure,
in the reports which follow registration. In both states, however, nondisclosure of general retainers or salaries by lawyer-lobbyists is
normal.

The Michigan law does not require periodic reports, but it does
demand that records containing the customary information on legislative expenditures be kept by the agent or his employer for six years
following the final adjournment of the legislative session in which
they were made. These records must be produced on subpoena issued
either by a court of competent jurisdiction or by a legislative committee which has been authorized so to act by concurrent resolution
of the legislature.[119] The last part of this procedure is, of course,
likely to be quite difficult to negotiate.

The Michigan statute also requires that if any legislative agent
has "any financial transaction" with a member of the legislature, he
must within five days file with the secretary of state a sworn statement of all the facts surrounding it. This officer must then furnish
a copy of the statement to the legislator involved.[120] California
similarly requires that any lobbyist who employs or causes his employer to employ a legislator or any other full-time state employee
must file a statement with the clerk of the Assembly and the secretary of the Senate showing the nature of the employment and the
consideration to be paid.[121]

The Michigan provision protects only the legislator, whose defenses
are already more than sufficient. To the public, whose need is infinitely greater, it can offer nothing. In the California provision, there
is at least the possibility of publicity, since the statements would be
subject to the same public inspection as the regular financial reports.
According to official records and memories, however, no such statement has ever been filed.

The Maryland act requires the usual detailed reports within thirty
days of the legislature's adjournment, but it also gives the governor
power to require "any or all legislative counsel or agents and their

employers to render him forthwith a full, complete and detailed statement . . . of all expenses paid or incurred by them" whenever he has reason to believe that untoward expenses have been paid or incurred in connection with any bill presented to him for signature.[122] While this provision presents obvious administrative difficulties, it could help to meet the objection that the regular reports are filed too late to be of more than historical interest. Here again, there is no official record or memory of the section having ever been invoked. It is no small irony that two of the most perceptive reporting requirements in all state disclosure law are among its deadest letters.

Penalties

State disclosure laws are remedial rather than criminal in spirit. Their dominant purpose is to illuminate certain activities assumed to be of consequence to the legislature and to the larger community. Their purpose is not to ensnare and punish those who, for their own reasons, prefer to live in darkness. But they are still laws, and they bear penalties for those either careless or willful enough to violate them. The range of these penalties is as wide as the range of reporting provisions is narrow. Of the twenty-eight states with registration laws—thirty if we include the vestigial Florida and Oklahoma statutes —a total of twenty either allow or prescribe stated terms of imprisonment for convicted violators.[123] In addition, Georgia deems violations of its registration law as misdemeanors, which may be punished by imprisonment, and New Hampshire holds those making false statements in their registrations or financial reports liable to trial for perjury, conviction for which may also result in imprisonment.[124]

The extremes of leniency and severity are truly that. South Carolina's law permits a maximum imprisonment of only thirty days, and this is optional with the court. Florida, on the other hand, provides that any witness who swears falsely to any material fact in the oath that he may be required to take by the legislative committee before which he appears shall be deemed guilty of "false swearing" and imprisoned not to exceed twenty years.[125] It goes without saying that this absurd toll has never been exacted within the memory of living man.

The penal provisions of the other laws are more nearly like South

Carolina's than Florida's. The most frequent maximum is one year. This is specified in nine laws and is in each case optional with the court in lieu of, or in addition to, a money fine. Ohio and North Carolina allow maximum terms of two years, Mississippi allows three, and in Kentucky a lobbyist who violates any provision of the registration law may be imprisoned for five years. Once again, these penalties and/or fines are optional with the court.[126]

Only four laws prescribe minimum terms of imprisonment: thirty days in Wisconsin, six months in Indiana and Michigan, and one year in Ohio. The minimum and maximum terms are generally specified for "any violation" of the laws. A few states prescribe imprisonment for only natural persons, but only Wisconsin has set forth different penalties for different violations (e.g., noncompliance, false reports, etc.). The other laws treat all violations as equal.

Logic, practice, and the nature of the offense suggest that fines are more suitable punishment than imprisonment, and only Georgia, Florida, and Oklahoma do not provide for their assessment.[127] Here too there is a wide variation, with the maximum set as low as $100 (in South Carolina) and as high as $5,000, which figure is found in nine states. Ten other laws permit fines up to $1,000, and Vermont and Wisconsin set the maximum for certain violations at $500. The most frequent minimum specified is $100, and this occurs in eight laws. Four others prescribe fines ranging upward from $200, while Wisconsin assesses lobbyists convicted of filing false reports no less than $500. At the other extreme, the minimum is only $25.00 in South Carolina and $50.00 in North Carolina and Virginia.[128] As with imprisonment, fines are usually specified for any violation of the registration or reporting provisions. Only Kentucky, Maine, and Wisconsin distinguish between the offenses for which fines may be levied. Fines are invariably optional with the court in those states where imprisonment is also possible. In nine of these states, both fines *and* prison terms may be imposed at the court's discretion, while in the other seven it must be either one or the other.[129]

The laws typically declare that any person convicted of violating any of their provisions shall be punished by the specified fine and/or imprisonment. Nine states, however, distinguish between agent and employer and have separate scales of punishment for each, usually with respect to fines.[130] Kentucky is especially stringent with employers who fail to register or report for their legislative agents. They may be fined $1,000 for the first offense, $2,000 for the second, and $3,000 for the third. If the employer is a corporation, it may additionally face forfeiture of its charter, hardly a likely eventuality.[131] Maine's law also reserves special treatment for employers by providing that "any person, firm, or corporation who shall falsely enter upon the docket . . . the name or names of any person or firm as his or their legislative agent shall be punished by a fine of $100 and shall be answerable in damages to the person or firm whose name or names has been so falsely entered."[132] This unique provision bears witness to the opprobrium that has so long attached to the lobbyist's calling.

Connecticut, Nebraska, and New York add another financial penalty to the fines specified in their laws by requiring that for each day after the end of the postlegislative grace period that an agent or his employer does not comply with the reporting requirement, he shall forfeit $100 to the state. The operation of these provisions has not greatly enriched the treasuries of the three states; there is no record of a single day's penalty ever having been collected.

A final penalty, found in the acts of nine states,[133] prohibits convicted counsel or agents from acting as such for three years or, in the more specific language of the California law, from "attempting to influence, directly or indirectly, the passage or defeat of any proposed legislation or from appearing before a committee of the Legislature in support of or in opposition to proposed legislation."[134] The three-year prohibition is mandatory in the nine states that allow it, except in Kansas and Massachusetts, where it may be imposed as an alternative to fine or imprisonment, and Montana, where the period of prohibition can be shortened at the discretion of the secretary of state.

This is usually called a "disbarment" penalty, but the term seems misused. Although many lobbyists are lawyers, lobbying has neither the professional standing nor self-policing organization of the bar, and it should not be treated as if it did. Further, disbarment for an attorney is usually a permanent penalty and not a finite one as it is here, and it is imposed not by the state but by his professional peers. Forced withdrawal from lobbying for a period of time runs more closely parallel with the requirements of conflict-of-interest statutes, although the substantive lines of comparison obviously diverge.

The name of the penalty is, of course, less important than its appropriateness and legality, and both of these are open to question. As the nature of the offense argues against imprisonment as a penalty for violation of a disclosure law, so too should it argue against denying violators the right to earn their keep. That they can be denied it is, at best, problematical. Although the issue has not yet come squarely before a state constitutional court, it is difficult to quarrel with the recent conclusion of a California legislative committee that "although a number of states have such a provision, it is probably unconstitutional."[135]

Enforcement

The imposition of these penalties depends on the vigor with which the laws are enforced. Vigorous enforcement, in turn, rests more on the initiative of responsible officers than it does on the bare statutory obligation to prosecute violations. This would be true under any circumstances; it is doubly true when the enforcement provisions generally provide only a sketchy basis for official action. The usual statement is nothing more nor less than this: "It shall be the duty of the attorney-general, upon information, to bring prosecutions for the violation of the provisions of this chapter."[136] This formula, or a close variant of it, appears in the laws of thirteen states.[137] The other laws do not specifically lodge enforcement responsibility with any officer, although it can be assumed to fall upon the attorney-general and subordinate public prosecutors.

Whether this officer is specifically or implicitly charged with authority to enforce the law is less important than the question of whether its special purposes can best be served by vesting supervisory authority in him at all. The attorney-general is the chief legal officer of the state. The meaning of disclosure laws lies in their being something more than ordinary criminal statutes. When they operate as they should, they are instruments of enlightenment and not of restriction. They can ideally inject a critical element into the making of public policy: information about who wants what, and how badly.

Those persons and groups unwilling to submit to minimal public scrutiny liable themselves to the penalties that the law prescribes. But these penalties measure the law's failure rather than its success; when they must be meted out, the essential values of the law have been lost.

This is not to say that the penalties are inappropriate to willful violations (although some of them are), or that they should not be imposed whenever these occur. But to conceive of these laws in purely criminal terms and to vest their enforcement in officials whose primary concern is with criminal prosecution is to miss their central purpose. The aim of enforcement should be to make the laws work to the maximum of their possibilities, and this is a task that calls more for a missionary than for a public prosecutor. By this test, which is an ultimate one, the typical statutory arrangement can offer little.

It is, therefore, only partly true and essentially irrelevant to argue, as some observers have, that "the major flaw" in state lobbying laws is "the failure to designate some agency responsible for enforcement,"[138] or "the lack of adequate enforcement provisions."[139] These offhand strictures neglect the fact that a near-majority of laws specifically designate the attorney-general as enforcement agent; the same responsibility ultimately falls to him even where the law is silent, so long, at least, as the law prescribes penalties for violations. The hard question is not so much who should act, but what should be done, and toward what end. That is to say, agreement on purposes should precede and determine the choice of agents. If the purpose of disclosure is to induce conformity through criminal sanctions—and these observers' preoccupation with the rarity of prosecutions would suggest this as their preference—then the state attorney-general is as much the appropriate enforcement agent as he is for any other criminal statute, and the enforcement provisions are not only "adequate" but necessary. If, however, the purpose of disclosure is to promote a more responsible and enlightened policy-making process by means other than criminal prosecution, then the attorney-general should have only a secondary role. The latter alternative is by far the one to be preferred. The true symptom of inadequate enforcement is too little knowledge, and not too few prosecutions, and its origin is more basic than imperfect administrative arrangements.

The claims of theory notwithstanding, the attorney-general is usually the principal administrative actor, and only a small handful of laws deviate from this pattern in any material way. The Connecticut law, for example, merely makes it the duty of the secretary of state to "promptly notify the Attorney-General of any violation . . . of which he may have knowledge."[140] This provision has a surface practicality since it is the secretary of state with whom registrations and reports are filed. Actually, the only violations of which the secretary could have official knowledge would involve delinquent financial reports. It is, of course, important that these reports be filed, but they are ancillary to the major enforcement problem, which is the securing of initial compliance, i.e., registration. This is a task which neither an attorney-general nor a secretary of state is ordinarily equipped to perform. The Connecticut provision, therefore, offers only slight and mainly theoretical advantages. Requiring the secretary to notify the attorney-general of violations merely makes explicit what should be standard administrative practice.

Much the same reasoning applies to the Virginia enforcement section, which makes it the duty of the secretary of the commonwealth to "take appropriate steps for the prosecution of any person violating [the law's] provisions." Prosecution may also be had upon the complaint of the attorney-general or any member of the General Assembly.[141] One commentator writes, with more enthusiasm than accuracy, that these provisions make Virginia the one state to have "concrete provision for detection and enforcement."[142] One can concede the possible value of allowing complaints to be initiated by legislators, although none have been so initiated. Legislators are, after all, in a position to have specialized information about lobbying. But the provision could also be used as a weapon of harassment against selected persons or groups.[143] It affords no procedural safeguards against misuse, and it otherwise fails to put enforcement on a reasonably systematic or "concrete" basis.

The Virginia provision for notification by the secretary of the commonwealth is as redundant as its Connecticut counterpart. The secretary has neither the authority nor the personnel to mount serious investigations of registration compliance. Again, delinquency in financial reporting would be the only category of violation of which this officer might be expected to have official knowledge. The only "appropriate steps" he could take for their prosecution would be to notify the attorney-general of their existence, and this he has been reluctant to do.[144] As in Connecticut, the law itself only affirms what should be normal administrative procedure. Neither provision treats enforcement as a positive and continuous process.

While the Wisconsin law also departs from the usual pattern, the departure is more in specificity than in substantive approach. The law makes it the general duty of the state attorney-general to bring prosecutions for violations, and it also vests authority in the district attorney of Dane County, in which the state capital is located, to bring actions for the revocation of individual lobbyists' licenses. Although the provision has rendered useful service since its enactment in 1947,[145] it lays no basis for administrative persuasion. Official effort is negligible until prosecution is at hand.

If there is any unique approach to enforcement, it is to be found in the 1950 revision of the California law, and even here there is some question as to whether the enforcement arrangements were not primarily designed to foster more efficient investigation and prosecution. The Joint Interim Committee which was responsible for the 1950 revision expressed dissatisfaction with the usual enforcement procedure when it reported:

> The study of the committee [sic] has revealed that one of the prime weaknesses of all existing legislation is the lack of an adequate enforcement agency and the inability of ordinary enforcement agencies to cope with this particular kind of enforcement.

To this chronic complaint it added this constructive note:

> Legislation, therefore, should provide for an agency to enforce the act which would have enforcement powers. Since knowledge of the activities of lobbyists is peculiarly within the province of the Legislature itself, the enforcing agency should be composed of members from this branch of government.[146]

In line with this sensible approach, the committee recommended the establishment of a "board with adequate powers"—which were not stated—"to act as the enforcing agency." This board should consist of four members from the Assembly and four from the Senate, with absolute bipartisanship to obtain in their selection.[147]

Although the legislature refused to accept the joint board proposal, it did eventually provide that each house could establish appropriate committees with the duty and power to grant, revoke, or suspend certificates of registration; "to investigate or cause to be investigated the activities of any legislative advocate or of any person who they have reason to believe is or has been acting as a legislative advocate"; to recommend amendments to the law; and to report violations to the appropriate law enforcement officers.[148] If these provisions are literally somewhat weighted in the direction of efficient prosecution, there is in them the basis for a more positive approach to the administration of a disclosure system. Standing legislative committees, properly staffed and with sufficient funds, ought to be uniquely well-positioned to collate and disseminate information, do original research, submit reports and statutory recommendations, conduct hearings and informally stimulate compliance, and generally exercise competent supervision over the law's operation. These functions might be even better managed by a permanent joint legislative committee—a proposal which the legislature has regularly rejected.[149] Although the California committees have failed fully to exploit either their statutory authority or their own resources, their continued existence has, at very least, contributed to the relative success of the California law and has, at very most, been mainly responsible for it.

California's administrative arrangements easily surpass those of other states, and if they fall short of the ideal, they afford at least a distant glimpse of the necessary and the possible. They suggest no more than this: There is no guarantee—there may, indeed, be only small chance—that disclosure requirements alone, however well designed and run, can much contribute to the eventual development of a political process where responsibility has at least equal weight with responsiveness. Law which remains opaque to the special administrative needs of disclosure, however, is not likely to contribute at all. Among these needs, none is more important than the establishment of a proper balance between enforcement and other kinds of official effort. Perhaps the key to the distinction is that disclosure will be well enforced only when its literal enforcement has become unnecessary. The distribution of disclosed data is the only legitimate end—as it is the best measure—of the disclosure idea.

Lobbying and Ethical Standards

PROBLEMS

Although lobbying unavoidably involves ethical questions, American state legislatures have on the whole demonstrated remarkable adroitness in avoiding them, not only when they were writing disclosure laws (in large part because prevailing ethical norms had been breached) but more generally as well.[150]

There is no need to frame elaborate operating definitions. By "public ethics" we mean those explicit and implicit normative constraints imposed by the community, or in its name, on more-than-voting participants in the political process. These constraints may be expressed in constitutional, statutory, or common-law proscriptions, such as those that operate against bribery, fraud, intimidation, threat, libel, deceit, and the like. They may also be expressed in those impalpable but deeply rooted and widely shared conceptions of right and wrong that are part of what Truman has described as "the rules of the game."[151] As a system of government is a distinctive process of social accommodation, a system of public ethics reflects a society's distinctive mood and the barriers it tries to erect around the conduct of the public business. Lobbying or any other variety of interest politics (which is to say, politics itself) becomes an ethical problem when its chosen means is to level the barriers. One of the chief hallmarks of a democratic society is that it is especially concerned with keeping these barriers intact—and high. No democracy survives by merely functioning. That "the rules of the game" are observed counts every bit as much as its outcome. If democracy is processes, only some of them conform to the logic and values of a democratic order.

For most of the ethical questions that lobbying raises or is associated with, we have not yet begun to devise either intellectual or legal answers. Some of these questions relate to the internal relationships between group memberships and their political representatives, and they pose no less prickly dilemmas of public policy for their ostensibly private character. To what extent, for example, can or should memberships contribute to the formulation of group positions on legislative matters? Is the proper relationship between group leaders and group memberships one of simple agency, or one of virtual representation? What are the standards of propriety, who should apply them, and by what means? These are not rhetorical questions. When a representative of the state federation of labor (or medical society, or chamber of commerce) claims to represent the united opinion of x thousand workers (doctors, businessmen), is it the business of the legislature to inquire into the devices by which this alleged unanimity was developed or ascertained? Some observers have proposed that disclosure laws should require evidence of how "democratically" group policies have been determined, and while these proposals generally reflect a simplistic view of the operating characteristics of group bureaucracies, they nonetheless reflect an appropriate concern, although one that may be beyond the immediate ability of the legislature further to pursue.

The legislature may be more seriously concerned with the end results of group decision-making than with its mechanics. An essential part of the supporting rationale for lobbying is that the complexity of modern legislation creates insatiable demands for information—fact and opinion—which it is both the right and the responsibility of interested groups to provide. But what happens when group "facts" are arguable, and group "opinion" either overstated or contrived, a possibility nicely suggested in Schattschneider's "first rule of successful pressure politics: to make a noise like the clamor of millions but never permit an investigation of the claims."[152] To what extent is it the business of the legislature to inquire into the legitimacy of group claims? To what extent can or should the law require that these claims be "honest" and "honestly" asserted? Are mere assumptions of ethical self-restraint sufficient to assure the integrity of the data on which the legislative process feeds?

If these questions are not difficult enough, there are others that are much more difficult, that have wider ramifications, and that cannot be answered by exhortations to do good. These questions involve the relationships between public officials and interest groups, group representatives, and group interests. They are questions of ethics in the most fundamental sense, and the continued viability of our political system may depend in considerable part on the answers that we find for them. When, for example, should a minimally civilized morality require that interest groups or their representatives be prohibited from offering—and public officials from accepting—gifts, hospitality, or services? How much is too much? For Senator Paul Douglas, any gift worth more than $2.50 is beyond the pale, but would the judgment of a Douglas be swayed by gifts worth one-hundred times as much? And how many state legislators would be willing to impose such stern ordinances upon themselves?

With state legislative salaries and expense allowances as they are, the bind is particularly tight with respect to entertainment. Havard and Beth describe one Florida lobbyist who is "famous for merely sitting around hotel lobbies . . . and for buying the breakfasts of rural legislators who arise before 6:00 A.M." They also quote a Florida legislator as saying that he "never worries about meal expenses during sessions because try as he will he can never spend over a dollar a day on them—'somebody always picks up the check.' "[153] Few legislators in any state buy all their own meals and drinks, but is there any ethical distinction between the Florida legislator who allows a lobbyist to buy him dinner, and the Wisconsin legislator who ate three meals a day at the finest hotel in Madison and signed a lobbyist's name to the tab?

The sums involved are not always so trivial nor the contact so direct. In 1959, for example, an Ohio Grand Jury examined (and substantiated) charges that a registered lobbyist had paid a state senator's $140 hotel bill, without complaint by the latter. Now this was not illegal under Ohio law, nor was it apparently uncommon, but was it "ethical" on either side? And is there any real distinction between a lobbyist paying for a legislator's hotel room and paying a prostitute to visit him there?[154] Again, these are not rhetorical questions, for these things happen. How much is too much, and for what objects?

As the provision of various creature comforts for legislators shades almost imperceptibly into putting money in their hands, the question of amounts shades into one of circumstances. Outright offers of cash to vote or "take a walk" still come to light, as they did in Maryland in 1963 during a battle to ban slot machines in the state. Such offers raise no ethical problems only because they are illegal, and legislators predictably respond to them with "shock" and "amazement," although, as one weary (and unbought) Maryland delegate put it, "Money does not surprise, shock, or amaze me. But it scares me at times."[155] Harder questions are posed by payments that are not in terms illicit, but for which the donors' expectations of return are often justifiably large. What of cash contributions, for example, made by lobbyists or groups to legislators' election campaigns? This was a standard tactic of the slot machine interests in Maryland, and of other interests everywhere. Or, what of the employment of legislators by interest groups, particularly when the services involved are few or undefined? Some interests—railroads have been prominent examples—are so organized as to require at least nominal legal representation in every corner of the state, and the services of attorney-legislators are seldom unavailable. Other interests with business to conduct before state agencies—alcoholic beverage licensees, for example—often find advantages in the same kind of arrangement. It was no accident that Artie Samish erected his California empire on precisely this foundation. Here again, it was legal but was it "ethical" on either side? Despite all the ferment that it caused, the California legislature did not find against it.

The most elusive ethical questions of all flow from those situations in which public officials are—or are made to be—unable to keep their private preferences and interests at a sufficient distance from their public responsibilities, but without direct consideration having passed. This is what the Douglas subcommittee generically described as "involvement," and it takes many forms. While few of these are directly attributable to lobbying, few are far removed from it, for the creation of involvement is both a common means and intended end of all group political effort. The distinction between involvement resulting from lobbying and involvement having more "natural" origins is apt to be tenuous indeed. When we discover (as we cannot but discover) that legislators are not detached arbiters but committed advocates, is there any functional difference between commitments brought about by group effort and those that spring from the legislator's personal values, interests, and group memberships? Does the latter somehow have purer consequences than the former because it was not brought about by external "pressure"? Again, these are not rhetorical questions, nor are there easy answers for them.

Some of these involvements fall under the rubric of conflicts-of-interest. One variety is demonstrated in the recent observation by a responsible California observer that "at least one-half" of the members of the legislature hold stock in state-licensed savings and loan associations. Some members are also officers or directors of banks or savings and loan associations, and are on legislative committees on finance or taxation.[156] For most of these members, the only lobbying that had to be done was that which they performed on themselves. However it came to pass, they are in the happy but questionable position of regulating institutions of which they are owner-managers.

Every legislator carries into office with him a full set of group affiliations and personal interests—economic, occupational, educational, geographic, and the rest. He responds more to some group appeals than to others. But legislators may also take more active roles in behalf of interests with which they are involved. The majority leader of the New York Assembly recently came under attack for pushing Governor Rockefeller's mandatory shelter bill at the same time that he held interests in a company specializing in shelter construction.[157] Nor is the direction of interest-group tactics by legislators at all unique. Havard and Beth describe how the president of the Florida Senate was once reported to have told the chairman of the Board of the Florida Power and Light Company (of which the president was himself a director) to "leave Tallahassee because he was 'such a colorful and well-known figure that he was attracting much attention to the power company's bills' and thus harming the cause."[158] The use of public position to promote or protect private financial interests is not ordinarily this overt or well publicized, but it happens. What, if anything, can or should be done about it? Congress and a few state legislatures have self-disqualification rules, but they are uniformly honored in the breach. If legislators were firmly to withhold their votes on every issue that touched their own group memberships or financial interests, how could any American legislature ever muster a quorum?

A legislator or administrative official may also use his public position after he has left office. The registration dockets in every state are liberally dotted with the names of men who have served their apprenticeships in public office and are now engaged in the more profitable business of group representation before the legislature or administrative agencies. Beyond the surface advantage of access to the floor of the legislature, ordinarily extended as a courtesy to former members, such men possess the more important assets of inside experience and established personal relationships. Should or can they be debarred from putting them to work?

LEGAL REMEDIES

These are some—and only some—of the ethical problems that flow from, or are related to, lobbying in the states. These problems are real, and, because they involve public confidence in the integrity of representative institutions, they are urgent. But the gap between plain needs and attempted remedies is wide, deep, and apparently unbridgeable. No more than a small handful of legislatures have sought to give their disclosure statutes an added ethical dimension, and their efforts have on the whole been unrewarding.

Wisconsin's 1947 revision, most of which was also adopted by Montana twelve years later, was determinedly and self-consciously concerned with ethical standards, its stated purpose being "to promote a high standard of ethics in the practice of lobbying," and "to prevent unfair and unethical lobbying practices." The route to this attractive destination was to license lobbyists, and to provide for the revocation of their licenses for "unprofessional conduct," defined as follows:

> a) A violation of any of the provisions [of the title], or soliciting employment from any principal, or instigating the introduction of legislation for the purpose of obtaining employment in opposition thereto, or attempting to influence the vote of legislators on any measure pending or to be proposed by the promise of support or opposition at any future election, or by any other means than a full and fair argument on the merits thereof, or by making public any unsubstantiated charges of improper conduct on the part of any other lobbyist or of any legislator, or engaging in practices which reflect discredit on the practice of lobbying or the legislature.

A second paragraph, enacted in 1955, applied the same sanction to lobbyists:

> b) Directly or indirectly furnishing or being concerned in another's furnishing to the Governor, any legislator, or to any officer or employee of the state, to any candidate for state office or for

the legislature, any food, meal, lodging, beverage, transportation, money, campaign contribution or any other thing of pecuniary value. This paragraph does not apply to entertainment by a non-profit organization at a bona fide social function or meeting of such organization.[159]

As noted earlier, this anti-free-lunch section was wrung by Governor Nelson out of a reluctant legislature as a condition to his approval of legislative salary and expense increases. The governor's proposal that lobbyists report legislative entertainment and other services emerged as outright prohibition, however, and the legislature showed its spirit and fine impartiality by extending it to the governor as well. The section is both pompous and nonsensical, with an escape hatch —"a bona fide social meeting or function"—almost ludicrously wide. The prohibition of even indirect group campaign support comes close to being other-worldly. In any case, it has had no discernible effects on Wisconsin politics.[160]

Paragraph (a) deserves to be taken more seriously, but its many values do not quite offset its limp one-sidedness. Although the second clause, for example, relates primarily to the conditions of the hired agent's employment, it quite properly condemns a vicious racket which should be of wide concern. But who is the racketeer? The lobbyist peddling shoddy goods, or the legislator who gives him the goods to peddle? If the lobbyist is guilty of "unprofessional conduct," then the legislator is guilty of a far graver breach of trust. The third clause is no less one sided. The state may deem it necessary to deprive a group representative of his livelihood if he says "November" in a legislator's presence, but is it either fair or realistic to leave legislators free to accept a group's political endorsement (if not a "thing of pecuniary value") while the group should have no right to ask anything in return?

The next two clauses strike at malpractices that clearly affect the larger public, but in terms redundant of the common law of bribery and defamation. "Full and fair argument on the merits," and "unsubstantiated charges of improper conduct," when placed in a section labeled "Unprofessional Conduct," are given a glossier setting than they deserve. What seems advanced and an innovation consists only of new descriptions for acts that have long been otherwise proscribed. The clause forbidding "practices which reflect discredit on the practice of lobbying," is a vague catch-all that could mean whatever a court would allow, but it is consonant with the rest of the law, which seeks generally to dignify and regularize private access to the legislature. That this might be a worthy enterprise does not necessarily make it one to inspire confidence; hortatory declarations are seldom effective means of reordering complex human relationships. As for the prohibition of "practices which reflect discredit on . . . the legislature," it should probably be sufficient to observe that if American legislatures have been discredited, it is mainly because they have regularly demonstrated a truly remarkable and bipartisan talent for discrediting themselves. Legislative ethics have seldom been considered a fit subject for legislative inquiry or action.

Support for the point can be adduced from Michigan's experience. After an ugly scandal in 1944 had resulted in the imprisonment of seventeen legislators, their outraged colleagues solemnly prohibited the employment of legislators for "fees in excess of the reasonable value of such service if the same was performed by a person not a member of the legislature." Robert Allen calls the provision "a joke,"[161] but there are probably better words to describe it. The legislature's action did not compare favorably with the position taken by the Michigan Bar Association, which in a formal opinion given in July, 1944, declared that "a lawyer after election to the State Legislature, or while serving in that office, may not accept or continue retainer or employment from a client directly or indirectly interested in action by the State Legislature."[162] Since the question of unethical financial involvement usually, but not always, concerns lawyer-legislators, the Association's opinion was far-reaching, and it has to all appearances been fairly vigorously enforced by the Michigan Bar. That this kind of injunction should have to be enforced by a private professional body, however, is no credit to the Michigan legislature, or to its counterparts in other states that have been equally reluctant to protect their own integrity and reputations.

California, last of the states to have acted in this general area, did not follow Michigan in attempting to fix the fees that legislators might accept, but it did provide for the filing of statements setting forth the nature and terms of such employment. Although this approach is probably more realistic than efforts to set reasonable levels of compensation for services which may often be only vaguely defined, the requirement, as noted earlier, remains completely unobserved.[163]

In addition to this provision, the 1950 revision of the California law included a section entitled "Obligations of Legislative Advocates," violations of which are cause for revocation or suspension of registrants' licenses.[164] These standards, like those in the Wisconsin law, apply only to the registered lobbyist and fail thereby to meet the ethical marginalia for which the individual lobbyist cannot reasonably be held responsible. But while the focus of the two sections is similar, the substantive content of the California law is the more supple and perceptive of the two. The "legislative advocate" must, first of all, register, and he must retain for two years the books and other documents needed to substantiate his financial reports. Beyond these administrative requirements, the advocate is forbidden from causing the introduction of legislation for the purpose of "thereafter being employed to cause its defeat." The language is different; otherwise, this fine stricture is no improvement over its Wisconsin prototype. Both are much too selective in their ascriptions of guilt.

With this exception, the California "obligations" diverge considerably from Wisconsin's standards of "unprofessional conduct." The California "legislative advocate" must refrain from putting any legislator "under personal obligation to him or to his employer"; he must never "deceive" a legislator on "any material fact pertinent to any pending or proposed legislation"; he must not "encourage the activities of or have any business dealings relating to legislation or the Legislature" with any person whose registration as advocate has been suspended or revoked; he must "abstain from any attempt to create a fictitious appearance of public favor or disfavor of any legislative proposal"; he must not claim, truly or otherwise, to control legislators' votes; he must not solicit employment "except on the basis of his experience, or knowledge of the business or field of activity in which his proposed employer is engaged"; and he must not represent "an interest adverse to his employer."

The last two of these obligations again concern matters of primary interest to the parties involved, and the condemnation of claims of improper influence echoes earlier prohibitions; only the setting and the penalties are new. The remaining standards are novel, however, and they are addressed to problems of large relevance. If one is to cavil at them it must be on the grounds that they do not do their job as well as they might, nor on all of the right people. The first cavil relates once again to language; terms like "personal obligation," "deceive," "encourage," or "fictitious appearance of public favor" are simply as elusive as the wind. They may not be beyond definition, but they have not yet been defined. For this deficiency, the remedies of more precise statutory language and/or administrative construction are at least available, if unused; for the one-sidedness of these injunctions, for their easy focus on the obvious villains, there is no remedy short of several basic changes of emphasis.

This one-sidedness has two aspects. First, the legislator is tacitly absolved of all responsibility for whatever "personal obligation" to the lobbyist the law was intended to prevent. We do not argue that the legislator is invariably a venal reprobate waiting to be corrupted. At the same time, there is nothing to be gained by not being candid; no lobbyist can put a legislator under "personal obligation" unless the legislator is somehow willing so to be put, or somehow unable to avoid it. The origins of easy legislative virtue are many and complex, but it exists.[165]

Second, it is by now abundantly plain that the lobbyist is only the intermediate agent for misrepresentation of public favor, or for deceit, or for creating obligations, or for all the rest of that long and dreary catalogue of vices for which lobbying and lobbyists are often held responsible. These are no longer purely personal tactics; they are, rather, tactics of which the group the lobbyist represents is both principal instigator and ultimate beneficiary, and they should be so understood. The Artie Samishes of this world are not unmindful of a quick buck for themselves, but their greater glory is a satisfied client. This is no distinction without a difference, for the contrast between individual and group-oriented laws lies at the heart of the difficulties which beset disclosure in the states. The standards of conduct specified in the California law are desirable enough. The misfortune is that they are incomplete and wayward in their aim, particularly in the one state law that could otherwise be group oriented to a major extent.

PROSPECTS AND PERSPECTIVES

It may turn out that the complex ethical problems generated by a modern politics of interest cannot be resolved by legislative action alone, but it is also quite unlikely that they will or can be resolved without it. Why then have so few legislatures acted, and why have their efforts been so insufficient to the need?

Part of the explanation doubtless lies in the fact that there has been no sustained demand for the development of appropriate statutory remedies. Frequently, the enactment of a disclosure law has blunted the edge of public concern, and in some states this has been precisely its intended consequence. This edge, moreover, rarely needs much blunting. Although there is obviously some diversity in "the public's" ethical preferences, it would probably not be too far from the mark to characterize them generally as spasmodic, uninformed, and weary. They are spasmodic in the sense that they are likely to take shape only in the face of revealed wrongdoing by lobbyists or legislators, if at all. They are uninformed in the sense that there is simply no persuasive evidence that the meaning and extent of lobbying are widely understood, and some that suggests that the contrary is probably true. And they are weary in the sense that a numbing surfeit of wrongdoing has already been revealed. In the atmosphere that surrounds most state legislatures, there are ethical grotesqueries enough for a hundred revelations, but such things have lost some of their ability to shock because they have too long been unaccompanied by legislative action that appears to guard against recurrence. What capacity for public outrage we have left tends to spend itself in banishments of evil men. Americans no longer clamor for institutional reform.

If there is apparently little public understanding of how far and how often lobbying and related activities may breach accepted ethical norms, and no widespread demand for stern preventive measures, the fault cannot be laid to public apathy alone. Part of it should also be assessed against a press that has been generally alert to public scandal, but has not ordinarily been interested in much less. The real configurations and mood of the legislative system, and the ethical strains involved in what we take to be its normal operation, are difficult to describe. Few capitol reporters do not understand them, however, and fewer still do not stifle their knowledge and their instincts and write of blander things. One reporter with a statewide reputation for probity and fairness once told the writer that the legislature in his state had "the moral tone of an abattoir" and described an assemblyman-turned-lobbyist as "a perfect swine who has never had so much as a parking ticket." But few hints of what he knew and felt deeply seeped into his columns. To the question "Why not?" his answer was an infinitely expressive shrug. If few things rouse us any more, it may well be because the press feels helpless to try.

Legislators' attitudes toward the ethical problems that surround or affect them are complex and diverse, but there are a few common threads. We need not concern ourselves with those legislators—and there are still a few—who are zestfully and cynically "on the take"; such men are not interested in ethical niceties but only in avoiding detection. More difficult to deal with are the many technically honest but overinvolved legislators who simply do not see any serious problems short of outright corruption in the assertion of group claims. The lives, the careers, and the interests of these men are too deeply interwoven into the group process to allow them the luxury of moralistic perspective. These men are inclined to be indifferent to philosophical arguments about their function as legislators, and to regard disclosure laws as burdensome and meddling. They do not see themselves as *de facto* representatives of group interests, but they believe in any case that these interests have a legitimate right not only to be heard but to be heard effectively, and from the inside. And if they are suspicious of disclosure laws for lobbyists, they are actively hostile to the application of the same principle to themselves. They similarly recognize no serious need for stringent conflict-of-interest requirements, for they may not recognize that conflicts-of-interest exist. As one of the shrewdest—and most moral—of Washington columnists wrote of the late Senator Kerr of Oklahoma, "More than any other man he symbolized the corrupting legislative conflict-of-interest which honeycombs Congress and is so taken for granted that a man like Kerr never even recognized it."[166] Kerr was a titan playing for grand stakes on a national stage, but his approach to legislation has unacknowledged adherents in every state legislature in the country.

Every legislature also has its members who are more than technically honest, who are deeply troubled by the morass that swirls around them, and who are outnumbered by those who aren't. Although such members typically generate or channel what little demand there is for lobbying and conflict-of-interest laws, it is the

Kerrs who write—or more commonly, fail to write—them. Recent events in California demonstrate the point. Despite an Interim Committee warning in late 1962 that new conflict-of-interest laws were urgently needed to maintain "public confidence," the legislature quietly buried a series of remedial bills in 1963. Speaker Unruh admitted that something needed to be done. His suggestion: a blue-ribbon commission to hear special cases and "give advice" to legislators involved in conflict-of-interest complications.[167] This was, at least, some improvement on the Minnesota statute of 1961 which proposed to deal with such complications by, in effect, exhorting legislators to avoid them, as of course they should.[168]

If the state legislatures have been too close to the group political process to either recognize or deal squarely with the ethical problems that it generates, political scientists have in the main been too distant and dispassionate to supply the deficiency,[169] or have sought to supply it by prescribing standard remedies without hard inquiry into the nature of the malady or the specificity and prospects of the cure. A few straight thinkers, on the other hand, have become so disenchanted with the remedies that they end by questioning the existence of the malady.[170]

These separate moods have several common origins. The growth of a self-consciously behavioral approach to the study of politics has been one of the most important of them, for it has plainly discouraged systematic concern with ethical values except as they can be identified and described as behavioral variables.[171] This approach may also make a virtue of the otherwise disabling fact that few political scientists have any real "feel" for the American legislative environment. What passes for detachment is too often only insensitivity.

This is not to say that political scientists are morally insensitive; most of the remedies in the political scientist's kit—the disclosure idea, structural reform, renovation of the party system, heroic leadership, and all the rest—look toward the essentially moral end of a responsible political process. It is to say, rather, that political scientists are ordinarily ashamed to moralize in public. Confronted with the grossest evidence of moral rot in public life, their inclination is to find politics no more aberrant than other social systems, to peddle their nostrums without regard for the enormous practical impediments that stand in the way of their adoption, and to wonder privately why men are not all angels.

.   .   .

Rough assessments such as these run the obvious risk of being called "impressionistic," but unless they are entirely off-target they may be of some help in accounting for the reluctance of state legislatures to define, punish, or prevent departures from "ethical" lobbying practices, and of other political participants and observers to demand more vocally that they should. They may also suggest how difficult this would be under the best of circumstances. Lobbying ethics are not strictly separable from legislative ethics or public ethics, for lobbying is not an isolated phenomenon; it cannot be understood apart from the larger political system that surrounds and supports it, nor is it likely to be remade in a purer image short of a renaissance beyond our present ability to conceive.

Summary Comments

What kind of balance should be struck on the textual aspects of state lobbying laws? On the positive side, these laws are relatively compact, no more complex than their subject, and no more archaic than their nineteenth-century origins. But the debits are both more numerous and more important. These laws lack precision, scope, and clear direction. They reach only individual lobbyists in an era of group politics. They reach only legislative lobbying in an era of expanding administrative power. They reach only personal confrontation in an era of indirect political persuasion. They contribute little to the erection of safeguards adequate to the scale and variety of modern political temptation. They are over-modest in their requirements, aimed at the wrong targets, and unequipped to serve their own unstated purpose, which is simply to inform. Although these laws should touch the heart of our collective experience, they operate, in Truman's description, "well out on the periphery of the political process."[172] This is a result of more than deficient laws alone, but it would not have been so had the laws not been what they are.

These deficiencies are not irremediable, although there is no widespread clamor to correct them. Indeed, the germinal disclosure idea represents an approach to the central problem of government that should be worth every effort to conserve. This problem is, as it has always been, to hold private interest at an optimum distance from the exercise of governmental power. If regulation of lobbying helps to define this distance, and to maintain it, then it will have fully justified itself.

Chapter 4

DISCLOSURE IN OPERATION

From a legalistic point of view, adverse judgment of state disclosure laws would have much evidence in its support. These are not finely chiseled statutes. No legislature has ever done all that it might have done when it wrote a disclosure law, nor is it likely that any legislature ever will. In an area so congested with political conflict, the remarkable thing is not that these laws are as bad (or as good) as they are, but that they get written at all.

The common tendency to regard state regulation of lobbying as primarily a statutory problem, of which the obvious solution is "better" statutes, has been both cause and consequence of a general reluctance in the literature to examine either the special origins and ritual character of state disclosure laws, or the massive impediments that the legislative system erects in the way of their operation and improvement.[1] It is not difficult to conclude that these laws in many cases do not conform to the niceties of statutory draftsmanship, but they cannot be understood from this perspective alone. Our concern should be no less with the operation of the law than with its language. Where, in sum, does state regulation of lobbying fit into the political process, and what does it accomplish there?

Data that might throw useful light on these questions are becoming somewhat more accessible. Comparative studies[2] and state political profiles[3] are more numerous and provocative than they were a generation ago, and some of these have marshalled evidence or suggested hypotheses of obvious relevance for an assessment of state regulation of lobbying. We still fall short of having all the raw materials that we might like to have. Ideally, these would include comparably exhaustive political studies of each state, studies that would grapple honestly with the hard questions: Who rules? By what means? To what ends? If this agenda covers most of the spectrum of political inquiry, it does so because disclosure systems are components as well as indices of more inclusive political systems. Disclosure laws work "well" or "badly" only with respect to the larger settings against which they operate.

In what follows, our concern is with disclosure laws at work. How well are they complied with, and by whom? What kinds of data does compliance produce, whom does it reach, and by what means? Does disclosure achieve its purposes, and are these realistic or sufficient to the need? Where, if any place, do we go from here? In attempting to answer these questions, we will draw on the available literature; on official commentaries and investigative reports; on the raw and processed data that the operation of the laws provides; and on interviews, correspondence, personal observation, and speculation. If after seventy years the evidence is still imperfect, it is more than time enough to assess such of it as is presently at hand.

Registration: Lobbyists' Census

The most palpable—and in many ways the least satisfying—kind of data coming out of the operation of state disclosure laws are the registration figures. As table 1 shows, we know how many individuals or groups have registered or been registered as lobbyists in given states in given years, but these figures do not mean much by themselves. They may, in fact, be positively misleading. It requires no survey research team, for example, to verify that the "0" after Georgia does not honestly reflect the number of working lobbyists in that sovereign state. What this figure really means is that an undetermined number of them neither saw, nor were persuaded to see, any reason to pay the $250 fee that the law exacts of those who would comply with it.[4]

Caution is also in order when comparing one state's registration figures with another's. Massachusetts and Virginia, for example, have registration provisions of almost identical applicability, and to all appearances the laws are reasonably well observed in both states, yet the Massachusetts registration total is regularly on the order of three times as large as Virginia's. Why do such states as California, Wisconsin, North Dakota, Indiana, and Kansas have relatively so many registered lobbyists and such states as Mississippi, the Carolinas, Virginia, Vermont, and New Hampshire have relatively so few?

TABLE 1
LOBBYIST REGISTRATIONS

State	Year	No. of registrants	Employers represented
Alaska	1960	71	90
	1961	58	69
	1962	58	53
California	1959-60	563	479
	1961-62	534	434
Connecticut	1959	371	288
	1961	369	290
Georgia	1961	0	0
Indiana	1961	300*	150*
Kansas	1959	384a	—
	1961	412b	—
Kentucky	1960	100*	75*
	1962	93	79
Maine	1961	131	216
Maryland	1959	232	—
	1961	247	—
Massachusetts	1957	307	—
	1958	292	—
Michigan	1961	240	239
	1962	221	223
Mississippi	1961	74	—
Montana	1961	208	199
New Hampshire	1960	70	—
	1962	88	—
New York	1961	140	148
	1962	129	134
North Carolina	1959	132	—
	1961	124	—
North Dakota	1961	280	—
Ohio	1959-60	387	—
	1961-62	348	218
South Carolina	1957c	23	—
South Dakota	1961	91	138
Rhode Island	1962	100	—
Vermont	1959	64	89
	1961	69	123
Virginia	1962	104	120
Wisconsin	1959-60	284	413
	1961-62	242	348

* Figures are estimates by responsible state officials.
a Consists of 260 agents and 124 counsel.
b Consists of 286 agents and 126 counsel.
c The figure is from Zeller, Belle, "Regulation of Pressure Groups and Lobbyists," *Annals*, vol. 319 (September, 1958), p. 95.

Of the many factors that could account for these disparities, differences in the requirements and administration of the laws are probably the least important. As the former are, with few exceptions, quite comparable, so too have official efforts at construction or enforcement tended towards a placid uniformity. If analysis begins, rather, with the provisional assumption that those subject to fair readings of the similar registration requirements generally comply with them, the registration data can serve as rough but useful measures of the level of group political activity in each state. Registration varies from state to state less because the laws are different or differently enforced than because group political systems vary from state to state. Although there are the usual exceptions—New York, for example— the registration figures usually run highest in the large, populous, ethnically and economically diverse industrial states such as California, Connecticut, Massachusetts, Michigan, and Ohio. It should be unnecessary to observe that social density and economic differentiation generate political interest groups.

Of a different order and more difficult to assess are the relationships between the size and functioning of each state's group system and the operating characteristics of the more "official" political institutions. Do the forms and prevalence of interest group action vary with changing conditions of party balance and control, and do the registration data reflect the variation? At first glance, it might appear that they do; in no southern state, for example, is registration as heavy as it is in most of the northeast and north-central states. But what is the significant variable here: one-party politics or basic differences in sectional economic development? And what is "one-party politics"? As Key and others have shown, many of the southern states are one-party in only the most nominal sense, with fluid factional warfare more than compensating for the absence of party opposition.[5] More recently, Jewell has demonstrated that a number of presumably two-party states have had long stretches of one-party dominance over both houses of the legislature;[6] and in some of these— Wisconsin, Ohio, Michigan, and Indiana, for example—registration has been relatively heavy.

If literal one-party dominance does not much help to explain differences in registration, the notion of *effective* control may be more useful. Where there is well-established party of factional control over legislative processes and agenda, the party or factional leaders become the major foci of group efforts to make themselves heard. Lobbying of the conventional variety with individual legislators—and this is the kind that disclosure laws are best equipped to reveal—tends to be relatively less prevalent. The existence of a disciplined and dependably large legislative majority may eventually have a dampening effect on the very process of group formation, as it appears to have had in New York; normally, however, it operates not so much to stifle groups as to present them with what Truman calls "stable and orderly channels of access."[7] One might also add that such channels are often narrow and publicly undefined, and that capriciousness and irresponsibility can be high prices to pay for order and stability.

Virginia illustrates rather well some of the effects that firm legislative control can have on group tactics, and consequently on lobbyist registrations under a disclosure law. Here is a relatively large and complex state with rapidly developing economic diversity, yet the pattern of legislative politics is quietly premodern. Since the basic accommodations are made outside of the legislature, much of the observable interest group activity in Richmond has a curiously *pro forma* quality to it. The main functions of many group representatives appear to be to remind backsliders of their obligations, and to keep an eye on other interests. Some groups, whose counterparts in other states work through their own permanent officers or employees, make their cases in Virginia through one of a dozen or so well-placed insiders—typically Richmond attorneys and/or former legislators or state officials—who know where the decision-making centers of Virginia government are, how to get there, and what to do when they arrive. Other groups with significant legislative interests have been deterred from going to Richmond by the belief that it would avail them nothing. Under the circumstances, consistently low registration figures come as no surprise.

At the other extreme are those states where politics is played free style. Here, conditions of dispersed or ineffective party or gubernatorial control of the legislature conduce to every-man-for-himself group efforts to reach and persuade individual legislators. The dispersion may be chronic, as it appears to be in California, or it may follow the accession of a new and relatively inexperienced legislative majority, as it did in Massachusetts after 1948. In such states as Connecticut, Illinois, Indiana, Iowa, Kansas, New Mexico, New Jersey, Ohio, Wisconsin, and Wyoming, the electorate's occasional recent penchant for mixing Democratic governors with Republican legislatures has tended to create "channels of access" more numerous than orderly. The origins and character of dispersed legislative control are somewhat different in each of these states, but its common consequence has been to enhance the values of direct legislative lobbying of the traditional variety, and eventually to increase lobbyist registrations in those states that require it. There is more lobbying where there is more need for it, and more lobbyists register to do it.

As for the effect on registration of such intangibles as the "tone" of a state's government or "citizen awareness" (whatever this means), one estimate is as good as another, and none of them is worth very much. One writer has ascribed the substantial registration in Wisconsin to the "generally high plane" of the state's government,[8] but quite a few states have achieved high registration figures without anything like the official attention that has been given to the Wisconsin law, and with governments that are, by the most tolerant standards, something less than "high plane." Without otherwise derogating the importance of these kinds of factors on the operation of a disclosure law, the most that can be said for them is that they are of incommensurable effect.

COMPLIANCE

The summary data on registration are only roughly comparable from one state to another. Each of the figures in table 1 is the product of a unique mix of variables, and the differences between them do not necessarily—or often—mean that one state's law is working better than another's. The more appropriate test of how well disclosure laws work is internal, i.e., do those who should comply with them generally do so? This is a test not easily applied; no one can estimate with complete precision how many persons are properly subject to a fair reading of any state's law, nor is there usually complete agreement as to precisely what this reading would require.

For all these obvious difficulties, the testimony of state officials, journalists, scholars, and lobbyists combines with personal observation to support the conclusion that compliance in most states is generally quite complete. The picture drawn by the responsible state officials, usually the secretaries of state, tends to be especially sunny. One secretary writes:

> I have reason to believe and do believe that there is 100% compliance with the law.[9]

Few officials are quite this sanguine, but their observations are usually on the plus side, although some add the small caveat of imperfect knowledge. A Michigan official observes:

> To the best of my knowledge, compliance with the act has been very good and the legislature has been quite insistent that lobbyists be registered and carry their cards when appearing in behalf of any particular piece of legislation.[10]

From South Dakota the reply is:

> We believe the law is quite effective and there is general compliance.[11]

And from New Hampshire:

> We feel the law is generally complied with and during the session the list is frequently referred to by members of the legislature or other interested parties to ascertain who employs the various lobbyists.[12]

From Vermont comes this appraisal:

> Relative to the matter of compliance with the law, I believe that practically every person who engages in lobbying registers under this law, but, of course, this office has no way of knowing that to be a fact.[13]

A Kentucky official states:

> We believe the legislation relating to lobbyists has been effective. Insofar as we know, the law has been fully complied with.[14]

Iowa registers its lobbyists under legislative rule rather than by statute, but the official view is no less optimistic:

> I might say to you that the lobbyists here in Iowa have been complying with this requirement I think to about 100%, many of them of course in a more or less facetious manner.[15]

If this is all too good (or facetious) to be true, it might be worth noting that secretaries of state are usually somewhat withdrawn from the tug and clash of legislative politics, and like most other officials are perhaps not entirely disinterested in defending their own works. And if they do not always know how well the laws they manage are being observed, it is not impossible that they sometimes take affirmative action not to know. Despite the obviously self-serving quality of these official appraisals, however, there is substantial external evidence in their support; if compliance is never "100%," it is commonly not much less.

Proof of the point is necessarily inferential. The rarity of prosecutions is, unfortunately, irrelevant, since it is almost wholly a function of the reluctance of prosecutors to prosecute and not of the prevalence of violations. More in point are the relative infrequency and negligible results of either serious charges of noncompliance, or major official efforts to anticipate or respond to them. That such diversions occur rarely and achieve little suggests that there is little for them to achieve in terms of improved compliance alone. Ohio's 1949 experience is in most respects typical. Following newspaper allegations of unregistered lobbying and the failure of the legislature to authorize its own investigation, Secretary of State Sweeney began a drive to bring what he called "sneak lobbyists" into the fold. It had been brought to his attention, he declared, that:

> . . . a number of individuals are lobbying at the current sessions who have not complied with the law. Unless they register and pay the $3 required by law, I will be obliged to ask the Attorney General to prosecute them for violation of the law.[16]

Although registration improved thereafter, the increase was only on the order of 10 per cent over the previous session.[17] There were no prosecutions, nor have Mr. Sweeney's successors emulated his efforts. The major subsequent concern with lobbyists in Ohio has centered on the more fundamental question of their financial relationships with members of the legislature.[18] Registration has continued to increase.

A similar flurry of interest in noncompliance was triggered in Indiana in 1949 by the appearance of a story in the *Indianapolis Star* alleging that "the record . . . disclosed that scores of illegal unregistered lobbyists are working the 86th Assembly." The *Star* did not say what "record" it had been reading; it pointed only to "the powerful county officials' lobby" which, although it was working prominently for the passage of what the *Star* called "salary grab" bills, had no lobbyists registered in its behalf.[19] This left scores-minus-one of non-registrants to be accounted for; the *Star* went no further in its accounting, however, and no corroborating investigation or other official action was undertaken.

Two years later, a front-page story in the *Indianapolis Times* scored the secretary of the Indiana Motor Truck Association for failing to register as he had in 1949. This gentleman's reply was nothing if not revealing:

> Two years ago, all the other lobbyists gave me a ribbing for registering. They said it wasn't necessary because there is a provision in the lobbyist law which says you must receive extra money for lobbying. Well, I don't get anything extra for coming over here. And I don't see why I should register. Maybe I should register. I don't know.[20]

Although the story strongly implied that many other lobbyists persistently failed to register, the *Times* adduced no evidence to this effect. One writer has guessed that if the law were "strictly construed and abided by, the number of registered lobbyists would be trebled," but he too offered no supporting details.[21] The estimate seems high. The present writer is inclined to believe that the great majority of those subject to the minimal requirements of the Indiana law comply with it, if only for the reason suggested to him by a thoughtful legislator: "They crave recognition." In Indiana as in most other states, the case for massive noncompliance is more easily asserted than proved.

Charges of registration noncompliance are sometimes aired as afterthoughts to more generalized or politically motivated outbreaks of lobby-busting. Typical of the latter was the statement by Governor Scott of North Carolina in 1949 that "the Third House is so strong that many sincere lobbyists are confused." The governor was aroused by legislative opposition to his program, which he believed was inspired by a cabal of four old-time lobbyists with "dozens of irons in the legislative fire." In its front-page coverage of the story, the *Raleigh News and Observer*, which played an important part in the adoption of the North Carolina disclosure law in 1933 and has followed it closely ever since, noted that "generally, lobbyists make a point of conforming with the law in the matter of registration."[22]

The next day, in another front-page story, the *News and Observer* found that the governor's attack had left most lobbyists "a little pleased by their newly won recognition." One of the four old pros named by the governor was quoted as saying, "Hell, it doesn't bother me." The story also declared that although eighty-six lobbyists had registered, there were "many others believed unregistered."[23] There were no specifications to charge, but they could have readily been made. Close observers of the legislative scene pointed out that educational, liquor, dog- and horse-racing groups, and a number of substantial trade associations had been active during the session but had not registered their representatives. These same observers agreed, however, that compliance was otherwise reasonably complete, if unenthusiastic. One registrant guessed that "at least ninety percent" of the professional lobbyists complied. His own motives were probably quite common: no great attachment to the disclosure idea, but a very great reluctance to risk the *News and Observer's* unquenchable curiosity.[24] Counterpart situations exist in several other states having comparably alert and aggressive capitol papers.

The events leading to the forced resignation of Wes Roberts as Republican National Committee Chairman in 1953 further underscore the view that charges of noncompliance with state registration laws can be used as tactical weapons. Largely as an outgrowth of factional infighting in Kansas, Roberts, a resident of the state, was accused of having received some $11,000 from the Ancient Order of United Workmen two years earlier for unregistered lobbying before the Kansas Legislature regarding state purchase of buildings owned by the Order. When a special committee of the legislature found unanimously that he had "deliberately and intentionally frustrated" the spirit and intent of the Kansas registration law—the committee was less sure that he had violated its letter—Roberts' position became untenable and he resigned it with the usual attitude of injured innocence, and the usual reciprocal expressions of regret.[25]

It is worth at least passing note that no other unregistered lobbyists were cast up in the wash of Mr. Roberts' travail. Registration in Kansas has increased steadily since 1953, but neither the Roberts case, nor official efforts, nor press concern appear to have contributed as much to the increase as the changing character of group and legislative interests. This applies with equal force to the handful of other states where registration noncompliance has emerged from time to time as either a main or secondary issue. The net is rarely cast wide, or with great vigor. The targets are usually carefully selected, and the effects on general compliance are usually slight.

Generally similar conclusions are also indicated for those states where the operation of the law has never seriously been in question. There are in *every* state a few obvious nonregistrants who could in all likelihood be successfully prosecuted for noncompliance.[26] In a few states—Georgia is the most obvious example—these cases assume majority proportions. But the impression remains strong that in most states compliance is at reasonably high levels. Given the nature of the requirements and the hostile torpor which commonly envelops their operation, registration works better than we have any right to expect. This is not to say that the laws reach as far as they might, or in the right direction, but only that those coming within reasonable readings of their registration requirements do, in general, comply with them.

Certainly the present picture is shades brighter than the gloomy canvases that were being painted twenty-five and thirty years ago. A few states, notably Massachusetts and Wisconsin, were regularly singled out for praise for the operation of their laws; most of the others were dismissed as ineffective.[27] Pollock wrote of lackluster results in Ohio, where there was supposedly a "good" law.[28] Zink found that of the 100 or more groups active during the 1937 legislative session in Indiana, only 47 were represented by registered lobbyists.[29] Other observers found little to applaud in the operation of the New York law,[30] or the registration rule of the California Legislature.[31]

That substantial improvement has occurred is plainly attested by the registration totals. Ohio's docket had 348 entries in 1962 as against 112 in 1937. Massachusetts has more than doubled its registration since 1943, as has California.[32] The Indiana, Kansas, Maryland, and North Dakota totals have all more than doubled in the past decade, and several other states have also shown marked increases. There are states, mainly in the deep South, where noncompliance remains a problem. In Georgia, for example, there have been no registrations since 1941, and only 31 since the $250 registration tax was enacted in 1927.[33] There are other states—Maine, Vermont, Virginia, North Carolina, Kentucky—where stable registration totals over the years reflect relatively stable political arrangements. But the central tendency has been in the direction of growing registration. This reflects the quickened pace of group formation and political involvement, the growing scale and urgency of state governmental problems, changing party balances, the disintegration of state political machines, and the general relaxation of legislative discipline and commitment. To some degree it also reflects the institutionalization of disclosure; that is to say, an established registration requirement is increasingly one that the great bulk of groups and/or their representatives are willing—if only reluctantly—to meet. If registration achieves little, it is for reasons more basic and difficult to cure than mere mechanical noncompliance with the law.

WHAT REGISTRATION TELLS

Within the limits of the law's language and its common conception of lobbying as a persuasive direct relationship between legislators and paid agents, registration develops at least a latent image of the persuaders. Does it develop anything more? Was it intended to?

A lot hinges here on what one believes to be the purpose of statutory disclosure. If the purpose is limited, then the latent image provided by reasonably complete compliance is enough. This view is demonstrated in the comment made by one secretary of state:

> I have reason to believe and do believe that there is 100% compliance, and that such compliance carries out to the full the purpose for which the law was enacted, namely, to identify principal and counsel.[34]

The argument is crisp; if it construes the ultimate purpose and possibilities of disclosure too narrowly, it does so because the law admits best of this kind of construction. The law "works" in the sense that it does what it was minimally meant to do: identify paid agents and their employers.

In this sense, the registration requirements commonly fail in only minor respects, and the failures are less of identification than of descriptive detail. The typical law requires that the registration include the name, address, and occupation of the employee; the name, address, and business of the employer; the date and duration of the employment; and, in the words of the Ohio statute, "the exact subject-matter pending or that might legally come before the General Assembly or either house thereof or before any committee thereof with respect to which such person, firm, corporation, or association is employed."[35] In Ohio and elsewhere, registrants usually list as the subject matter of their employment "any matter of interest to employer," or "any legislation that might affect property owners," or "legislation pertaining to labor," or some other equally ambiguous variant. One Ohio lobbyist has solemnly declared that he was employed in "matters pertaining to specific legislation." The California representative of the American Hypnotists Association similarly stated in 1961 that the legislation he was employed to support or oppose was "Support and Oppose," later amended to the no less cryptic "Hypnotic Legislation" (of which, in all justice, the California Legislature passes no more than its fair share). In Kentucky, where registrants are asked to state separately the legislation they are hired to support and the legislation they are hired to oppose, one finds such illuminating entries as "Favor—Health Legislation; Oppose—Anti-Health Legislation" (whatever that might be). The legislative representative of the *Louisville Courier-Journal* once proudly attested that he was for "equitable legislation" and against "inequitable legislation."

In most states, only a handful of registrants disclose their legislative interests with any precision. During typical recent sessions, 4 of 119 North Carolina registrants specified the numbers or titles of bills in which they were interested. In Wisconsin, 17 of 239 gave this kind of detail, as did 2 of 178 in Indiana, and 15 of 276 in Ohio. Six of 84 Virginia registrants and 2 of 86 in Kentucky cited bill numbers or titles, while 13 of 95 in South Dakota gave this or other reasonably specific descriptions of their areas of interest.

The language of the requirements in part accounts for the response. The usual statement is only that the "subject matter of the employment" be divulged, and, although there has been no litigation on the point, it is unlikely that courts would construe this to require great detail. This assumption is reinforced by the fact that vague docket entries have been the rule in Massachusetts since the state attorney-general held that the requirement was satisfied by an entry stating that the lobbyist was employed "on all matters of interest to employers."[36] Registrants in other states have reached the same conclusion by themselves.

If this kind of disclosure is not revealing, it is at least understandable. Registration is usually required before any lobbying services are performed. Since the majority of registrants in most states comply during the first week or two of the legislative session, they may be unable to state their legislative interests specifically. For the many agents, especially those representing well-established groups, whose main functions as capitol watchdogs are to look for statutory jokers, keep an eye on less well-positioned competitors, and generally oil squeak-points as they develop, the subject matter of employment is quite literally "all matters of interest to employer"; there may at the time of registration simply be no details to describe.[37]

But then again there may be, in which event the Maryland approach has much to recommend it. Although the law itself requires only the usual disclosure of the "special subject or subjects of legislation" with respect to which they are employed, the registration form instructs registrants to "give the full and exact title of each measure." During recent sessions, approximately half of the registrations have referred to bill numbers or titles. If abstract descriptions of legislative interest are a serious problem, Maryland's experience suggests that simple and sufficient administrative means are available to meet it.

Registration, then, identifies agent and principal; on its face it does not reveal much more. The requirement that the duration of the agent's employment be disclosed usually harvests two kinds of response: "indefinite," or "for legislative session," neither of which much advances our knowledge. The requirement that the date of employment be disclosed, on the other hand, yields answers ranging from "today" to "thirty-five or forty years ago," with considerably more tending toward the latter pole than toward the former. The registration rolls in every state are dotted with the names of men whose capitol experience reaches back to the Wilson era. Until quite recently, the seniority record probably belonged to the Kentucky registrant who began working the legislature for Southern Bell Telephone and Telegraph in 1907. The case is only slightly extreme. For longer than we realize, there has been a general and marked disparity in experience between members of the first two houses and the group officials, attorneys, publicists, research personnel, and contact artists who make up the third. These gentlemen are numerous, they are skilled, and they stay put. Most of the textbook shibboleths are true; tenure and talent in the state legislatures are such that the hypothetical "average" member is typically outnumbered, outpaid, and outlived by the lobbyists—and in qualitative terms he may also be outclassed. Implicit support for this view is one of the unattended consequences of registration.[38]

As registration serves mainly to identify principal and agent, it affords only a shaky foundation for more general speculation about the sources and structure of group political activity. Among other things, registration may be a most inaccurate measure of the relative power of competing groups; a large number of registered lobbyists may actually reflect the weakness of a group's position rather than its strength. In Indiana, for example, 74 of 178 individual registrants in 1949 represented various labor organizations, thereby giving rise to excited newspaper essays about the "swarm of CIO lobbyists," an "army of propaganda agents," and the "largest and most extensive so-called pressure group ever registered in Indiana legislative history."[39]

If the figures didn't lie, they could have been interpreted quite differently. Legislators of both parties agreed that labor interests were not then (nor are they now) dominant in Indiana politics. Given the usual rural-business domination of the legislature, labor's outgroup status, and the frequent concern of labor groups with legislation that would have changed the status quo, massive labor lobbying activity was less a matter of self-conscious muscle-flexing than a competitive necessity. The institutional sluggishness which Truman has aptly labelled "the defensive advantage" is rarely swept away by the most energetic group exertions.[40] A "swarm" of lobbyists is seldom the working equivalent of one sympathetic committee chairman.

Nor did labor speak with one voice. The seventy-four lobbyists represented twenty-five different and, in part, antagonistic organizations. The depth and bitterness of some of these cleavages not only had a dispersive effect on the total effort, but also required determined leadership to keep memberships intact and satisfied. In several cases, unnecessary compliance with the registration law was deliberately used as a means of demonstrating to the members that they were getting something for their money.[41]

Labor organizations and their representatives are generally scrupulous in their compliance with state registration laws, and for reasons other than internal necessity. In Indiana, as elsewhere, such groups usually face a hostile press, ready to damn them as a "super-lobby" if they comply with the law, and an "illegal lobby" if they do not. Of the two alternatives, the first is not the best but only the least unattractive.[42]

Registration dockets, then, may give distorted impressions of group strength, or of the real constellation of forces that converge on the legislature. Although these dockets overstate the significance of labor groups in many states, they understate it in others (as appears to be the case in Michigan and New York). Most dockets also suggest more extensive efforts by insurance companies and associations than can be corroborated from other evidence. During 1961-1962, for example, Maine and Michigan had fifteen registrations in behalf of various insurance interests; New York had sixteen, plus fifteen others for individual medical care plans; California had seventeen; Virginia had twenty-one; and Connecticut, home state of numerous insurance companies, had fifty-four. Here, in fact, is the classic defensive interest group: well represented, usually by substantial capitol attorneys, but active mainly in the relatively few situations where its interests are directly threatened. In these situations, however, its efforts are not too often wasted.

As the dockets sometimes suggest too much, they may also tell too little. It is, for example, quite unlikely that the power and influence of the Ford Motor Company in the Michigan legislature is accurately expressed in the one representative registered to speak for it in 1962. In this same year, neither the AFL-CIO nor the United Auto Workers had registered agents in Lansing, and General Motors had only two; something plainly was missing. The powerful Virginia Farm Bureau Federation had only one registrant in Richmond in 1961, as did the entire tobacco industry. During the 1962 session, there were only three registrants for agricultural interests in New York. There are few if any states in which the registration dockets do not fall comparably short of accounting fully for interests that figure significantly in the state's politics.

If the dockets are often incomplete or skewed indices of group political power, they may nonetheless come fairly close to reflecting the balance of interests that obtains within a state. In Kentucky, for example, transport, mining, beer, liquor, and tobacco interests are most prominent on the docket, as they are in real life. The docket balance in Nebraska tips in the direction of the railroads and the utilities, public and private, and here too the image is, by all accounts, a faithful one. Registrations in Maine reflect the special importance of paper, timber, and power interests in that state. Alaska's small registration—fifty-eight in 1962—suggests the prominence of oil, mining, fishing, timber, and construction groups in that outpost commonwealth. In Maryland, there is usually a generous sprinkling of registrations for horse breeders and racing groups, watermen's and pilots' associations, and distillers—interests that weigh heavily in Maryland politics. The disproportionate numbers of insurance company representatives in Connecticut, noted earlier, is in line with the significance of insurance interests in that state's legislative affairs.[43]

In sum, registration dockets may reflect a state's special pattern of interests; the smaller and less complex the state, the clearer the reflection. These patterns change somewhat from year to year. *Ad hoc* groups, organized around emerging issues, may loom large for one session and then drift quietly out of business; or they may achieve permanent existence in broader or different areas of interest than those that prompted their creation. Withal, the balance among groups is relatively stable from year to year, and the registration dockets tend to mirror this stability.

By themselves, however, the dockets can only begin to speak to the key question: Who rules? This is especially true in those states where registration seems to work best; the more registrations there are, the less they are likely to reveal of where the real power lies. In California, for example, one can spot and largely discount the cultists, faddists, naturopathic physicians, nudists, ethical hypnotists, and the like, but this still leaves five hundred-plus agents representing a bewildering variety of more substantial interests. Which of them really matters? The situation is much the same in states like Massachusetts, Michigan, Ohio, and Wisconsin, where there are hundreds of registrations annually, but few self-contained clues to their meaning. It is doubtless comforting to know that there are a lot of cheese-company lobbyists in Wisconsin, a lot of automobile-company lobbyists in Michigan, and a lot of insurance-company lobbyists everywhere. It may satisfy our sense of balance and proportion to know that the Ohio AFL-CIO and the Ohio Manufacturers Association confront each other on even terms in Columbus (eleven registrants each in 1961). This is the kind of gross data that registration can supply, but fifteen minutes with a good capitol reporter or candid legislator will reveal much more. What does registration suggest of the special advantages conferred on groups holding basically defensive legislation positions? Of the distribution of formal or *de facto* group memberships within the legislature? Of groups so deeply entrenched as not to require formal representation before the legislature? Of the effects of malapportionment on legislative preferences? Of the extent and consequences of working arrangements between groups and other groups, and between groups and political parties? These questions are neither rhetorical nor unimportant, and the answer to each of them is painfully obvious: Registration suggests little and tells less. It can summarize a state's complex of interests, sometimes rather completely; it cannot by itself indicate which of these interests weigh most heavily on the political process, or the means by which they make their weight felt.

REGISTRATION AND POLITICAL STYLE

If registration is no analytical master key, it is not without value as an index to the structure and operation of state political systems. As these systems vary, the registration data tend to vary with them.

The great majority of registrants in every state are either attorneys on special or general retainer, or permanent group or corporation officials or representatives; the remainder—probably no more than 10 per cent in the aggregate—consists mainly of self-employed individuals, free-lance agents, unpaid representatives, and public relations counsel or consultants. Of the latter type particularly, there are relatively far fewer active and registered in the states than in Washington, although many state groups conduct activities that would come within any reasonably functional definition of "public relations."

While attorneys and group representatives or officials account for the bulk of registrations, the preponderance of one or the other varies considerably from state to state. In Virginia, attorneys on regular or special retainer regularly comprise about three-fourths of the registration. With a docket more than three times as large, Wisconsin's attorney-registrant ratio runs only slightly less (usually on the order of 60 per cent). Such otherwise diverse states as Alaska, Maine, Maryland, New York, North Carolina, Rhode Island, South Dakota, and Vermont show a comparably high proportion of attorneys on their registration dockets. In Kentucky, Michigan, and Ohio, on the other hand, attorneys generally account for 15 to 30 per cent of total registration, with the remaining majority consisting principally of executive secretaries, managing directors, legislative directors, or other permanent officials or employees of associations, corporations, companies, unions, and other groups. The balance is similar in California and Indiana, although somewhat less uneven.

A high incidence of attorney-registrants is commonly accompanied by a comparably high incidence of what might be called "multiple agency"—that is, individuals registered in behalf of more than one employer. Maine's 1961 docket illustrates this tendency in extreme form: of 216 employers of record, 110, or slightly more than half, were represented by 8 of the 131 individual or firm registrants. Each of the 8 was an attorney, law partnership, or firm, and their clients ranged from local improvement associations, through the largest paper companies in the state, to (significantly) the American Mutual Alliance. Similarly, 20 per cent of the registered employment in New York in 1962 was reported by 5 attorneys or firms, less than 3 per cent of the total registration. The Virginia and South Dakota data are comparable, with approximately 20 per cent of the registrant individuals or firms in both states accounting for well over half of the employments of record. In Wisconsin, which has many more registrations, between 15 and 20 per cent of the registrants regularly represent more than one client, with such employments comprising from 35 to 40 per cent of the total registration. Although the judgment is somewhat impressionistic, multiple agency in all of these states is typically in behalf of interests that can fairly be deemed substantial: insurance companies and associations, large manufacturing concerns, limited membership trade associations, and the like.

Multiple agency is obviously less frequent where group officials outnumber attorneys on the registration dockets; in these states there are usually at least as many registrants as there are principals, and it is more common for groups to have more than one registered representative than for individual or firm registrants to represent more than one group. In Ohio in 1961, for example, 338 individuals or firms registered for 229 employers. Only 10 registrants, all attorneys, represented more than one client, while 60 employers were represented by more than one registrant. Fifteen of the 60 accounted for 73 individual registrations. In Michigan in 1962, 20 of 221 registrants were active for more than one principal, but 35 of 223 employer interests had two or more registered representatives. During the 1962 session in Kentucky, only 3 of 93 registrants represented more than one employer, while 18 of 73 employers had more than one agent. As few as 4 registrants have had more than one client during recent sessions in Indiana, while 30 to 35 per cent of the employers of record have regularly had more than one agent. The data are more or less comparable in such states as Connecticut, Massachusetts, Kansas, and North Dakota.

Now these differences in docket make-up, registrant types, and registrant-employer ratios cannot be accounted for solely by the state's human or economic diversity, by the prevalence or character of political interest groups, by legislative workload and complexity, by the availability of bill-drafting or legislative reference services, or by the substantive requirements or administration of the disclosure law itself. Although every registration docket reflects to some extent the operation of these and other purely local variables, more general covariants also appear to be present and at work. These can best be described impressionistically: By and large, a predominance of lawyer-registrants and a relatively high incidence of multiple agency by them go with smaller dockets. These, in turn, tend to be associated with comparatively undeveloped group complexes and comparatively passive group politics. A premium is likely to be placed on a personalized group approach, typically through experienced insiders, to the "real" centers of political decision (which may not be exclusively located within the legislature). The legislative process tends to be informal but quietly well disciplined, with a variety of constraints available against obstreperous back-benchers, who are expected to know their place and wait their turn. And seniority matters for groups as well as legislators, the oldest interests generally holding the preferred stock in the enterprise.

In other states, a predominance of group officials or employees on the dockets and a lower incidence of multiple agency by attorney-registrants go with larger registrations, more registrants than employers, and a discernibly different kind of politics. Groups tend to be more numerous, to have larger memberships, to be more professionally staffed. Group access to the legislature is more nearly equalized, and it is typically sought through the group bureaucracy. There is more frequent resort to explicitly political group sanctions against members of the legislature, along with a relative deëmphasis of the inside approach (although this is still used wherever it can be). Legislative tenure tends to be short, programmatic leadership of the legislature is relatively widely dispersed, and party lines are often fracture-prone on critical issues. The legislative process is better described as a politics of decision than as a politics of ratification.

These political "styles" are obviously far from pure and the relationships between each of them and the operation of registration laws are obviously more concomitant than casual; it would require much investigation and, as they say, "empirical verification" before they could be labeled systematic. They are noted here only to illustrate the kinds of inference that registration statutes can provide a modicum of data to support.

In the strictest sense, these inferences are comparative, and they are thereby somewhat irrelevant to either the purposes that disclosure statutes are supposed to serve, or a realistic assessment of these statutes' operation. State legislatures have not ordinarily passed disclosure laws merely to provide political scientists with tools to elaborate or verify hypotheses, and the criteria that ought to govern judgment are principally internal; that is, disclosure operates and justifies—or fails to justify—itself *within* states and not *between* them. There is, however, nothing to be gained, and possibly something to be lost, by rejecting comparative speculation out of hand. If registration is no master key to an understanding of the system, there is no canon against using it to open, however slightly, whatever doors it will.

THE PROBLEM OF IDENTIFICATION

The minimum purpose of registration is to identify lobbyist and principal. Although it leaves much unsaid, registration in most cases sufficiently identifies employing interests by recording them as such; front groups in state legislative politics are more common in fiction than in life.

This is less true for the lobbyist. There is more to know about him than who he is; what he *was* may be of greater relevance and interest, and to this kind of knowledge there is no direct statutory route. Proof of the point lies buried in every state's registration dockets. In California during 1961-1962, for example, 14 former members of the legislature, one former United States Representative, and 6 former state department heads were included among the registrants. Two of the ex-legislators had been speakers of the Assembly; a third, registered for 5 major railroads in the early 'fifties, actually resigned as speaker to become a lobbyist.[44] This kind of information might have probative value to a reasonable man.

The discovery that interest groups employ men who know how legislative decisions are made (because they have made a few themselves) should neither startle nor offend. As Truman puts it, "access to the institutions of government is basically a matter of relationships with individuals who occupy governmental positions."[45] The group hazards little in assuming that the former legislator or official will have kept *his* relationships alive; he is not expected to work miracles or cross itching palms, but only to be himself and continue cultivating his friends.[46]

The former public servant owns skills for which there is usually a brisk market, and he owns them from one corner of the nation to the other. A random scattering of examples may help to make the point. North Carolina's 1949 docket included at least 33 former legislators, one former governor, and one former United States Senator.[47] Former Governor Roberts was registered in Rhode Island in 1962,[48] and the ex-lieutenant-governor of Colorado was among the compliants with that state's legislative registration rule in 1960.[49] One week after the new Texas law went into effect in 1959, 3 former legislators were on the docket.[50] Two major national insurance associations are represented in Virginia by a former member of the

State Senate and chairman of the Virginia Constitutional Convention of 1945. The busiest registrant in Maryland in 1951 (9 clients) had been state attorney-general under Governor O'Conor (whose son was also registered as counsel for two groups). Almost as busy (5 clients) and much better paid was Joseph Wyatt, Balitmore political leader and former judge.[51] Ten years later, Mr. Wyatt was still doing quite well, with reported receipts of more than $33,000 from 4 client associations. Other Maryland registrants for 1961 included another former attorney-general (listed as counsel for Bowie Race Track), and a member of the Public Service Commission.[52] Former U.S. Senator John Bricker's law firm has been registered in Ohio in behalf of the Sperry and Hutchinson Company, and the firm of Tydings, Sauerwein, Benson, and Boyd (whose late senior partner was former U.S. Senator Millard Tydings), has been registered in Maryland.[53] Several former legislators and heads of state agencies have appeared on recent dockets in Ohio, Maine, Connecticut, Massachusetts, and Wisconsin. For the latter state, particularly systematic data are available; Leon Epstein has found that 151 of 863 ex-legislators registered as lobbyists at some time between 1921 and 1955, including more than a third of all attorney-legislators during the period.[54] Comparable studies of postlegislative careers in other states would undoubtedly result in comparable findings.

Political events may also thrust this kind of data to the fore, at least momentarily. In 1949, for example, the legislative session in Ohio was enlivened by an Assembly battle over a proposal to amend the public utility laws to include commodity belt transportation lines. This would have given the latter certain rights of eminent domain and enabled the construction of a belt line to link Lake Erie with the Ohio River. If the project had its science fiction aspects, it also had a very down-to-earth array of talent marshalled in its support. Registered in behalf of the belt interests were two former speakers of the Ohio House, a former clerk of the House, and a former assistant attorney-general. A second former House clerk and his opposite number in the Senate were also believed to have been on the belt payroll, although they were not registered.[55] All of this effort worked to the eventual detriment of its sponsors when antagonistic newspapers discovered and revealed its existence; the enterprise lost both its color of legitimacy and its legislative support, and the amendment was defeated.

. Group resort to the "inside" approach is seldom this concentrated or unproductive, but the case is not otherwise unique; the same theme reëchoes elsewhere, the principal difference being whether or not there is a registration law to provide at least indirect amplification.[56] And while even intendedly neutral recitation of the facts inevitably gives off an aroma of raked-over muck, there is nothing inherently objectionable in political interest groups hiring men with public service backgrounds to represent them, although it can and does raise a number of prickly ethical and political problems. But it should be known, for this is the kind of supporting detail without which a registration docket is neither meaningful nor complete. The examples given here demonstrate that it can be known, but these came to light in only two ways: tactical utilization of registration data by competing interests; and, more often, a working newsman's estimate of political significance or journalistic value. Nowhere does the law demand that such data be revealed, or aid at all in the revealing. Law that leans so heavily on accident or private choice is something less than whole.

IS IDENTIFICATION ENOUGH?

What should registration do? If its function is only to identify agent and principal in the simplest terms, then registration does what it was intended to—no more and not much less. But if simple identification does not sufficiently inform either public or legislative judgment—and can, indeed, do considerable mischief by encouraging the assumption that it does—then both the purposes and values of registration cannot but be in question.

Few of the commentaries on state registration laws have found much good to say about them. Most of the criticism, however, has been levelled at semantic phantoms rather than at the more serious operating limitations of identification as a guiding principle. There is admittedly much to criticize. The coverage of registration requirements is typically vague in the law and incomplete in practice. The status of persons paid in lump sums for the performance of both lobbying and nonlobbying services is a common problem, although it is met in a few states by the exemption of attorneys rendering purely professional legislative services, or of other individuals whose legislative services are only a minor part of their total employment. When the laws make employment to influence legislation the main test of their applicability—as almost all of them do—the surprising thing is that noncompliance among multifunctional group representatives has not been more widespread.[57] The pecuniary-interest test of applicability has also served to reduce compliance by representatives of nonprofit groups, although again to a lesser extent than the law might literally allow.

But registration labors under heavier burdens than mere gaps in statutory coverage. The standard law requires only that the registrant disclose his name, address, legislative interests, date and duration of employment, and his employer's name and address. This is simple identification, and it is simply not enough.[58] At best, it piques the appetite but withholds satisfaction; at worst, it reiterates the obvious. If identification is to be more useful, it must first be more complete. What does more complete identification entail? A few of the elements have already been suggested: minimal information on such matters as the background of the agent, and on the precise conditions of his agency. Information on employing groups—their structure, membership, management, and sources of financial support—is no less urgently needed. The hired hand is an inviting target, but it is the group that gives him life.

How is the law that would provide this kind of information to be obtained, and what grounds could be used to support it? Nothing can be gained by resort to the parallel between groups and parties. McKean, for example, has written:

> If the legislature is to take official cognizance of [these organizations] by requiring that they register, it should undertake to ascertain what or whom the groups represent. It is not enough to demand that a lobbyist reveal the name of his employer; the names and addresses of members of the organization and the financial affairs of the group should be included to give legislators any true picture of the sources of the pressures upon them. [As] the groups have now at least as important a place in the legislative process as the parties, and as the state found it necessary to regulate by law the internal affairs of the parties, it may find it necessary to regulate the internal affairs of the pressure groups.[59]

If more information is needed about interest groups, it is needed for the precise reason that the groups are different from the parties and not like them. Proposals to "regulate the internal affairs" of the two in similar terms, whatever other values it might promise, founder both on this essential dissimilarity and on the deep shoals of constitutional privilege that protect the right of men and groups of men to come to government with their needs.

It is at least conceivable that registration could be made to yield a richer harvest, although the law to do it is nowhere yet in prospect. And were it to be written, we should be under no illusions as to what it would achieve. Under the best of circumstances, many salient aspects of the group process would remain beyond its reach. The subtleties of personal influence and legislative involvement, for example, would predictably elude the most enlightened registration law, the very passage of which would itself require such profound changes in the total political environment as to be presently unimaginable.

Reporting

As the registration aspect of disclosure is concerned with the *dramatis personae* of group politics, the reporting aspect is concerned with the cost accounting. The simple assumption here is that, in politics as elsewhere, money talks. There are no doubt those who believe that it talks too often, too loudly, and for the benefit of too few, and that a reporting requirement should provide the evidence to prove it. Unfortunately, neither the purposes nor consequences of financial reporting under state disclosure laws are quite so virile. Reporting is no more than a small logical extension of the modest bias toward open dealing embodied in registration. The law assumes only that if it is useful to know who seeks to affect legislative decisions, it should be no less useful to know the scale and manner of their exertions.

The reporting requirement trails registration in point of time, but not in significance. That a number of states require registration without reporting does not alter the fact that registration by itself may be inconclusive and misleading. The most recent California docket shows, for example, that the United Patriotic People of the U.S.A. and the Southern Pacific Railroad were each represented

before the legislature by a single registered agent. But was the legislature equally attentive to both of them? Were they equal in resources,
prestige, skills, entree? In the magnitude and variety of their interests?
In what they spent to advance or protect them? Because the answer
to each question is so obviously "no," registration by itself is incomplete, however well it seems to work.

Since financial reporting adds the flesh to what is otherwise a
skeleton, it is important that it operate with maximum effect. The
most obvious standard of judgment—and, as with registration, one
of the least satisfactory—is formal compliance with the requirement.
Reporting compliance of course relates to registration compliance;
there cannot be more reports than there are registrants, but ideally
there should not be less. The optimum ratio is one to one, and this
is not always achieved.

As might be expected, reporting compliance is usually (but not
always) at the highest levels in those states where there is reason to
believe that registration compliance is also relatively complete. Registration is to all appearances well observed in Indiana, for example,
and reporting noncompliance is rare; for three successive recent
sessions combined, only one employer failed to submit the required
report. In Kentucky, where the employer also reports, complete compliance is the rule. New Hampshire, North Carolina, and Virginia
have also had good compliance records over the years.

For the most recent general legislative sessions, reporting compliance has also been very nearly complete in Ohio and Maryland.
This has not always been so. In Ohio in 1949, 31 of 276 registrants
failed to submit end-of-session reports, despite the secretary of state's
well-publicized crackdown on "sneak lobbyists." Again in 1951, 17
of 242 registrants did not comply. In the same year in Maryland,
50 of 129 registrants had not filed reports five months after the
expiration of the thirty-day postsession grace period allowed in the
law. Ten years later, however, reports had been received for all but
3 of the 247 registrants within two weeks of the grace period's end.[60]

These are all states in which the available evidence suggests that
registration compliance is reasonably complete, and reporting compliance follows nearly apace. In several others where registration
levels appear to be comparably high, reporting compliance consistently lags behind. In South Dakota, as many as 30 per cent of

registrants have failed to report. Although compliance in New York has appreciably improved since 1955, as many as 66 of 111 registrants (in 1951) have withheld financial statements. Wisconsin has in some years had no monthly reports from nearly half of its individual registrants; less than 10 per cent of the single postsession reports required of employers are usually withheld, however.

California has had large individual registrations since 1950, but compliance with the individual monthly reporting requirement has been spotty at best. The Assembly Interim Committee on Legislative Representation reported in 1961 that of some 8,588 individual reports literally required during the preceding legislative biennium, only 2,943, or 34 per cent, had been received. Many of the missing reports would doubtless have indicated that there were no reportable receipts and expenditures, particularly for those months when the legislature was not in session, but the committee was safe in concluding that substantial noncompliance was also involved.[61]

There are finally a few states where reporting noncompliance is easy to describe because it is complete. None of Mississippi's 74 registrants submitted reports in 1961, nor were any received in Georgia—understandably, since there have been no registrations since 1941.

In sum, registration and reporting compliance are generally—but not invariably—related, and something less than complete reporting compliance is not uncommon. Most of the gap can be accounted for by the character of enforcement, which, despite the obviousness of violations, is in most states rather relaxed. Although reporting compliance is better than it might be, the notion that law need function only 75 or 80 per cent of the time is hardly acceptable.

As was also the case for registration, scattered evidence from a few states suggests that compliance with the reporting requirements has improved somewhat in recent years. Ohio, New York, Indiana, and Nebraska all do better than they used to do, although in none of these could the improvement be described as striking.[62] Data are lacking for too many states to support more systematic comparisons.

Under what kinds of circumstances and for what kinds of groups is reporting non-compliance most frequent? Although it would be difficult to support statistically, the impression persists that the *ad hoc* groups—temporary organizations with limited and immediate legislative objectives—are the most likely to avoid reporting. Many such groups find either success or failure sufficient reason to stay around and try again; others fold up shop when their business has been disposed of, and there may be no one left to clean up details like a financial report thirty days later—particularly when the group has failed to get what it wants.

There is also some tendency for late registrants to be delinquent in reporting. Late registration usually indicates the emergence late in the legislative session of an issue or issues which are "hot" for the group concerned, whereupon a spokesman is hustled up to the capitol to do whatever he can as quickly as he can. His reportable receipts and expenditures may be small, and if, as is often the case, he is a lawyer, he is quite likely to treat them as *de minimis*— beneath his dignity to report or the law's to require. In California, where the records are ordered to facilitate this kind of analysis, January registrants are about twice as likely to file monthly financial reports as later registrants. During the general session year of 1959, for example, approximately three-fourths of all January registrants filed reports for each of the first six months of the year. Forty per cent of February and March registrants and even fewer of those registering in May and June—about one-third—filed similar reports for the months following their registrations.[63] Figures of this order appear to hold for a number of other states as well.

Group identities or interests do not appear to be as closely related to reporting noncompliance as the factors noted above. There is some tendency for representatives of labor groups to be somewhat less delinquent in reporting than representatives of other major interests, but the evidence is far from conclusive. In 1949, in fact, six of the thirty-one noncompliants in Ohio represented labor organizations. Four others were active for the commodity belt proposal discussed earlier, and one of these four represented the Special Transportation Committee, the *ad hoc* group that was formed to promote the belt idea.[64] Where relatively so few groups are involved, however,—and in this respect the Ohio figures are typical—general patterns are nearly impossible to detect.

REPORTING: PROBLEMS OF COVERAGE

There is little to be drawn from the raw reporting figures beyond the obvious conclusion that they are not always what they should be. More significant than widespread noncompliance is the fact that compliance yields less than it might. The purpose of a reporting requirement is to inform; the goal is not often achieved.

The laws themselves create many of the difficulties under which they labor. The typical reporting section requires only that "every person, corporation, or association whose name appears upon the legislative docket" shall file "a complete and detailed statement . . . of all expenses paid or incurred" by them "in connection with promoting or opposing in any manner the passage by the General Assembly of any legislation."[65] Under this language, there may be a real question as to who should file; either principal or agent, or both, can qualify as "person, corporation, or association." A similar problem exists with most reporting sections; conspicuously few of them clearly assign responsibility for meeting their demands. The problem can easily enough be solved by a simple administrative decision; that this has been made differently in states with otherwise comparable provisions underscores the ambiguity of the language.

In the end, somebody reports. The more difficult questions are raised by the substantive requirement that there be filed a "complete and detailed statement" of expenditures paid or incurred in connection with legislation. Although the details required vary slightly from state to state, only Indiana specifically limits the employer's report to expenditures made in connection with the employment of registered counsel or agents; elsewhere, complete disclosure ("all expenditures") is the statutory rule. Where the agents files, this will generally mean only his own expenditures; where the employer files—and this is the more common arrangement—"all expenditures" should often include more than payments to registered counsel and agents alone. At very least, it should include these completely.

The language seems to provide a broad enough net, but self-serving interpretation and official lassitude have in most states combined to punch it full of holes. Many groups, for example, prefer not to report the fees paid to their counsel and agents for, among other things, telling them how to avoid complete compliance with the law. As a Nebraska official has observed:

> The large corporations declined quite generally to state the amount of money paid to their lobbyists on the ground that such persons were not employed as lobbyists but were regular full-

time employees of the corporation whose casual duty it was to appear as lobbyists before the Legislature.[66]

The situation is not unique to Nebraska, nor to representatives of large corporations, but wherever and for whomever it exists, it reflects an excessively restrictive reading of the law. The Nebraska provisions, like those of most other states, require detailed accounts of all receipts and expenditures "directly or indirectly [received], paid, incurred, or promised in connection with legislation."[67] For the employer, this obviously includes payments made to registered agents; the agent's registration, however cautionary or superfluous, creates an obligation for the employer to report all payments made to him. In most states the applicability of registration sections usually hinges (as it does in Nebraska) on employment for the purpose of influencing legislation. If agents are not specifically employed for this purpose, then it can reasonably be claimed that they need not register at all. Once they have registered, however, payments to them should be reported. In theory, the Nebraska corporations and their counterparts in other states are making the right objection to the wrong requirement; in practice, they are meeting the easy requirement—registration—and ducking the tough one—reporting.

The rationale for this kind of evasion matters less than its result, which is that relevant information is withheld. The extent of the withholding varies with the language of the law, patterns of compliance, and levels of enforcement, but there is in most states widespread reluctance among multifunctional group or firm officers, counsel, or agents to disclose either their total fees and salaries or the parts of these that should be allocated to their legislative efforts. In Nebraska, approximately one-sixth of the registrants' reports do not state receipts, and one-quarter do not reveal expenditures, usually on the stated ground that nothing was received or expended for the specific purpose of influencing legislation. This kind of nondisclosure is even more common in states like Kentucky and Ohio, where group officials outnumber attorneys on the dockets; as many as three-quarters of the reports filed in both states have declined to state salaries, expenses, or both. A few Ohio registrants report that their receipts come from "dues"—a response doubly vexing since it indicates how the money came in but stops short of revealing how much of it did, or from whom. In North Carolina, roughly half of the reports regularly fail to state the registrant's salary or fee, as do approximately one-third of those filed in Virginia and Connecticut.[68]

The loophole is there even when it seems to have been closed. The Indiana law specifically charges the employer with reporting all expenditures made in connection with the employment of registered counsel and agents, "including the salaries of each such counsel and agent."[69] Despite the plain language of the law, nineteen of eighty-six principals during one recent session reported neither expenses nor salaries for their agents, and twenty-eight others reported only the former—the reports in several cases being accompanied by disclaimers to the effect that the registrants were not paid for lobbying alone, and that, therefore, their salaries need not be disclosed. This is not what the law says, but it can be read this way with practical impunity.

Only Massachusetts and California have attempted to deal with this kind of tortured construction—Massachusetts by statute, and California by administrative rule. A 1913 amendment to the Massachusetts law charges principals with reporting their registrants' salaries and expenses, but when these are "included in an employment by annual salary or retainer, the statement shall specify the amount of the salary or the retainer apportioned therefor." If apportionment is impossible, then the total salary or fee must be disclosed.[70] There is no way out here. The law can be read in only one way, and the evasions that persist arise from desultory enforcement.

The California law lays no basis for apportionment, but the registration form asks registrants, "How much are you paid . . . for legislative representation (if total compensation is not for this purpose)." Responses to this item are usually used as a point of reference in the subsequent monthly reports, which do not themselves require apportionment of registrant receipts into legislative and nonlegislative categories. That many of these responses are given with obvious reluctance does not render them less informative.

Failure to report all payments to registrants is at least derived from a literal interpretation of the law. A more common and important omission, and one for which there is no interpretative warrant, is the reporting of such payments and nothing more. It might be argued that since the typical law defines the employer in terms of his agents, his reports need only detail those expenditures involved in their employment. But if the argument is plausible above the surface, it is spurious below, and quite unnecessary in the bargain; groups simply report for their agents (when they report at all), and this is almost gratefully accepted as full compliance.

This universal shrinkage of the law's broader language, accomplished with the tacit consent of all concerned, has kept financial reporting immobilized on the level of the hired lobbyist; political interest groups, the proper target of disclosure, remain beyond its reach. One can examine thousands of reports—the writer has—without finding more than a small and inadvertent handful which give any meaningful detail on group receipts and expenditures not directly attributable to the employment of registered lobbyists. If such things as group headquarters and field expenses, research and public relations costs, gifts or services to public officials, and political contributions and activities cannot often be fairly subsumed under "all expenses paid or incurred . . . in connection with promoting or opposing in any manner the passage . . . of any legislation," then the words have lost part of their meaning. Seventy years ago, "in any manner" meant hired lobbyists. It means very much more than this today, but groups, legislators, officials, and the press remain content to accept it at no more than its original value.

These problems of coverage and applicability are compounded in their effect by what might appear to be a trivial matter: the almost unrelieved inadequacy of the official reporting forms. If there are to be the "full and detailed" reports that the law demands, the report form should not only accommodate but encourage them. The typical form does neither. A few actually negate the plain language of the statute they purport to serve. The Connecticut law, for example, requires the conventional detailed report of "all items paid, incurred, or promised, directly or indirectly, in connection with the legislation pending at the last legislative session."[71] The report form, however, asks employers to report only the "Persons Paid or Promised (Names of Lobbyists)," and "Amounts Paid to Lobbyists." In other words, the state accepts the view that payments to registered lobbyists exhaust the possibilities of reportable group expenditures. This may simplify the reporting burden and ratify group preferences, but it sells the law short.

In Connecticut the report form explicitly limits the range of the reporting requirement; in other states the same end has been achieved with forms that are merely ill devised. The most common faults are as easily remedied as they are obvious: lack of space, sparse (if any) instructions, and headings either vague or undiagnostic. The Ohio form typically gives the registrant two lines under the general heading "Receipts" for the full and detailed account of all money received by him that the law requires. The results are dismal, one registrant after the other replying "Dues," "Income," "Regular receipts," or some other laconic synonym. This might happen with the most carefully designed form, but then again it might not.

A few states have set up categories of expenditure on their report forms. This has made for consistency of reports, but it has also restricted their scope, for the categories are usually either vague or trivial. Virginia asks both principal and agent to report the following kinds of expenditures: "Hotel bills, etc."; "Traveling expenses"; "Expenses of correspondence, including messages by telegraph or telephone"; and "miscellaneous." This is all appealingly systematic, but like the Connecticut form it gives official sanction to a limited construction of "all expenses" paid or promised in connection with legislation, which is what the law itself requires to be reported. In practice, the "miscellaneous" category has been the one most heavily used, and it has provided a convenient blanket under which reporting groups can disclose large lump sum expenditures without otherwise describing them.

Registered lobbyists in Wisconsin are required to submit monthly expense reports. These need not include "personal living and travel expense," but they must include "expenditures made or obligations incurred . . . in behalf of or for the entertainment of any state official or employee concerning pending or proposed legislative matters," even though the furnishing of such entertainment ("food, meal, lodging, beverage . . . ") is elsewhere in the law deemed "unprofessional conduct" and made cause for revocation of the registrant's license![72] Living and travel expenses were excised from the reporting requirement in a useful effort to avoid the usual tired recitations of subsistence items that clutter reports. Entertainment reporting was added in an effort first to demonstrate and then to curtail the extent and cost of what is usually called "social lobbying." Again, the form fell short of fully supporting the law; it called only for the date, amount, and recipient of the expenditure (under the headings "Meals," "Refreshment," and "Entertainment") without requiring either separate disclosure of each entertainment or the names of the officials entertained. While the sums reported prior to 1958 lent no substantial credence to capital rumors of lobby-sponsored bacchanalia, they were large enough to suggest that the story about the legislator who ate three meals a day at the Lorraine Hotel and signed a lobbyist's name to the tab was not apocryphal. To prove the point would have required a subpoena, however, since the form did not compel disclosure of the "entertainee," and the deficiency was never voluntarily supplied. He may have been more hungry than venal, but this is something that the public should have had a chance to decide for itself.[73]

It is unrealistic to assume that reporting can somehow be "better" than the instruments with which it is accomplished; nobody loves disclosure that much. With the possible exception of those used in California, the report forms commonly evidence the most hasty and thoughtless preparation, and they are rarely revised. That these instruments reflect so little concern with the potentialities of the law points again to the listlessness that pervades the administration of disclosure in the states.

REPORTING: THE GOLD AND THE DROSS

Indifferent report forms and a general reluctance to read the law as it is written have combined to fix the focus of reporting on the hired lobbyist. If the shadow cast by this kind of disclosure is smaller than life, it is still preferable to no shadow at all. Within these limitations, reporting can give at least a beginning indication of how much money reporting groups spend to influence legislation. Table 2 summarizes the available data for selected states in recent years.

The most obvious conclusion to be drawn from table 2 is that in some states quite large aggregate expenditures are now reported. This has not always been so. A generation ago, Pollock found that every expense report filed in Ohio declared: "Received nothing, spent nothing." The sums reported in several other states ranged from the suspiciously to the absurdly small.[74] Clearly, there has been a change in the direction of more extensive reporting.

TABLE 2
REPORTED EXPENDITURES IN SELECTED STATES

State	Year	Total expenditures reported by or to registrants
California	1952-53a	$ 808,788
	1960-61a	1,000,000b
	1962-63a	1,046,983
Connecticut	1947	100,807
	1961	167,274
Kentucky	1950	55,991
Maryland	1951	66,392
Massachusetts	1958	307,886
Nebraska	1949	119,277
	1961	185,000b
New Hampshire	1951	68,930
New York	1961	324,785
	1962	302,397c
North Carolina	1949	37,662
	1961	80,000b
Ohio	1949	156,618
	1957	70,000d
South Dakota	1951	72,651
	1957	80,000d
Virginia	1950	78,687
Wisconsin	1949	282,433
	1957	320,000d

a Includes only first six months of odd-numbered year; reporting period is eighteen months.

b Approximate figure drawn from press or official source. The California figure includes only registrant expenditures, and not receipts (fees, salaries, etc.)

c Incomplete figure.

d Source: Zeller, Belle, "Regulation of Pressure Groups and Lobbyists," Annals, vol. 319 (September, 1958), p. 95. The Ohio figure includes only reported registrant receipts.

There are logical reasons why it should not have occurred. As Truman has observed, the reporting of large expenditures should present obvious tactical advantages to groups representing opposing interests.[75] But this view greatly overvalues reporting laws as weapons; as patterns of relatively innocuous compliance with them become established, groups can disclose rather substantial expenditures without seriously compromising their competitive positions. An appearance of compliance is not dangerous so long as one does not comply alone. Groups commonly file reports not from any deep devotion to the disclosure idea but because they see no threat in it.

Table 2 shows a rising level of reported expenditures, not only over the long run, but during the past decade. Beyond a growing candor in the reports, this is a natural reflection of two facts: There are in every state more political interest groups than there were, and the competition among them has become more intense, diversified, and costly. This has probably happened to a greater extent than reported expenditures, largely limited to the costs of maintaining registered lobbyists, might alone suggest. Rising expenditures must also be partly laid to inflation, which affects the group as consumer just as it does the rest of us.

Although reported expenditures have generally increased, it is difficult to compare one state's total with another's. Each figure reflects a different combination of the same common variables that affect registration: the requirements and administration of the law; compliance habits; the character and dimensions of the group complex; political issues; the state of legislative control; press coverage; and half a dozen others. Even more than registration, reporting yields a peculiarly localized result that does not readily lend itself to comparative analysis. Total reported expenditures and the number of competing groups do not appear to be dependably related. Similarly, reported expenditures do not vary systematically with differing patterns of legislative control. One might expect higher reported expenditures in a two-party, high turnover milieu, and lower expenditures where legislative control is more stable, but the facts do not always—or even often—fit the expectation. Nor is there any necessary relationship between reported expenditures and state wealth, major interests, or heterogeneity. In sum, each state total is unique; comparisons between them do not reveal whether the law is doing well—or at all—what it was intended to do.

If the totals are unique, the individual reports of which they are compounded have much in common. Almost without exception, the expenditures reported in every state by principal and agent alike are confined to those involved in hiring registered lobbyists and maintaining them in the style to which registered lobbyists have become accustomed. Allowing for the unquenchably Statlerian preferences of many political practitioners, in and out of office, the reports could, in fact, serve as an informal Baedeker to the more attractive hotels and restaurants in the various state capitals.[76] This is hardly their purpose, but it suggests the character of the expenditure information they convey: hotel, restaurant, club, and liquor bills; train, plane, and cab fares (lobbyists never travel by bus); postage, telephone, and telegraph bills; and the inevitable "miscellaneous." While a knowledge of where registered lobbyists live and take their meals may not be vital to the safety of the republic, such matters are not totally devoid of interest. So long, in any case, as the usual reporting requirement is given its usual restricted meaning, it is most of what we can expect to see revealed.

The main value of this kind of reporting is that it might throw some antiseptic light into those tenebrous corners of the system where group politics and the free lunch coalesce. The light at least flickers in California; it has elsewhere been almost thoroughly extinguished. Individual registrants in California are required to report monthly the recipient and purpose of each expenditure larger than $25.00 made by him "in carrying on his work." As in Wisconsin, neither the law nor the report form compels identification of such legislators or other public officials as might raise their cups at the lobbyist's board. Notwithstanding this tantalizing omission, the reports continue to give a better-than-surmise glimpse of what "social lobbying" means in Sacramento.

California registrations, employer authorizations, and monthly reports are photoprinted verbatim for each legislative biennium. For 1960-1961, this material filled a six-by-nine-inch volume, four and one-half inches thick and weighing more than four pounds. There was much chaff, but also much wheat. The reported expenditures were, in the aggregate, larger than they had ever been in California or any other state. Although no official totals were announced, the *Sacramento Bee's* informed estimate of $1,000,000 in registrant expenditures alone—neither their fees and salaries nor expenditures made directly by their employers were included—was, if anything, conservative.[77]

If the total was problematical, the individual reports were reasonably explicit, and in some cases suggested a prodigal open-handedness. Monthly expenditure reports of three-to-four thousand dollars and more were not uncommon, with the largest single monthly total being reported by Ben H. Read, longtime executive secretary of the Public Health League of California ("organized to protect the public health by the preservation of ethical medicine, dentistry, and allied health services").[78] Mr. Read reported spending $4,984.62 in February 1961, including $3,079.54 to the Hotel Senator for "hotel service." Mr. Read must have been comfortable at the Senator; for the first five months of the year, his bills there came to $12,097.16 (of total expenditures of $19,154.71 for the same period). For the four months that he filed reports, Monroe Butler, representing the Superior Oil Co., reported expenditures of $11,859.11, including $9,267.05 to the Senator Hotel.

Also prominent among the spenders was former Assemblyman James Garibaldi. Representing the Hollywood and Del Mar Turf Clubs, the California Beverage Distributors Association, the Pacific Outdoor Advertising Company, and the California Association of Highway Patrolmen, Mr. Garibaldi reported disbursements of $15,061 for the legislative year. Former Assembly Speaker Gordon Garland ("public relations and legislative counsel") spent $12,804.17 on behalf of nine clients between February and June,[79] and ex-Assemblyman Jefferson Peyser reported sessional disbursements of $13,603.35 for the Wine Institute and two other clients. Comparably large—and, in a few cases, larger—expenditures were reported by representatives of several major oil companies, liquor interests, utilities, the California Railroad Association, the California Real Estate Association, the State Bar, Ginn and Company (textbook publishers), and the Cities and Counties of Los Angeles and San Francisco.

At least two score other registrants each reported spending more than $5,000 during the five months of the session. The bulk of this spending was reported under such general headings as "lodging," "food," "beverages," and "entertainment." One can only guess at the proportion that went to satisfy the creature and social needs of the reporters, but it would almost certainly not account for all that was reported. Approaching the matter from another perspective, the expenditures reported by registered lobbyists to keep the glasses, plates, and empty hours of legislators full aggregated at least $2,500 for each of the 120 members of the legislature. Purely business-related expenditures—travel, car rental or maintenance, secretarial and other office expenses, and the like—were also quite substantial, but appeared to have been outweighed by those of a more convivial nature.

Not only does reported spending run higher in California than elsewhere, but it is also reported for a wider variety of objects. Beyond personal subsistence and business or office expenses, and the run-of-the-mill luncheons, dinners, banquets, and cocktail parties for legislators, California registrants have reported the costs of such things as "crabfests," river excursions, chartered air flights to Nevada, theater tickets, golf fees and equipment, flowers, wedding presents and baby shower gifts (for legislator's wives), and vitamins for legislators. In Sacramento, the glad hand picks up many tabs.

The main point of this dilation on the California experience is that it represents expenditure-reporting at its present best. The law is among the most demanding (monthly reports and enumeration of expenditures in excess of $25.00), compliance by regular registrants is well established and reasonably candid, the requirement is relatively well administered, and the reports indicate larger and more diversified expenditures than is anywhere else the case. Even in California, however, there is much that eludes analysis. That a registrant reports a monthly bill of $3,000 for "hotel service," for example, is revealing and perhaps suggestive, but it is not descriptive. The *way* of it is beyond the ability of this kind of financial report to capture. This is not primarily because the reports are deliberately incomplete, or because, as Graves once put it, "far more is spent than ever finds its way into the published reports."[80] The fundamental difficulty is the lump sum, offhand kind of reporting which prevails to a considerable extent in California and almost totally elsewhere. Substantial enough sums are reported in several states, but they are usually completely undifferentiated, or are grouped in several ambiguous categories. The net effect is to disclose but not to inform.

This may, of course, be enough. History and necessity both lend support to the view that the only and intended purpose of financial reporting by registered lobbyists was precisely to disclose in summary terms only what is spent by or through them in efforts to influence legislative action. But if this was, and is, of legitimate public concern, so too should be the deeper identities of both the spenders and those for whom they speak. It should by now be unnecessary to reassert that the hired lobbyist has become no more than a replaceable instrument for the achievement of group purposes. Of the group proper—what *it* is, what and how *it* spends—reporting reveals too little to be responsive to modern needs. In California, where the law explicitly requires group reports (in section 9903) and a reporting form has been provided to accommodate them (Form 1), the grand total of two organizations compiled during 1960-1961: the Northern California Committee, Californians against Capital Punishment, and the Friends Committee on Legislation. Without in any way derogating the value and sincerity of these groups, one can fairly observe that they did not bulk large on the Sacramento scene. Group compliance per se is no better in any other state, which is to say that it is even worse.

If the reports everywhere lack detail and group orientation, they usually specify at least round expenditure figures. The reporting of receipts, which, in the absence of true group reports, means registrant fees and salaries, suffers from somewhat different deficiencies. As noted earlier, registrants are frequently reluctant to state what they receive for legislative services, particularly when these are rendered as only part of a more comprehensive employment, and when neither the statute nor administrative practice requires an apportionment. When fees and salaries are stated, however, the results can be revealing.

Among other things, they are often quite high. Here again, the California data are especially apposite. Of the 534 individual or firm registrants during 1960-1961, 107 reported annual salaries or retainers of between $10,000 and $15,000. Eight of these indicated apportionments to legislative services in this range; their total earnings were larger. Another 35 registrants, including 3 who apportioned this amount, reported receipts between $15,000 and $20,000. Twenty more (3 by apportionment) reported between $20,000 and $25,000 in receipts, and 12 (2 by apportionment) were earning more than $25,000 a year. These figures are, of course, not completely reliable. On the one hand, they include the total receipts reported by many registrants who could have reasonably apportioned less than $10,000 of their earnings to lobbying services but who, for one reason or another, failed to do so; on the other hand, they do not include many registrants earning more than $10,000 a year who apportioned sometimes questionably small amounts to compensation for lobbying. These biases probably come close to canceling each other.

To these figures should be added the reports of those 15 registrants who worked on a per diem basis and earned in excess of $10,000 for lobbying during the year. Rates varied, but the modal figures were $25.00 an hour ($40.00 was high) and $150 the day ($300 was high). The reports filed by former Assemblyman Garibaldi were not untypical of the group; working on a $156.67 per diem, Mr. Garibaldi reported payments amounting to $12,562.25 for the first five months of 1961.

Among those registrants working on a regular salary, fee, or retainer basis, the highest earnings were reported by Albert Shults, agent for five major oil companies ($3,350 of total monthly retainers of $5,030), and former Assemblyman Elmer Bromley, now representing seven utility companies ($3,333.33 of total retainers allocated monthly). Former Speaker Garland reported regular retainers from seven assorted clients totalling $6,125 per month, not all of which was attributable to legislative services; his actual monthly receipts averaged only $4,824 during the 1961 session. Former Assemblyman Kenneth Ross reported annual retainers and expense allowances of $50,000 from his six clients (four cement companies, the Los Angeles Turf Club, and Associated General Contractors), and former Assemblyman Kenneth Redwine, active for five trade groups, reported annual retainers of $37,000 and actual receipts during the 1961 session of $23,750.

There are two main conclusions to be drawn from this material, and they largely draw themselves: Many lobbyists do quite well in Sacramento, and former officeholders do particularly well. The average monthly earnings reported by the fifteen ex-legislators registered during the 1961 session were $2,111, and this figure, calculated on the basis of the registrants' own apportionments, was pulled down significantly by the small fees reported by the two former members whose legislative activities were limited and brief.

The only unique thing about the California data is their magnitude. Fees and salaries are generally more modest in other states,[81] and the proportion of former officials to total registrants is generally somewhat higher, but the distribution of rewards follows much the same pattern everywhere: Men with public service backgrounds can usually be found at or near the top of the reported income lists. This should neither surprise nor offend. Such men have much to offer groups seeking knowledgeable and effective representation, and they have an obvious right to work at what they know best—the business of politics.

If the discovery that lobbyists are often well paid, particularly when they happen to be former legislators, is one of the principal kinds of intelligence to result from the reporting requirement, it has not been widely shared. Newspaper stories occasionally compare lobbyist earnings and legislative salaries (to the inevitable disadvantage of the latter), but since the number of legislators attempting to live on their official stipends is in most states quite small, such comparisons usually have the air of exercises in strained irrelevance. The root of the matter is that in this respect as in others, any serious effort to find meaning in the reports needs more than the reports alone to sustain it. The earlier discussion of the 1961 California filings, for example, was literally built from scratch; the raw materials included the official compilation of reports, one newspaper story, a set of California Blue Books, and one man-day's work. The work may or may not have been wasted; if, however, this kind of analysis supplies a useful complement to the reports proper, the question is whether or not the writer should have had to do it. The answer may be "no," but there were no alternative doers, even in the state (California) where disclosure works "best."

There is one last respect in which the reporting by registrants of their expenditures and receipts adds to more than the sum of the component parts. The reported expenditures are often trivial, undifferentiated, or incomplete, and fees, retainers, salaries, bonuses, and expense allowances often go unreported. For all these and other obvious limitations, however, the reports can yield a latent but revealing image of the relative effort and resources that competing interests bring to bear on the state's governmental process. The image may lack contrast and detail, but it is all that we have.

Table 3 ranges reported expenditures and/or registrant receipts under major interest headings for recent legislative sessions in a number of states where reasonably complete data are available. For greater comparability, the results are given in percentages of totals rather than in dollars. The headings are not entirely satisfactory, for there are groups that do not fit squarely under any of them. The overall picture is clear enough, however, and again there are few

TABLE 3
REPORTED EXPENDITURES BY MAJOR INTERESTS IN SEVEN STATES

State	Business a	Transport b utilities, communication	Labor c	Farm	Loan, banking, insurance	Misc. d	Total
Indiana	11.9	15.8	36.8	1.7	4.5	29.3e	100.0
Kentucky	28.4	29.4	23.1	4.9	12.4	1.8	100.0
Nebraska	43.5	28.7	18.9	5.0	2.3	1.6	100.0
North Carolina	58.2	13.8	11.4	6.3	0.0	10.3	100.0
Ohio	44.0	21.2	17.6	1.7	2.9	12.6	100.0
South Dakota	28.2	32.9	5.3	5.0	18.9	10.0	100.0
Wisconsin	54.2	11.2	9.1	4.7f	9.0	11.8g	100.0
Seven-state Average	42.9	19.6	15.4	4.0	7.1	11.0	100.0

a Includes retail, wholesale, and manufacturers' trade associations; individual partnerships, firms, and corporations; mainly business-supported cause groups.

b Includes construction and associated concerns and interests.

c Includes public employee groups, but not public officials, which are included under "Miscellaneous."

d Includes professional, reform, tax, citizens', educational, and veterans' groups.

e Forty-three percent of this total ($8,622 of $20,013) was reported by an *ad hoc* tax assessment group deriving its support from diverse sources and individuals.

f Includes expenditures reported by coöperatives and other nonprofit groups.

g Consists exclusively of expenditures reported by cities, counties, and other public agencies.

surprises in it. Groups in the "business" or "utilities" categories generally report the largest expenditures, and the imbalance becomes more pronounced when these categories are lumped together, as they logically can be. In terms of common legislative interests, the "insurance and banking" category could be added to the first two without strain; all three are "business" in a broad sense, and the summary impression has to be one of business dominance, at least so far as reported spending is concerned.

What this means in practice is nicely demonstrated by the Wisconsin reports of a few years ago. The fourteen highest spending groups were, in order: Wisconsin Railroad Association, Wisconsin Motor Carriers' Association, Petco Corporation, City of Milwaukee, Associated Public Works Contractors, Wisconsin Wine and Spirit Institute, Wisconsin Mutual Insurance Alliance, Wisconsin Automotive Traders Associations, County of Milwaukee, Northern Paper Mills, Wisconsin Electric Power Company, Tavern League of Wisconsin, Wisconsin Association of Osteopathic Physicians, and Wisconsin Association of Real Estate Boards. The "business," "utilities," and "insurance" categories account for all but three of the fourteen—and two of the three exceptions are public agencies, which, under the laws of Wisconsin and several other states, are required to report on the same terms as other groups.

This kind of result only adds substance to standard expectations. Short of a total economic reconstruction, business interests in the United States will predictably spend more for political purposes than other sectors of society. They have more to spend, they have more in the way of legally defined status to protect by their spending, and they have the eminent good sense to protect themselves. The political posture of organized business and the widening scope of its interests are explanation enough for the figures shown in table 3.

Some of the same considerations applied in reverse account for the generally lower expenditures reported by labor and labor-oriented groups. Their ability to support massive political expenditure has, until recently, been relatively limited. It takes no great prescience, however, to predict that as the material resources of labor groups grow, and as these groups gradually see their objectives take statutory form, their efforts to protect their gains will inevitably increase (as witness the intensity and general effectiveness of labor campaigns against right-to-work laws in the late fifties).

The comparatively small expenditures reported by agricultural interests in most states are also in line with what one would expect. The political power of such groups depends less on superior material resources, or threats of electoral reprisal, or skilled lobbying, than it does on the representative structure of the legislature itself. It is unnecessary here to state the shibboleths of malapportionment and rural legislative dominance; it is enough to say that most of them are true.[82] With a built-in guarantee that their voices will be heard, agricultural groups are under no compulsion to engage in the conventional varieties of lobbying to the same extent or with the same urgency as less privileged interests. Although the major farm organizations are rarely without some kind of capital representation, substantial legislative expenditures by them should be, and are, unusual.

The expenditures reported by groups representing other interests are ordinarily quite small. California is the only major exception, with spending by medical interests, the State Bar Association, diverse professional, semiprofessional, and trade associations, educational groups, public agencies, counties, municipalities, and other jurisdictions consistently running far above that reported by counterpart groups in other states. In all of the states, veterans, patriotic, reform, and cause groups are conspicuously less active than they are on the national level, as the relatively small "miscellaneous" percentages in table 3 would suggest.

These interest-spending profiles admittedly leave much unstated, but they are not without their values. While they may not speak conclusively to the question of who rules, they can at least provide clues to the answer, lend substance to what might otherwise be unverifiable surmise. Without counting the hours that went into their preparation, however, it should be sufficient to observe that these profiles did not draw themselves. If this kind of analysis can serve any useful purpose—as we obviously believe that it can—then it should have been undertaken by the states. The point cannot be overstressed: Meaningful disclosure requires something in the way of public effort. For all its apparent simplicity, the disclosure idea cannot fulfill itself.

REPORTING IN PERSPECTIVE

The reporting requirement is the heart of state regulation of lobbying, and, in many respects, its most conspicuous failure. Full compliance is uncommon, and, where it exists, unilluminating. The expenditures reported are usually for standard personal or business items, or are reported in bulk without significant detail. Information about such matters as group sources of support, or group expenditures for purposes other than the employment of registered lobbyists, is rarely reported at all. These difficulties are capped by the belatedness of the reports. Except for California, Nebraska, and Wisconsin, where monthly statements are required, the reports drift lazily in from thirty-to-sixty days after the legislative session's end (if at all) when, as Walker once put it, "any damage that may have been caused is beyond repair."[83]

Each of these objections is separately valid, but they do not add up to the conclusion reached by one writer that reporting is "fruitless."[84] The fact is that with it we know more about lobbying than we could hope to know without it; reporting is "fruitless" only if this means that its potentialities remain largely unrealized. Working far short of maximum effectiveness, the requirement has at very least justified itself. Its problems point not to the futility of the procedure but to the need to apply constructive intelligence to its improvement. And, although it is not likely to happen in very many places in the recognizably near future, reporting could be substantially improved. Such improvement would not require major statutory change, and in many states it would require none at all. Nor is it even necessary that the general purpose of reporting be reconsidered *de novo*. This purpose should continue to be nothing more nor less than the periodic disclosure of information deemed relevant, without advance assumptions that disclosed information will be put to specific uses or have predictable consequences. This view of the disclosure process would rule out the idea that expenditure reports have value only as weapons, implied typically in the criticism that such reports are filed too late to "repair" any group-inspired "damage." Postsessional or even monthly reports may not be filed in time to prevent ill-considered legislative action, but this is not in any case a problem to which reporting is, can, or should be addressed. If "damage" is to be repaired and mischief in the legislative process prevented, measures more fundamental than more frequent or diagnostic reporting will be required.[85]

The key to improvement in reporting is not to demand more of the requirement than it can deliver, but to point it more directly at what should be its intended target—the political interest group. A requirement that groups report lobbying expenditures beyond those involved in the employment of registered lobbyists should be routine. In most states, furthermore, it could be established administratively and justified under the present general language of the law. There is no significant demand in any state that such a requirement be established, nor would the general operation and likely consequences of the disclosure process necessarily be greatly altered if it were. Nevertheless, some relative shift of emphasis away from the hired lobbyist and toward the group remains an indispensable necessity for more meaningful reporting. The lobbyist is an important political actor and we need to know all that we can about him, but not at the cost of distracting our attention from the groups for which he speaks. If there is no more to "lobbying" than what lobbyists do, then we might well undertake to redefine the term.

Chapter 5

ENFORCEMENT, ADMINISTRATION, AND PUBLICITY

Disclosure laws present two alternatives to the responsible official. He can regard them as conventional criminal statutes and enforce them as such. Or he can regard them as remedial in spirit, less proscriptions of conduct deemed unlawful than attempts to inject certain values into the political process. In this event, a quite different official attitude and procedure will be required. The first alternative calls for enforcement in a literal sense; the second calls for positive administration. These two approaches are related but separate. The former has the advantage of being stated in the law. Although the latter may more fully express the underlying purposes of the law, it is not supported by statutory imperative. These purposes can be achieved without criminal enforcement; they cannot be achieved by it alone. Flagrant or deliberate violations may warrant the imposition of appropriate penalties, but these penalties by themselves inform no one.

Most treatments of disclosure in the states have defined the enforcement problem in purely criminal terms without seriously questioning whether or how much this could advance the ultimate ends of the disclosure idea. From this perspective, the evaluation of enforcement tends to become a mechanical matter of counting prosecutions and convictions; the more there are, the "better" it is.[1] The more appropriate criterion, of course, is not how many people are caught in various postures of violation (although this may reflect how seriously the law is being taken on both sides), but how well the law performs its educational function. The penalties involved in effective disclosure are of another order.

Enforcement

On the side of criminal enforcement, the conclusion is inescapable that state disclosure laws have not often been put to work. It is not true, as Allen has asserted, that "there has never been a single prosecution under these laws."[2] It is true, however, that under the great majority of them, including many that date back more than sixty years, there have been no prosecutions. Although the data are not altogether dependable—official memories are short, and court and newspaper records are unavailable and/or obscure—it would appear that formal prosecutions have been undertaken under registration and reporting laws in just four states: Kentucky (twice), Missouri, North Dakota, and Wisconsin.

The character and outcome of most of this litigation is in itself instructive. The North Dakota case is marginal, involving conviction of a registered lobbyist for contempt of the Senate for having lobbied on the floor.[3] The Missouri case (State v. Crites, decided in 1919) centered on a contingent fee contract violating a provision of a disclosure law passed twelve years earlier. The Missouri Supreme Court not only sustained a lower court decision quashing the indictment, but found the law unconstitutional on the ground that it violated the requirement that a law contain no more than one subject, "clearly expressed in its title."[4] In the first of the Kentucky cases (Campbell v. Commonwealth, 1929), the Court of Appeals found the disclosure law constitutional but reversed on technical grounds the conviction and fine of a lobbyist for having gone uninvited onto the legislative floor.[5] In the second, a life-insurance company was indicted for failing to file the required expense report for an employee who, without the knowledge or consent of the company, had registered as a lobbyist in its behalf. A verdict was directed in the company's favor by the trial court, and this judgment was affirmed on appeal.[6]

Prosecutions for substantive violations of state disclosure laws have actually been successful only in Wisconsin, and this state's experience has been so unique as to deserve special comment. Wisconsin has always taken its disclosure law relatively seriously, as the frequent amendment of the original act suggests. There have also been more legislative investigations of lobbying and related phenomena in Wisconsin than there have been in any other state, committees of inquiry having been active in 1905, 1929, 1931, 1933, 1945, 1947, and 1957. The first major enforcement efforts, however, followed the extensive revision of the law in 1947. New provisions giving the district attorney of Dane County (in which Madison is situated) authority to prosecute certain violations were used against two lobbyists who had failed to register as such until two days before the end of the legislative session. The two men were barred from lobbying for three years, and fined $250 each.[7]

In 1949, newly elected District Attorney Robert Arthur—"a young, crusading county attorney,"[8] as one journalist described him—brought criminal actions against the Petco Corporation and two of its agents for having paid and received fees contingent on legislative action, a violation of the Wisconsin law. The case was first dismissed in Superior Court on grounds that the law empowered the district attorney to bring actions only to revoke lobbyists' licenses, and that a prosecution for contingent payments would have to be brought by the state attorney-general. Subsequently, however, Circuit Judge Reis issued a mandamus to the Superior Court ordering it to try the Petco case, which eventually came before the Wisconsin Supreme Court on the main question of the district attorney's authority under the law. The court not only upheld the constitutionality of the statute but also affirmed that a district attorney had both the right and the duty to bring actions whenever information of *any* violations occurring within his county reached him.[9]

Arthur also brought revocation actions in 1949 against lobbyists representing the Wisconsin Road Builders' Association, the Wisconsin Wholesale Beer Distributors' Association, and the City of Milwaukee, the complaint in each instance charging that the registrants' expense report was incomplete or false. The Beer Association representative had his license revoked for having failed to report some $7.05 spent by him in entertaining members of the legislature. It was the first revocation in American regulatory history. Several months later, the Beer Association was fined $300 in a separate civil action. The Milwaukee lobbyist was brought to book for failure to report certain items of expense which were billed directly to, and paid by, the city, and the revocation of his license stood up on appeal. The Road Builders' agent had his license revoked for false reports, and the revocation was affirmed on appeal, with the court rejecting allegations that the statute was so vague and indefinite as to violate due process.[10]

The direct results of this brief flurry of enforcement—it was not continued in 1950 or thereafter—were of no great significance in themselves. Its greater value lay in the impetus it gave to reporting compliance and candor, which in turn served to further the objectives of the law. The fees and expenditures reported by and for registrants in 1949 were substantially higher than they had ever been before, and doubtless one of the principal factors involved in this improvement was a widespread belief that Mr. Arthur, a normally ambitious man, meant business. But the change also reflected more than momentary caution, as Belle Zeller once found to be the case in New York under somewhat different circumstances;[11] indeed, its relative durability can be counted as the most important consequence of Mr. Arthur's efforts. Improved compliance means more information, which means more raw materials for effective administration to exploit. This is all that criminal enforcement can do. It will not control "undesirable activities" unless these are defined strictly in terms of registration and reporting noncompliance, and those who look to disclosure laws as means of "control" usually make it unmistakably clear that their criteria of the undesirable are considerably more inclusive.[12]

The Wisconsin experience suggests that occasional prosecution, or threats thereof, can have at least indirect value, yet counterpart efforts in other states have been infrequent, shallow, and lacking in conviction. Violations are common, especially of reporting requirements, but they are generally tolerated—which is to say, encouraged. It is news when responsible officers even entertain the possibility of prosecution. In Virginia in 1948, for example, two groups failed to submit the required postsessional reports. The *Richmond News-Leader*, a prime mover in the passage of the Virginia law, asked the secretary of state, who is charged with informing the attorney-general of violations, what would be done about these palpable examples. The answer was illuminating: "It was indicated that neither employer would be prosecuted, although [the secretary] said she intended to confer with the attorney-general within a few days on the matter." Whether the conference took place was not reported, but no prosecutions were brought, nor were the delinquent reports ever filed. Two years earlier two other employers had failed to file reports and at that time the attorney-general had specifically advised against prosecution, observing that "prosecution of unincorporated associations is most difficult."[13]

It is apparently most difficult in other states as well. Blatant violations are occasionally discovered and publicized by the press, but there are simply no prosecutions. In most states, nothing whatever is done to prevent, discover, or punish violations. In a few, the secretaries of state take tentative steps to minimize the most frequent kind of violation (i.e., failure of registrants or their employers to submit reports) by sending dun letters to noncompliants after the thirty- or sixty-day postsessional grace period has elapsed. In Alaska, Kentucky, Maryland, Massachusetts, North Carolina, and Indiana, these usually succeed in bringing in nearly all of the outstanding reports.[14] Nothing happens if they fail, however, beyond *pro forma* notification of the attorney-general, which closes the matter.

What accounts for this common unwillingness to act? Part of the explanation can be found in the widespread official belief that the penalties specified in most laws are inappropriately severe. Technical violations, or even deliberate evasions, are not, in one writer's words, considered "sufficiently heinous" to warrant prosecution and possible imprisonment.[15] The attorney-general of Ohio on one occasion advised against prosecution for a clear violation of his state's law since "he thought that a jury would not convict for an act involving no moral turpitude."[16] A companion view was expressed to the writer by the secretary of another state. He goes to considerable pains to persuade (or "pester," as he put it) all registrants until they have filed reports, which he personally believes are "a farce." He seldom has any delinquents, and he does not initiate any action through the attorney-general when he does. A lawyer and a former member of the legislature, he feels that the law deals largely with the lawyer-client relationship, which is difficult and perhaps "improper" to regulate. Although he is certain that no court would convict for violation of his state's law, he does nothing to put his certainty to the test.

The separate parts of this explanation are somehow more persuasive than the whole. Granting that violations of disclosure laws are not recognized as heinous offenses, that the maximum penalties are too severe, and that most courts would be reluctant to impose them, why are prosecutions so rare even where the penalties provided by the law are minimal? Clearly, there are deeper causes for nonenforcement than mere concern for appropriate sanctions.

It is, of course, true that the provisions of some laws would be impossible to enforce under the best of circumstances. To enforce the occasional prohibition against all but written and printed appeals to legislators, for example, would require that "a detective be stationed at every member's elbow all the time."[17] Nor would it be conducive to well-considered legislation to read such requirements literally; state legislators are not yet equipped to live and work in hermetically sealed voids.

It has been argued that the "vagueness" of most state disclosure laws has been a bar to their vigorous enforcement, but this explanation also fails to satisfy. Enforcement is most needed where violations are most frequent, and this is at the reporting stage. There may be some question as to whether an individual should register. There may also be some question as to what he or his employer should report. But there is no question whatever that, once registered, he should report, and there is nothing vague about the official's responsibility if he does not. Yet every year hundreds of reports are simply withheld, and they are withheld with impunity. Since *Campbell* v. *Kentucky* over thirty years ago, there have been no reported cases in which states have acted against violations of this character. Nor has any individual or group ever forfeited the $100 per day penalty that a few states exact for delinquent reports.[18] One writer has observed that prosecutors are reluctant to prosecute and courts are reluctant to convict except where there have been "flagrant violations accompanied by wide publicity"[19]—to which one might add, "and even then they are reluctant."

Walker has offered still another explanation for desultory enforcement: "Public opinion in most of the states has been satisfied by the enactment of the antilobbying statute, and there is little demand for its strict enforcement."[20] These are not "antilobbying" statutes, of course, although it may be true that "the public" thinks that they are. There should, however, be no cavil with the view that there is "little demand" for their enforcement. Has not the legislature, in its majestic wrath, banished "the interests" from the temples of the commonwealth? Not only does the enactment of the law settle everything, but it is also perpetually self-executing—a proposition than which none could be more soothing and less true.

As much as public apathy may contribute to the nonenforcement of state disclosure laws, active hostility from another quarter weighs even more heavily in the calculus. The plain fact is that the laws could and would be enforced if the legislatures wanted it that way. Here is the heart of the matter. The bright image of the legislature as citadel of the public weal against a darkening swarm of "special interests"—the Alamo of democracy, only this time we win—may warm the heart but it should repel the intellect. For the legislator defines his constituency in group terms; he is what his own group life has made him; now overtly, now tacitly, he represents something more than undifferentiated people. One can argue on rational grounds that the legislator misconceives a disclosure law if he reads menace in its lines, but if he does read it this way he can easily perceive in it a threat against himself and against the cluster of interests that shape his political universe. Nosey reporters, frustrated governors, or other upstarts may from time to time stir up the natives with yeasty allegations of corrupt or excessive lobbying, and these may require reassertion—brief, loud, and public—of the legislature's determination to preserve its own integrity; the enactment of a disclosure law or the demand for more stringent enforcement of existing laws can serve these necessities nicely. Apart from such occasional excitements, however, most legislators are prone to regard anything but the most limited or selective disclosure with deep-grained suspicion. We can grant that the penalties are often absurdly severe, that the laws are unenforceably vague, that "the public" is indifferent, but in the end enforcement founders on the same shoals of legislative hostility that made the laws what they are to begin with, and regularly strand any serious efforts to improve them.

The shoals were especially treacherous in 1953. Bills or resolutions to amend or study their states' law were introduced in at least seven legislatures during the year, and all of them vanished without a trace.[21] These were, in the main, efforts at improvement. The course and content of a quite different California proposal of the same year may be even more instructive. A bill sponsored by Senator Abshire of Sonoma County would have abandoned the requirement that registrants disclose their salaries or retainers. Allocation for legislative services was sometimes difficult to figure. "Besides," argued Senator Abshire, "the reports might show that one lobbyist makes more than another, and this might cause the lesser paid man to demand more money from his employer." And the senator did not believe that the legislature should "pass laws which cause friction among employers." Senator Donnelly replied that this was the "feeblest excuse" he had heard in his nineteen years in the legislature, and the *Sacramento Bee*, a family newspaper, merely observed: "What rot and nonsense! And what a philosophy."[22] The end of the story must by now be predictable: The Abshire bill and two others that would have reduced the reporting requirements were passed by the legislature but vetoed by Governor Warren.[23]

This happened in California, which has the best and best-administered state disclosure law in the country. It had happened before: An attempt in 1951 to amend the law to prohibit lobbying by registrants whose credentials had been denied was gutted by the Assembly before a gallery that "resembled a convention of lobbyists."[24] And it has happened since: Under a bill debated by the Assembly in 1961, state departmental executives associated with the development of state policy would have been prohibited from seeking or accepting employment to work against it for a period of two years after leaving state service. The most noteworthy thing that happened to the bill in the course of its defeat was the removal from it of a similar prohibition that would have operated against members of the legislature.[25]

These California episodes are unique only with respect to their frequency, their overtness, and the comparatively favorable disclosure background against which they unfolded. They admit of no other conclusion than this: It is profitless to assume that the dominant elements in the typical state legislature want or will permanently tolerate vigorous, impartial enforcement of disclosure statutes. It is equally profitless to assume that the attorney-general can or will enforce the law irrespective of the legislature's wishes. Of course he should, but the system just doesn't work this way.

These considerations argue against the view that improved administrative arrangements would by themselves produce more active enforcement. It has been urged, for example, that some official be made specifically responsible for enforcement, for "what is everybody's business is nobody's business."[26] Most laws do, of course, vest responsibility in someone, usually the state attorney-general, and while it may be true that a "busy attorney-general and his deputies cannot be expected to go through a mass of records to search for violations,"[27] it is nothing short of naive to assume that the attorney-general's reluctance to act derives wholly from inadequate information or from the many competing demands on his time. It might be feasible to lodge the secretary of state's present function as repository for registrations and reports with the attorney-general, as the channels of communication between the two are ordinarily quite ambiguous. This would give the attorney-general easier knowledge of violations, but it would not give him more authority to act, or more reason for doing so, or more support if he did. Logic, experience, and the nature of the case still argue for legislative administration of disclosure requirements, although this obviously could erect formidable difficulties of its own in the way of evenhanded enforcement.

Aside from their negative character, the main objection to these and other proposals for improved criminal enforcement procedure is not that they are technically unsound but that they are so unlikely to be adopted. Their adoption depends on the legislatures. As these bodies have been disinclined to broaden the scope of disclosure laws, so too have they shown no disposition to strengthen their enforcement provisions. The need is not for administrative devices so much as it is for a means of overcoming legislative distrust of the disclosure idea, and the administrative inertia that feeds upon it.[28]

The need is more easily perceived than met, and so long as our political affairs and the men who conduct them remain basically as they are, the prospects for the development of the required order of legislative tolerance and administrative energy are less than dazzling. The worst despair may be the best hope, and the recurring scandal that has in the past given rise to the enactment of disclosure laws may yet move the legislatures to become interested in their more effective operation. Although there is no certainty that we shall have to pay it, the price might be excessively high.

Positive Administration: The California Approach

A common preoccupation with the enforcement—or more properly, nonenforcement—of state disclosure laws misconceives their deeper meaning but coincides with prevailing administrative practice. An essay on what might be called "positive administration" does not have far to range. It can begin by saying that the goal is not prosecutions but knowledge; it can end by saying that except in California, official efforts to achieve this end are practically unknown.

California's experience with its disclosure law has been brief (as these things are measured) and in many respects disappointing. What has been done there, however, is at least suggestive of both the possibilities and limitations of positive administration. The events that led to the enactment of the law in 1949-1950—the banishment of Samish and virtue's inevitable triumph—have already been described. What followed the sound and the fury? How was an administrative superstructure erected on the foundations of a potent but ill-considered law? The original act of 1949 made no provision for administration or enforcement except to designate the clerk of the House and the secretary of the Senate as recipients of registrations and reports, a procedure borrowed from the parent federal statute. If Governor Warren had not called an extra session in 1950, principally to consider "improved lobby control," the legislature would probably have been content to leave things as they were. Warren called the session, however, and after several days of backing and filling, the legislature enacted administrative provisions. The most important of these stated that the legislature, through appropriately established committees, had the duty and responsibility of granting, denying, suspending, and revoking lobbyists' certificates; of investigating, through hearings and otherwise, the activities of such lobbyists; and of reporting violations to the appropriate officers. The committees, when established, would also be responsible for recommending statutory amendments to the legislature.[29] The establishment of a licensing system resembled the action taken by Wisconsin in the 1949 revision of its law; the California law went considerably further in providing for overall legislative control *plus* specific investigative authority. Beginning in 1951, both houses established the committees authorized in the law, and they, along with occasional interim study groups, have since operated continuously.

The existence of these Committees on Legislative Representation, as they have been called, has probably counted for more than their concrete achievements, but the latter have not been altogether negligible. At the outset, the Assembly Committee formulated a careful set of procedures to be used by it in the granting, suspension, and revocation of licenses, and in the investigations incident to these,[30] while the Senate Committee took the lead in the processing of individual applications for registration certificates. During its first year (1951), the Senate Committee denied eight applications, including those of an unabashed Artie Samish, four representatives of the California Institute of Social Welfare, and one of the Communist Party of California. Such denials, it should be noted, were (and are) less than catastrophic for their victims; the legislative counsel has from the beginning taken the position that registrants do not need certificates so long as they file their reports regularly and refrain from appearing before committees of the legislature.[31] Since Mr. Samish had not made such an appearance in years, the loss for him was not a great one, although other applicants have doubtless been more seriously inconvenienced.

In recent years, primary responsibility for the issuance of credentials has drifted to the Assembly Committee, with its Senate counterpart sitting quietly in the prompter's box. This arrangement was nicely demonstrated in April, 1962, when the credentials of the American Federation of Teachers' Sacramento representative were held up in the Assembly Committee on the complaint of Senate Majority Leader Burns.[32] The case was uncommon only in that the withholding was based on allegations concerning the applicant's background; forty-to-fifty certificates are usually withheld on more mundane grounds—technically defective or incomplete applications—each biennium.

If the case for legislative administration rested solely on the committees' control over credentials, there would be none. The values of continuous legislative involvement in the disclosure process are more prominently displayed in the intermittent hearings that the committees and their interim counterparts have conducted, in the analyses and interpretations of the law for which they have been responsible, and in the statutory recommendations that they have from time to time brought forth. At their hearings, the committees have sought both the counsel and criticism of lobbyists, enforcement officers, and other interested persons. That the counsel has not always been wise nor the criticism fair is of less consequence than the simple fact that it has been sought and aired.[33]

The several reports issued by the Committees on Legislative Representation have also been uneven in quality, but again their issuance counts for more than their substantive value. The best of them, aided materially by the assignment to the committee of a first-rate legislative intern, was very good indeed,[34] and the worst of them was no worse than merely pedestrian.[35] Although proposals for alterations in the law have come from other sources, these reports have also been the principal vehicles by which suggested changes have come before the whole legislature. The suggestions have not been unfailingly constructive, but the legislature has responded to the good and the bad alike with fine impartiality and nearly complete indifference. While the three amendments that have been enacted since 1950 owe their success to committee sponsorship, none of these can fairly be described as significant.[36] The thoroughgoing revision proposed by the Assembly Committee in its 1961 *Report* was never in danger of serious consideration by the whole legislature.

Although the California law, like the Federal Act from which it was drawn, remains to many a wallow of confusion (largely self-made), it has actually been more fully and precisely interpreted than other state laws, and for this too credit is due the Assembly and Senate Committees. The Legislative Counsel has issued at least fifteen separate opinions on the requirements and applicability of the California law, all but one of which have been in response to questions submitted by committee members.[37] These opinions have in no case enlarged the law; they have in several, however, had the result of clarifying its language to require greater detail in individual compliance.[38]

All this is to the good, but there are also debits to be entered. The first of these should by now be familiar: The Committees on Legislative Representation have done virtually nothing either to demand or to stimulate group compliance. They have not lacked the opportunity. At a hearing before the Assembly Committee in September, 1956, then-Attorney-General Brown reported two palpable violations of section 9903 (the group reporting provision). Why had he not acted against them? Because there had been "no active compliance with the law by any other persons subject to the provisions that had been violated."[39] There had actually been some; in either case, the committees were at fault because there had not been more, for bringing about "active compliance" should have been an important part of their *raison d'être*. It still should be, at least until such time as the group reporting requirements are excised from the law (as the Assembly Committee tacitly recommended in its 1961 *Report*).[40]

There is also no compelling reason why a committee from each house *plus* a legislative staff agency (the Legislative Analyst—recipient of registrations and reports) should all be involved in the management of the disclosure system. Legislative supervision would be more effective and more complete if it were in the hands of a joint committee with adequate staff of its own. To their credit, the separate committees have since 1950 regularly proposed just such an arrangement, and in its latest report the Assembly Committee additionally observed that "sound and thorough administration requires a full-time administrator."[41]

Although there is no widespread legislative interest in the joint committee approach and even less in the appointment of an administrator, at least the Assembly leadership appears to be willing to experiment with new administrative arrangements. Early in the 1963 session, in fact, Speaker Unruh sought (and thought for a time that he had won) Senate agreement on a joint committee, but at the last minute the Senate leadership decided to continue to go it alone.[42] Later in the year, and for reasons not entirely germane to the merits of the case, the Speaker disbanded the Assembly committee altogether and transferred its functions to the Rules Committee. Since the latter body already carried heavy burdens, the transfer in effect left the Senate committee to occupy the field alone. It also went a long if inadvertent way toward meeting the objection that the Committees on Legislative Representation had not always attracted the strongest members of either house; beginning with the 1963 session, the Senate committee was chaired by Alvin Weingand of Santa Barbara who, although only a freshman (of 58) at the time of his appointment, had already won unusually high marks in Sacramento for his intelligence and honesty. Later in 1963, the committee began to live up to its promise with a series of hearings designed principally to develop statutory recommendations for submission to the legislature at its next general session in 1965.

Some observers have suggested that from time to time in the past, the committees have been used as both protective weapons and instruments of personal harassment by their members. If such assertions are true, the circumstances that give rise to them would in all probability not be much altered by the two houses pooling their efforts in a joint committee. However and wherever they are mounted, investigations of lobbying are invariably selective as to their targets.[43] For this inherent bias, however, procedural remedies are obviously available, if generally unexplored.

The ultimate test of the California system, of course, is not whether it is orderly, well staffed, or even fair, but how effectively it processes and distributes the torrent of information that flows in regularly from more than five hundred registrants. In comparative terms, the system works well. Every year, under the imprimatur of one or both of the committees, the state prints an alphabetical "List of Legislative Advocates and Organizations" (i.e., registrants and employers). Every two years, all of the registrations and reports for the preceding legislative biennium are arranged alphabetically, photoprinted, and bound for distribution. No other state goes to anything like this trouble or expense, yet much of it is wasted because the materials stand completely alone. They are presented without classification, without analysis, without commentary, and they are not distributed widely or systematically. Here, in effect, are the facts; come get them and make of them what you will. As noted earlier, this is availability in the best sense, but it is not positive administration and it is certainly not publicity. Without any preliminary arrangement of the data, the effect of the biennial compendium on he who would find meaning in it is likely to be overwhelming. And without deliberate effort to put the data in the hands of those who could put it to use—principally mass and group media—the enterprise loses much of its distinctiveness and validity. Effective disclosure requires more than a slow gravitational trickle of disclosed data to whatever public exists for them; they have also got to be pumped, and the main task of administration is to do the pumping. In California, this extra effort has not yet been exerted.

After thirteen years, it is still difficult to strike a judicious balance in evaluating the California experience. Artie Samish and his works have become historical curiosities, but his spiritual legatees are still around to pick up the tabs and render other services to the commonwealth. Lobbyists register and report, the Committees on Legislative Representation go their separate and usually desultory ways, and the

Sacramento Bee's capitol man does his thoughtful best to find some news in their printed trail. Interim committees contribute intermittent reports, none of which have much altered or advanced the requirements or administration of the law. There is little general legislative interest in the operation or improvement of the system, and no evidence to suggest that this disinterest is not widely shared in other quarters. Measured against the experience of most other states, disclosure in California has been a triumph. Measured against the advantages with which it began—basically strong law, potentially viable administrative structure, and substantial press and public support— it would have to be adjudged a constructive disappointment.

THE DESIGN OF POSITIVE ADMINISTRATION

Precise structures are less essential to positive disclosure administration than agreement on the purposes disclosure laws should serve. If this could be reached—and it has not yet been reached anywhere —the details of administrative organization and procedure would in large part develop themselves. The end to be sought is, in all its complex simplicity, the widest possible dissemination of whatever relevant intelligence the law can be made to provide; the appropriate agencies and techniques are those that can help to achieve it. Criminal enforcement should be regarded as a second-effort sanction, to be invoked only where persuasion and publicity have failed.[44] Although the balance of official action will obviously vary from place to place and time to time, it should always hover around this central concern.

This kind of disclosure administration would require an agency for which there are presently no exact counterparts. Above all else, it should be an agency concerned exclusively with disclosure, unable to defend mal- or nonadministration on the grounds of press of other business. The nature of the problem and the generally dismal record of nonlegislative control suggest the values of general legislative oversight. The California experience does not encourage the view that this should be exercised through separate legislative committees, however, and joint committees, unless they were more amply staffed and autonomous in operation than is reasonable to expect, would represent no great improvement. The most promising arrangement yet proposed calls for a semi-independent agency, operating under the general supervision of a joint legislative committee responsible for "overseeing its methods and determining its policy."[45] Aside from the enormous difficulties of building "independence" in *any* agency that an American legislature is regularly called upon to support, and particularly in one that could cause the legislature such great discomfiture, the proposal has much to recommend it. The Securities and Exchange Commission affords at least a distant parallel, although it obviously deals in goods much less volatile from the legislative point of view.

Were it to be established, such an agency should have binding authority to interpret, subject to the usual judicial controls, the substance and coverage of the statute under which it worked. This implies some degree of discretion in granting and denying exemptions, and in determining the form and contents of registrations, authorizations, and reports. It should also have authority to mount inquiries into compliance, and independently to impose minor sanctions for noncompliance. It should finally be competent to institute appropriate civil or criminal actions against palpable or persistent violations of the law, or of its own regulations. The agency's main concern, however, should be to collect and analyze and throw to the four winds whatever data come its way; this would make the game worth the candle.

The main difficulty with this kind of administrative charter is that it is unlikely to be written in the recognizably near future. After seventy years, the need is plain enough, but there is no reason to believe that the legislatures will soon recognize that it exists. Until they do, the disclosure idea will remain essentially untried—and thereby fresh and new for those in whom the sanguine hope still springs.

Publicity

The ultimate end of a disclosure law is to convey special facts to plain people. This does not necessarily involve the assumption, that if "people are free and have access to the 'facts,' they will all want the same thing in any given political situation."[46] It assumes only that certain facts are relevant to public judgment, and that the public, therefore, should have them, reacting however their preferences or intellectual ingenuity may dictate.

While their underlying rationale assumes the competence of public judgment, state disclosure laws reflect no great concern with the ways of opinion formation in a modern society. The laws provide a means to get certain "facts," which are assumed to be both self-evident and self-propelled; they are, unfortunately, neither. The difficulty is partly of statutory origin. The typical requirement is only that certain information be filed at stated times and held open to public inspection. Beyond a few provisions for the publication of all or part of the disclosed data in legislative journals, and a few more calling for the distribution of lists of registrants to members of the legislature, this is "publicity" as the laws provide for it.[47]

It is not enough. There are two sides to the disclosure process: getting facts, and making them known. Registration and reporting—the investigative side of the process—can work to perfection, but without active dissemination of the results, the point of the law is lost. Notwithstanding our attachment to sentimental conceptions of vigilant citizenship, widespread public interest in these results cannot be vouchsafed in advance. It has got to be built, and since neither the laws nor prevailing administrative practice provide for the building, the keystone in the arch is the willingness of private disseminators of information to give the disclosure idea a voice that the laws neglected to provide. They have not often been willing. Press coverage varies from state to state and city to city, ranging from none to some, with the mode probably closer to the first extreme than to the second. In some states (Virginia, North Carolina), segments of the capital press have been instrumental in the enactment of disclosure statutes and have continued to follow their operation with faint and weary pride. In others (Ohio, Kansas), allegations of excessive or illicit lobbying have briefly drawn press attention to the operation of existing laws, or have prompted proposals for their revision or strict enforcement. There are a few states where major daily papers regularly give some attention to registrations and reports (California, Wisconsin, Texas, Rhode Island, Nebraska, Maryland, Indiana, South Dakota), but this usually consists of sporadic inside-page coverage in one or two papers. There are, finally, states where the operation of the law is usually— the temptation is to say "systematically"—ignored. New York is probably most conspicuous in this group.

Even at its infrequent best, press treatment of disclosure is not of the headline variety except where some sort of explosion has occurred. Wilson put it well when he observed that registration and reporting stories in Nebraska are "relegated to positions which normally escape the public eye."[48] Much of the responsibility for this kind of result must be laid to torpid administration. In most states, the responsible officials—usually secretaries of state—do nothing to make it easier for the press to function. Registrations and reports are often kept in forbidding disorder, without the simplest effort being made to arrange or collate them.[49] Mimeographed lists of registrants are no longer as uncommon as they were, but counterpart lists of reported fees or expenditures are rare. Still rarer are routine press handouts on the filings.[50] The reporter, scholar, or citizen bold enough to think that these filings might somehow be important is conducted to the records with unfailing courtesy; once there, however, he is strictly on his own.[51] Granting that the secretary of state has many responsibilities, that his office is usually understaffed, that the function ought to be lodged elsewhere, the conclusion is irresistible that publicity in the sense of active dissemination is more hampered than advanced by this officer's ostensible administration. The law gives him little to do, and he ordinarily does this no better than he has to.

The general failure of the press to put disclosure in 64-point type has origins more fundamental than official inertia. Principal among these is the fact that, again in Wilson's words, "the filings have comparatively little news value."[52] Disclosure stories in any of the ten or twelve papers that do a reasonably thorough job with the filings leave the curious common impression that their authors are straining for meaning, are threading their way around the periphery of something they know is gripping and important but beyond the ability of the filings alone to reveal. The stories are by now so worn and predictable that they almost write themselves: "Lobbyists Outnumber Solons 3 (or more) to 1." Or: "Lobbyists' reports on file at the State House reveal lobby spending of $ ———— . The highest fees were reported by former Senator ———— , representing ———— groups. The largest expenditures were reported by the ———— Association in opposition to the ———— Bill, which was defeated. Reports have not yet been received from ———— registrants." Are these things important? To whom? And can they be made gripping to anyone?

Special circumstances surrounding the law's operation occasionally call for variations from the standard format. The *Atlanta Constitution*, for example, regularly makes of nonregistration under the Georgia law what one of its editors calls a "cute" feature.[53] In South Carolina, light registration and no reports at all periodically move the *Charleston News and Courier* to give "prominent display" to the inadequacy of the law and its enforcement.[54] As noted earlier, this approach has also from time to time been followed in other states where the game was less fair.

If the displays are sometimes "prominent" in Charleston, they are not ordinarily either prominent, regular, or frequent elsewhere. Standard capital newspaper coverage calls for two stories a year—the first early in the legislative session dealing with the initial rush of registration, and the second after the session dealing with the financial reports then on hand. Even in those states where monthly reports are required, regular monthly stories are not the rule. The one well-established exception appears to be in Maryland, where the *Sun* of Baltimore includes lobbyists' filings in its daily "Legislative Routine" section. The *Sun* additionally carries relatively frequent news stories on filings of more than routine interest, and gives considerable space to the most interesting financial reports.[55] In terms of both frequency and total inches of space, the *Sun's* coverage of the Maryland law ranks high. That it still falls short of the easily possible underscores the difficulties of making disclosure more than nominal.

This is so in Maryland, where the *Sun* is the only daily paper of any consequence and has effective circulation through much of the state. Few papers blanket their states as thoroughly as the *Sun* blankets Maryland, however, and most of those that do have been relatively inattentive to the operation of disclosure laws. Capital papers are almost by definition more attentive, but they do not typically have statewide circulations. Although the *Sacramento Bee's* disclosure coverage, for example, is far and away the best in California, neither the size nor the spread of its circulation compares with those of the *Los Angeles Times* or *San Francisco Chronicle*, which do not ordinarily devote much space to lobbyist registrations and reports. The *Albany Times-Union* has also done a respectable job with the New York materials, but the major metropolitan dailies in Buffalo, Rochester, Syracuse, and New York—including even the good, gray *Times*—rarely give them space. Similar situations exist in Ohio, where coverage is more extensive in the *Columbus Citizen-Journal* than in the much larger *Cincinnati Enquirer* or *Cleveland Plain Dealer*, in Wisconsin, where the *Madison Capital-Times* outdistances its Milwaukee competition; in Michigan, where the *Lansing State Journal* gives better coverage than the Detroit papers; and in several other states where the contrasts in size between capital and big city papers are substantial but less extreme. One might well conclude that the possibility of effective disclosure is most present where the capital is located in the state's first or second largest city, where the largest paper in this city has influential circulation throughout the state, and where this paper is seriously interested in disclosure. The first two conditions are met in perhaps eleven states, the last in only a few of these.[56] With the exception of the *Baltimore Sun* and *Louisville Courier-Journal*, noncapital papers of statewide importance have rarely much concerned themselves with disclosure.

If coverage is only fair in most capital papers and slight in papers in major cities, it is practically negligible in the small-town press. Lobbying is apparently regarded here as filler news of limited importance, distant down- or upstate stuff not fit to take space from Little League box-scores, or Elks' lodge picnics. We might yet write better disclosure laws and administer them with verve and imagination, but there is no certainty that the predilections of both the owners and clientele of the American provincial press would not remain what they are, less resistant than indifferent to the disclosure idea.

It is difficult to argue that the press should not be indifferent, for there is no way around the fact that filings under present disclosure laws lack drama and "news value." A $25.00 bribe offer to a Washington legislator makes Seattle headlines, while a $3,000 "hotel and entertainment" item in a California lobbyist's report passes quietly unnoticed.[57] How can the report be made as newsworthy as the bribe? The answer, of course, is that it can't be. More diagnostic and demanding laws would yield a fuller harvest to intelligent administration, but the working newsman and his editor might well continue to prefer a story highlighting peripheral aberrations to one of real significance. And this is as it should be. It is no proper part of the disclosure idea to depend upon or demand alterations in the newsman's scale of values. His choices can, within narrow limits, be aided; they remain his alone to make.

The presumptive effects of disclosure are no less extraneous. The real criticism of our present laws is not that they are intrinsically inadequate, or that they "fail to strike directly at any lobbying evils,"[58] but that they have been allowed to operate in near privacy. This confusion of criteria has been nowhere better demonstrated than in the *Report* of the California Joint Interim Committee on Lobby Regulations. Limned against the setting of a uniquely useful law by men who should have known better, the *Report* confidently asserted that "all of these disclosure laws have proceeded on the common principle that undesirable activities can best be controlled by publicity."[59] No. Publicity itself is the only—and the only legitimate—end. Control of "undesirable activities" (whatever these are) is not a common principle but a commonly unfulfilled and irrelevant expectation.

But publicity, in the committee's view, could "open the door to what might be called concealment by over-disclosure."[60] Although the precise meaning of the language was enveloped in a misty haze, it seemed to suggest that all manner of sinister transactions ("undesirable activities"?) could with wide-eyed innocence and perfect safety be buried in the always copious reports. In reality, of course, the reports are seldom copious and would certainly reveal no irregularities if they were. The committee came to the unexceptionable conclusion that "the publicity given to undesirable activities by the various acts now in effect throughout the country is more illusory than real," but doggedly added this curious caveat:

> . . . the danger always exists that any special publicity for the mass of detailed material required to be filed would result only at times when certain groups come under attack by adverse interests. Deliberate or even careless use of such information without being properly analyzed and evaluated creates a constant threat for the use of false and distorted conclusions as a weapon injurious to legitimate enterprise.[61]

The argument is speculative, overblown, and ultimately self-defeating. Financial reports have rarely been put to use by competing interests, largely because the detailed and presumably damaging materials "required to be filed" are quite different from the undetailed and harmless materials that *are* filed. If the use of disclosure as a weapon injurious to legitimate or any other kind of enterprise is a problem, it is one not much to be feared in any case, for the objective of disclosure administration should be precisely to analyze and evaluate disclosed data so that "false and distorted conclusions" could not easily be drawn from them.

Essentially the same spectral banner has been furled against the application of the reporting requirements of the Federal Regulation of Lobbying Act to certain categories of group and corporate public relations expenditures. One writer fears that this kind of disclosure might become a political football, "bandied around by the press and subjected to every conceivable misinterpretation."[62] Surely it might, but in a free society does the distant possibility that intelligence will be misused justify its suppression?

The intent here has not been to take issue with the Joint Committee, which did a generally constructive job under trying circumstances, but rather to illustrate a view quite widely held of the box of dangers that more systematic disclosure is assumed to lid. The committee decried "illusory" publicity, but shied away from recommending steps that might have made it real. Most observers do not come this far, preferring to subordinate publicity altogether to more active enforcement, or institutional renovation, or other methods of direct control. The preference is not difficult to understand. The ultimate disclosure system cannot promise an end to lobbying, or to group conflict, or to the pressure of involvement in our public men. It can promise only a muted and continuing test of one aspect of the democratic thesis. This is little enough, but if interest groups are dragging the polity into a deepening mire of attrition and decay, it remains the most tolerable approach at our disposal.

And it still remains untried. The true measure of disclosure and publicity is not whether they have had demonstrable effects, but whether they have been intelligent, vigorous, and unflagging. No state has yet come close to meeting these criteria, and to say when, where, or whether they will be met would require large prophetic gifts—and uncommon optimism.

If the future of disclosure is cloudy, at least the shape it might ideally take is reasonably clear. The main requisite is administration that would promote the widest possible dissemination of disclosed information. This requires an appropriate administrative structure, the possible configurations of which have already been described. It also requires a distinctive procedural emphasis, of which the main components should be orderly management, intelligent analysis, and imaginative public relations. Orderly management means simply the maintenance of records so that they are readily accessible and understandable to someone other than the maintainer. Intelligent analysis means arranging and collating disclosed data in clear and meaningful ways. The compilation of expenditure totals, for example,—by major interest, by legislative interest, and in gross—should be routine.[63] Imaginative public relations would center around the single objective of getting the data to a maximum audience with maximum clarity and impact. It would involve writing handouts and releases, developing and servicing mailing lists, cultivating relationships with the press and other interested groups, and generally breathing life into the great mass of undifferentiated data that now goes listlessly to seed.

Improved administrative arrangements, like more diagnostic statutory requirements, are at least remotely possible through legislative action. For the final and indispensable ingredient, however, we are back again to the judgment and values of mass media managers.[64] However probing the law may be, however fully its resources may be harnessed, the whole enterprise hinges in the end on what these men think is news. All that has gone before distills to this: A public policy of full disclosure can only be privately fulfilled. If the process is agonizing and incomplete, we have yet to find a better way.

Chapter 6

DISCLOSURE IN PERSPECTIVE

Let us try to draw the salient features of the terrain we have covered into summary perspective. Where do we stand after seventy years of statutory disclosure? What kind of law is it? Where has it succeeded and where has it failed? Are better alternatives realistically available?

Questions of statutory language and technique are not our principal concern, although adverse judgment on these grounds would have much evidence in its support. State disclosure laws are uniformly imprecise in language, selective and uncertain in their application, and dotted with internal contradictions. Their relationship to other statutes is, at best, unclear. They state requirements and penalties, but generally fail to specify appropriate administrative or enforcement procedures. They make distinctions that are artificial and unobserved. Some of the more obvious of these flaws would be relatively easy to correct if the will to correct them existed. To remedy others, however, would involve disabling sacrifices of breadth and flexibility. There is nothing to be gained by seeking immaculate solutions here. While the failure of some state lobbying laws can be at least in part ascribed to their technical deficiencies, no law has yet succeeded purely—or evenly largely—because of its technical superiority, and no law ever will.

More in point are the formidable conceptual and operational burdens under which state regulation of lobbying has labored. The characteristic origins of disclosure statutes account for much of the burden. These laws have for the most part been enacted in direct response to charges or evidence that the legislature had yielded, or was about to yield, too much, too easily, to too few. Drawn hastily and from archaic models as retrospective declarations against sin, state disclosure laws have commonly been written without serious effort or intention to come honestly to grips with the more complex problems of which such overt activity as legislative lobbying is no more than an arresting surface symptom. And although most of them creak painfully under their nineteenth-century origins, these laws are rarely amended, and almost never improved.

Within the limitations imposed by their common conception of lobbying as a direct persuasive relationship between lobbyists and legislators, the laws operate. They operate, however, with little administrative support, and with few discernible consequences. The clear majority of those subject to current or defensible readings of the requirements *do* register and file reports, and we know in consequence far more about lobbyists and the groups for which they speak than we did before. But the "we" means principally journalists and scholars interested in such things, and we have had to travel routes to knowledge barred by circumstance or preference to others who might wish to share it. The few newspapers that have been even sporadically attentive to the operation of state disclosure laws have had to rely almost wholly upon their own resources in imposing some kind of order on the profuse clutter of undigested data that the laws wash up. The results have not been impressive. Press coverage has been shallow, infrequent, and largely confined to capital city papers. With every few exceptions, noncapital papers with substantial statewide circulations have been glacially indifferent to the existence and operation of disclosure laws. What is left of the provincial press has not improved on the performance, which is to say that it has fallen even short of it. With government and private groups no more than passively involved, disclosure as public policy has had to depend for its fulfillment on private estimates of disclosure as news, and these have generally been low. Whatever other values may accrue from the operation of disclosure laws, they have not yet drifted into the mainstream of community opinion, nor have they been pushed.

Here, in sum, are laws that David Truman, with his customary cool accuracy, could describe as operating "well out on the periphery of the political process."[1] They are on the periphery for a number of reasons, not the least of which is that they have never been anywhere else. Even as the first disclosure laws were being written, the political system had already begun to accommodate itself to the rapid and spontaneous growth of political interest groups. By the end of the first two decades of this century, the outlines of what Schattschneider has called the "associational universe" had settled into substantially their present form.[2] Writing soon after the first World War, Robert Luce could observe that no phase of political reconstruction was comparable in significance with the "planting at the nation's political center of the administrative headquarters of the 'interests.' "[3]

Luce was writing about national politics, but essentially the same development was taking place in the states, although on an obviously smaller scale. The major statewide associations, or state affiliates of national associations, had by then been formed and were making their presence felt. Lobbying of the traditional variety was—and still is—a more prominent aspect of state than of national politics, but the main actors in the new group politics were in many ways a new breed of men, engaged in varieties of activity that Hurst has well described as

> . . . almost wholly alien to the stereotype of the 'lobbyist.' The staple work of the representatives of major interests concerned with legislation began to center around detailed, technical craftsmanship in the drafting of bills, the gathering of statistics and descriptive material, collection and analysis of legislation and legislative documents from all over the country, the careful bill-by-bill scrutiny of all that was fed into the legislative hopper session by session, the assembling of briefs on pending proposals and the formal appearance before legislative committees, the preparation and dissemination of large quantities of printed material presenting a point of view for the education of the members of an interest group itself or of the general public. The conduct of this sort of work required both more professional and more routine skills than the old-style lobbyist possessed. Hence there arose a bureaucracy of interest group representatives. In its turn, this bureaucracy, by its own concentration of effort and its own ambitions, tended to strengthen the individuality and coherence of the various groups which it served.[4]

If state disclosure laws operate on the political periphery, it is in considerable part because they have from the outset been aimed at peripheral targets. Political interest groups do more than hire lobbyists to represent them, but this remains a fact that no disclosure law sufficiently reflects.

The development of political interest groups has been accompanied by gradual but cumulatively significant changes in the uses and objectives of private political action. As groups realize their objectives, their political preoccupations are often subtly transformed. Group goals tend to become protective rather than acquisitive; that is to say, while they still stand ready to accept whatever they can get from governments that still have much to give, many well-established groups want mainly to be left alone, a proposition of which state and national medical associations would appear to offer particularly obvious, but by no means unique, proof. Such changes in the character and texture of group demands have both reflected and fostered changes in political technique, and these in turn have greatly complicated the operation of disclosure laws. That lobbying methods are generally "cleaner" than they were eighty years ago can only partly be explained by such self-congratulatory factors as "an enlightened citizenry," or "an alert press," or "higher standards of public morality," although such factors have not been entirely without influence. The relative circumspection of present-day group activity, however, may be even more significant as an index of past political success; not only are relatively satisfied interests no longer able to corrupt entire legislatures with virtual impunity, but they no longer have sufficient reason to try. Capitalizing on the procedural lacunae of the government process, on their access to decision-making vantage points in legislatures and administrative agencies, on their electoral power, and on that institutional sluggishness that Truman has immortalized as "the defensive advantage," major groups increasingly play a quiet politics of stalemate, attrition, and delay to head off threats from competing groups whose interests lie in upsetting established equilibria. Such tactics are inherently less costly, less disrupting, and less visible than overt action in behalf of positive objectives, and they are also inherently less susceptible to the requirements of disclosure statutes (as these are ordinarily interpreted).

The relative visibility of the political process is also related to the failure of disclosure in a more general way. The bigger government becomes, the more difficult it is to see it whole or recognize how profoundly it has changed. This applies with special force to the legislature, not only because we customarily associate bigness in government primarily with expanded administrative power, but also because changes in the legislative environment have had a more elusive quality. Administrative agencies proliferate; legislatures do not. One can, however, point to such palpable developments as the unremitting growth of legislative workloads, with their attendant pressures for competence and professionalization in the legislative process; the decline of locality as the legislator's primary point of reference; the erosion of the legislature's representative cachet as its members have been increasingly obliged to assume the role of middleman between constituent interests and administrative agencies. These alterations have obviously and significantly affected group-legislative relationships, and, more generally, the representative character and function of the legislature itself, but there is no evidence to suggest that they are widely understood.

In a real sense, the legislature has drifted out of public view. We are sensitive to intimations of legislative misbehavior, but we are not continuously concerned with the normal operation of a legislative system that staggers under increasingly complex and insistent problems. We demand that revealed miscreants be punished, but fail to sense subtler varieties of corruption. We want "better" men in office, but do nothing to establish more positive standards of legislative performance. We are unaware of what the legislative system really looks like behind its institutional façade. Senator Clark of Pennsylvania recently observed that when Americans look at their legislatures—all of them—"we react to what we see with scarcely concealed contempt."[5] This might be true for those who look. One could also argue, however, that the dominant attitude of Americans towards their legislatures contains elements of apathy, alienation, and cynicism as well as deep and justified contempt. "Invisible government" used to mean covert domination of the political process. In modern perspective, it may mean something much more deadly: government so large, so technical, so complicated that men can no longer comprehend it, and hence no longer try. Confusion about government and plain distaste for it produce essentially the same result: withdrawal from continuous and committed participation in political life. Against this kind of background, mute disclosure laws have had little chance to operate as their supporting rationale assumes they will. Men should care enough about reality to seek it out unaided, but they do not.

Neither the shrinkage of the political public nor changes in the visible configurations of the political system conclusively account for the failure of state disclosure laws, however. The heart of the matter is this: If these laws have always operated "well out on the periphery of the political process," it is mainly because the legislatures have put and kept them there. We have already described the typical reluctance of state legislatures to enact disclosure laws. They have been no less reluctant to revise them except to weaken their requirements. In several states, the guise of improvement has actually cloaked efforts to dilute or scuttle laws enacted earlier, and these efforts have come mainly from within. We need not again restate the shibboleths of legislative involvement except to say that most of them are true. While there are, of course, the usual exceptions, most state legislators are prone to view disclosure laws through their own group memberships, preferences, and involvements, which they can reasonably perceive as threatened by demanding disclosure requirements. The real impediment to improved disclosure laws is not the technical difficulty of the task, but the general unwillingness of legislatures to take it on.

This applies *a fortiori* to systematic, rigorous extension of the disclosure idea to the legislature itself. Without this kind of parallel requirement, disclosure of group political activities is simply less than whole, but as American legislatures have not ordinarily regarded legislative ethics, interests, or behavior as fit subjects for inquiry or candor, they have been no less disinclined to fashion weapons that might achieve the same end indirectly. Evidence to support the point is inferential but abundant. It might include the nearly complete absence of requirements that legislators divulge their financial interests and relationships, the one-sidedness of recent legislative proscriptions of conflicts-of-interest, the arrogant piety with which a few legislatures have formulated codes of ethical behavior for other participants in the political process whose ethical perceptions were no more cloudy than their own. If American legislatures have not been more beguiled with externalized disclosure than they have strictly had to be, they have rejected it out-of-hand for themselves.

Beyond their failure to write "better" laws and to apply disclosure to themselves, the legislatures have also been at least initially responsible for the failure of the press to give the present laws a voice they do not independently possess. Both at and after their enactment, these laws have been consigned to a patchwork existence, unsupported by the kind of administrative structure and approach of which they are peculiarly in need. The problem is not so much that the legislatures have failed to establish appropriate criminal sanctions against non-compliance as it is that they have not concerned themselves enough with either stimulating more compliance or systematically and vigorously diffusing whatever data this might bring to light. The last of these is the real objective of disclosure, and it is primarily the legislature's responsibility to achieve it. As they have been unwilling to extend the reach of disclosure laws, however, so too have the legislatures been unwilling to assume any important responsibility for their effective operation. And with the possible exception of California, they have nowhere shared or sponsored efforts to move disclosed data into the mainstream of community opinion. Although many other factors—the laws themselves; the formation of political interest groups, and the development of group bureaucracies and political techniques; changes in the texture and insistence of group demands; the enlargement and dispersion of government; group and media preferences; public apathy and political withdrawal—have doubtless contributed something to the result, the conclusion is irresistible that the desultory record of state regulation of lobbying derives in largest part from legislative nonsupport. In the end, disclosure fails because here is no legislative zeal for it.

The Values of Disclosure

Hard assessment of the states' experience may not inspire total confidence in the future of the disclosure idea, but men continue to find values in it. For some observers, disclosure laws are essentially what they were to Governor Russell over seventy years ago: instruments for the prevention of improper conduct by representatives of private interests. A California legislative committee recently expressed its belief that the "fundamental purpose" of that state's act was "to protect the legislative process from being influenced by improper or unethical lobbying practices, and to expose to public scrutiny all expenditures that might be either actually or potentially abusive of the legislative process."[6] The difficulty here is that the ordinary operation of a disclosure statute cannot reasonably be expected to provide evidence of impropriety, unless this is narrowly defined as group expenditures or activities deemed excessive after the fact by an electoral consensus registered against candidates or proposals publicly associated with them, and this kind of test would be difficult to apply in most situations. There is even less reason to assume that disclosure requirements can reveal violations of the less elusive juridical standards (bribery, fraud, intimidation, and the like). This at least is true of such laws as we have managed to enact, and the prospect of more demanding ones is exceedingly remote.

Other observers have found related but more extensive values in disclosure. The authors of one widely-used college text assert:

> The theory behind such regulation is that if vital information concerning lobbies is made a matter of public knowledge, the people will be able to evaluate the propriety of the pressures which are brought to bear upon government officers. In particular, it is hoped that legislators will thereby be able to resist pressures which in the past they have submitted to because of fear that public opinion would not support them if they stood their ground.[7]

Efforts to distinguish between legislators and "the people" as consumers of disclosure have much to recommend them, but neither group has often used disclosed data as "the theory" argues that they should. There is, for example, a wide gulf between the sunny possibility that that "the people will be able to evaluate the propriety of pressures" and the realistic probability that they will. As Bertram Gross has shrewdly pointed out:

> The answer hardly lies, as some of the ardent advocates of disclosure have maintained, in the possibility that large numbers of people who might be described as 'the public' will have time or interest to read, understand, react to, or act upon this information.[8]

The possibility exists, but it is rarely realized.

The hope that a disclosure law will stiffen legislative backbones relates to David Truman's observation that it can serve as "a political asbestos suit." But where for Truman disclosure was a means of "protecting the claims of the legislative group itself against overly insistent group demands,"[9] it becomes here a means by which legislators will "be able to resist pressures." The argument is more irrelevant than it is untrue. The pressures that count come from within, and the kind of legislative self-revelation that would be required to lay them bare is simply beyond our present ability to achieve. The image of a politics where uncommitted men can hammer out agreement on the anvil of dispassionate debate still summons forth a warm response, but the burden of creating it is more than mere disclosure laws can bear.

The legislature also figures prominently in another cluster of perspectives on the disclosure idea. Here, disclosure requirements are regarded as means of "improving the legislative process,"[10] or of preserving its "integrity,"[11] or of enabling the legislature "to identify pressures and be guided thereby in making its decisions."[12] The purpose of disclosure is to keep political discourse civilized, open, and on the merits between plainly identified competitors. The authors of these views generally assign the legislature a more creative function than that of merely serving as a battleground where the myriad interests of a free society can have it out. For Chief Justice Warren,

> . . . full realization of the American ideal of representative government by elected representatives depends to no small extent on their ability to properly identify pressures. Otherwise, the voice of the people may all too easily be drowned out by the voice of special interest groups seeking favored treatment while masquerading as proponents of the public weal.[13]

The guiding assumptions here are that there is a discernible public interest in every political situation, and that it is the legislature's job to find it, declare it, and see it through. But "the public weal" is rarely this self-evident, and American legislatures rarely take so constrained a view of their competence. In the face of the unquenchable pluralism of American political life, it rings faintly hollow to assert that the ideal of representative government may require that protective mantles of disclosure be thrown around legislatures that may not need and do not often want them. There was greater wisdom, candor, and humility in T.V. Smith's description of legislation as ". . . a business in which you do something, then wait to see who hollers, and then relieve the hollering as best you can to see who else hollers."[14] No disclosure law alone can amplify the voice of all the people, or preserve the "integrity" of the legislative process, although it might yet help to test the need and bona fides of him who hollers loudest.

In the more "group-oriented," "tough-minded," and "operational" views of the disclosure process, there is no room for any sentimental nonsense about "the public weal," or "the voice of the people," or legislative integrity. Truman caught the most of it with his passing reference to disclosure statutes or proposals as "minor weapons in group politics and . . . reaffirmations of 'the rules of the game'."[15] Writing later and from a closer vantage point, Gross observed in similar vein that a "complex mass" of disclosed information would probably be

> . . . of greatest use to those participants in the legislative process whose sources of information are meager and whose power might be buttressed by facts of this type concerning other participants. In short, the information could, to some extent, serve to deprive some participants, particularly the stronger ones, of the advantages achieved through more complete secrecy and add a minor increment to the power of the weaker participants.[16]

The logic is impeccable, but it was probably no accident that Gross used conditional language to express it. Apart from a scattered handful of temporary exceptions, the state experience, as we have seen, points only to the conclusion that groups persist in their reluctance to use disclosure laws as logic argues that they should.

There are, finally, those who seek no more from the disclosure idea than a small measure of progress towards that "civilized morality" that Stephen Bailey called the key to the survival of democracy.[17] Of this view, the report of the Douglas Committee remains the most notable representative:

> Disclosure is like an antibiotic which can deal with ethical sicknesses in the field of public affairs. There was perhaps more general agreement upon this principle of disclosing full information to the public and upon its general effectiveness than upon any other proposal. It is hardly a sanction and certainly not a penalty. It avoids difficult conclusions as to what may be right or wrong. In this sense it is not even diagnostic; yet there is confidence that it will be helpful in dealing with questionable or improper practices. It would sharpen men's own judgments of right and wrong if they knew these acts would be challenged.[18]

If the statement rings, it also troubles. The difficulties involved in the assumption that "the public" will put disclosure to effective use have already been discussed. They are compounded here by a benign and hands-off optimism as regards technique. If any lesson can be drawn from the state experience, it is that the disclosure idea cannot be expected to fulfill itself. It requires management. While it may be in accord with democratic values to assume that there can be disclosure without it, that men care enough about "the facts" to seek them independently, it flies in the face of all that we know about the gathering clouds of cynicism and indifference that cast a pall over our political life. No disclosure law can ignore them, or operate freely in their presence.

The modest notion that disclosure can be "helpful in dealing with many questionable or improper practices" is an improvement on the usual moralistic cant, but it raises questions of its own. Since 1890, disclosure has been valued as a means of discouraging impropriety from without. For the Douglas Committee, the men whose judgments needed to be sharpened were not private citizens who had overreached themselves, but public men unable to distinguish their private preferences from their official responsibilities. No disclosure law will help such men to hone their ethical sensibilities to keener edge until they have also placed themselves within the law's impartial reach, and this they have been disinclined to do.

For the "general effectiveness" of disclosure, the committee adduced no evidence, for there was—and is—none. More in point was the committee's observation that disclosure "can do no harm to the public, and the long-run effects may be helpful."[19] And even here there is room for doubt; disclosure laws could do considerable harm if they were widely accepted as final solutions to whatever problems one believes they were designed to meet. That these laws were intended more as demonstrations than as remedies does not prevent men from imputing to them more curative powers than they actually possess.

"Real" Values and Dim Alternatives

Statutory disclosure is not without potential values, but we should have no overripe illusions as to what they are. Although the line between circumspection and deviousness often is, and will be, difficult to draw, there is at least scattered evidence that disclosure requirements can operate to modify group tactics to some degree, particularly when their operation is accompanied by actual or threatened legislative investigation, changes in distributions of power within the legislature or administration, or widely aired charges of noncompliance or other forms of covert conduct by groups or group representatives. These laws may also have internal values for group leaderships interested or compelled to demonstrate to their constituents that the latter are getting something for their money. Disclosure can buttress and, in a sense, legitimize group attacks on competing interests, both within the legislature and without, and it might conceivably make some residual contribution to wider public understanding of the real configurations of the political process.

If these are slender benefits, our present laws cannot be expected to produce more substantial ones. And if the promise of the disclosure idea rests on the adoption and enlightened management of more exacting statutes, then it has small promise indeed. Although guidelines to improvement are not difficult to draw, "better" laws are simply not in prospect, and might well alter nothing if they were. The mere enactment of nominally superior statutes would predictably reflect no more than further reluctant concessions by the enacting legislatures to the same kinds of potentially explosive demand situations that have ordinarily generated the laws we now have. We might also administer these superior laws with intelligence and verve, but there is no great likelihood that mass or group media would be responsive to the change, or that it would seriously impede the process of group formation, or induce major or unnatural shifts in the character and targets of group political effort, or populate state legislatures with a new breed of tenants.

There is, in sum, no reason to assume that disclosure laws alone can bring about significant alterations in the shape and texture of the system. They have appeal as low-key reminders that a bias for open dealing is part of the American political tradition. They also have appeal for their simplicity; unlike the more ambitious solutions for the "group" or "lobbying problem," they involve no institutional renovation, with all of its attendant uncertainties. But they are not worth enacting as mere expressions of distaste for the disorderly tugging and hauling of the system, or as intended means of pumping into it enough balance and restraint to wash away the presumptive taint of interest. Whatever else these laws may be and do, they are badly overloaded as vehicles of political reconstruction.

The question that remains before us is whether state political systems stand generally in need of the kind of reconstruction that disclosure laws cannot provide. Specifically, does an inherently expansive web of group political activity present such serious threats to the practices and values associated with the American representative system as to require more fundamental corrective measures? There should be fifty separate answers to the question. One could, however, probably defend the general proposition that state governments have survived crises and convulsions in the past, and the unprecedented problems, demands, and expectations that now converge upon them do not yet appear to have brought them to the edge of total paralysis and dissolution.

But survival has had its costs—in plunder, waste, and privilege; in public disenchantment with the political process; in too many solutions too long deferred—and the fact that we have met them in the past offers no permanent assurance that we can meet them in the future. The capacity of state political systems for grinding out limited consensus under relatively normal conditions may not be sufficient to enable them to manage situations that demand more than small sacrifices or delicate adjustments. As Gross has noted:

> When few victories are ever complete, when power is widely dispersed among many "veto groups," when every solution is a compromise that is objectionable to many, and when every settlement itself creates new problems, you have the makings of a stalemate.[20]

It may be the height of tragic folly to assume that the system can indefinitely hold a lid on the explosive potentialities of legitimate group claims too long unsatisfied, a proposition of which the changing mood of the American Negro offers the most obvious and disturbing proof. Although dark visions are "an inevitable part of the sales kit of anyone with a panacea to peddle,"[21] the enormous problems of urban growth and social change that now confront the states may add a deeper note of urgency to the old alarms. We might, therefore, consider briefly the remedial prescriptions that accompany some of the more somber diagnoses. One can envy Justice Holmes the cold urbanity that prompted him to write, "I have no faith in panaceas and almost none in sudden ruin," but ruin can also come slowly and on cat's feet. If concern with remedies is often vain, it is always timely.

Almost without exception, these prescriptions involve either direct or indirect alterations in what their authors take to be the present role and functioning of political interest groups, principally as by-products of more ambitious renovations. Although they generally accept interest groups as inevitable in a free society, advocates of the more wide-ranging varieties of political reform suspect that these groups are "cutting the community's life-lines," or exercising "undue power," or exploiting the apparent inability of political majorities to govern.[22] It follows that we must "organize public power adequate in strength yet responsibly exercised under public control for the reconciliation of group-group conflict and the imposition of programs promotive of the public welfare."[23] Whatever else this may mean, the use of the word "imposition" is probably no accident, for after all, "there is no escape from the pressure of organized power"[24]— except, of course, more power, differently organized.

Beyond such general strictures, the highroad chosen to a politics devoid of group conflict, pressure, and involvement hinges largely on the preferences of the analyst. If a presumptive excess of group political power is laid to dispersed or insufficient programmatic leadership, emphasis is likely to be placed on the development of more cohesive and disciplined legislative parties, improved legislative-executive arrangements, or strengthening the executive's hand. If it is laid to inequitable geographic representation, legislative reapportionment will probably have considerable appeal. If group influence is ascribed to the legislature's lack of expertness, information, or time, expansion of staff, research, bill-drafting, and constituent service facilities may claim priority. If diffuse governmental structure and procedure looks to be the villain, reorganization and rationalization are likely to be favored. And if the problem smells like simple moral rot, there are always codes of good behavior.

Although no one of these approaches is by itself likely to produce major changes in state political systems—nor, for that matter, are they likely to be adopted without substantial compromise, except under the press of events presently unforeseen—there is nothing to be

gained by dismissing them all as no more than rival intellectual exercises.[25] To magnify the barriers that block the way does not alleviate
the need for change. Too many social scientists "know" that reform
is always a chimera, and are resolved, as one of the best of them has
remarked, "to prove the accuracy of their knowledge by their collective inertia."[26] If remedial proposals are unlikely to survive un-
altered or do all that has been claimed for them, we should at least
reckon with the possibility that doing nothing may involve greater
risks than pinning too much faith on avowedly imperfect solutions.
For a polity committed to democratic values, listless survival should
not be good enough.

It is, of course, equally possible that time will obviate the need
for direct solutions. The winds of change still blow across the land,
and some of them will inevitably alter the present configurations of
the group process. The forced elevation of legislative reapportionment to the top of the states' political agenda portends profound
alterations in established patterns of power, and the continuing reorganization of state governments in the face of growing complexity
and scale should work more modestly to the same end. The acceler-
ated erosion of one-party politics in some states and the tipping of
traditional two-party balances in others will unavoidably involve
significant redistributions of group political influence. Although it
should give pause in some respects, the hardening of group-party
alignments appears already to have injected stabilizing elements into
the system. Looking to the groups themselves, there is some evidence
that the maturing of the society and a spreading fatigue with associational life may operate jointly both to slow the pace of group
formation and to limit the depth and potency of member-based group
participation in the political process.

The best that can be said for these varieties of undirected change,
however, is that countervailing tendencies have not yet developed
sufficient momentum to arrest them. There does not appear to be
any long-run likelihood that they will produce major readjustments
in the established web of relationships between interest groups and
state governments, nor do they promise to correct any of the more
serious malfunctions associated with these relationships. Since the
prospects for designed reconstruction of state political systems are
even more remote, the survival that should not be good enough may

have to be. This does not argue for a mood of helpless resignation; stasis may not be satisfying, and it need not be permanent, but it is easily preferable to unchecked deterioration. It may also require determined effort to maintain.

Such effort can only begin with realistic understanding of the disturbances and disequilibria that the group process can generate or reflect. These have little if anything to do with assertions that political interest groups speak for "selfish" minorities, or undercut the representative system, or resort to "improper" tactics, or that government yields too much to them too easily—although all of these things to some extent have been, are, and doubtless will continue to be true. We get closer to the mark when we hold some groups occasionally guilty of complicating that dispassionate search for political accommodations defensible as "in the public interest" that lies at the center of any viable democratic mystique. This does not contradict Truman's observation that in developing a group interpretation of politics, it is unnecessary "to account for a totally inclusive interest, because one does not exist."[27] Nor is it inconsistent with Schubert's judgment that "the public-interest concept makes no operational sense."[28] What appears to be mere shadow-play becomes operational reality when men believe that it is; and when men believe that government is acting in behalf of interests that transcend their own, their belief sustains democratic institutions. Willard Hurst touched the heart of the matter when he described the American legislature's loss of its "title of legitimacy, its claim upon the people's trust and obedience as the agency most representative of their common interests" as being largely rooted in its having been "too often proved unable to set up against the divisive pressures of particular interests a positive, working idea of the general welfare."[29] This says more about the real nature and problems of American politics than volumes of "operational" debunkery. The central problem remains what it has been from the beginning: the establishment and maintenance of visible and sufficient separation between private interests and the exercise of governmental power. It is primarily a problem of and for the legislatures, and it should be so understood—all the more because so few American legislators have recognized that it exists.

There is no shortage of available solutions, and some of them— stringent conflict of interest, disqualification, and financial disclosure requirements, for example—are at least intellectually promising. To choose among them, however, is at the moment no more than an abstract exercise. Their adoption depends on the legislatures, and these bodies cannot be expected to take action until they can no longer avoid it, or until, as we stated earlier, they have been repopulated with a new breed of tenants.

If the paper panaceas are reduced, in the end, to a handful of dust, we are not without resources more substantial than mere pious exhortations to do good. The gulf between the real and the visible political systems need not be unbridgeable. There is no reason to abandon the alienated citizen, or to accept his political withdrawal as inevitable. Why not, rather, proceed from the assumption that public reengagement in political life is not beyond our ability to encourage and direct? To such a process of renewal, a political science conscious of its opportunities and obligations could make a useful contribution. More ethically sensitive studies of the group process, or the formulation of more realistic approaches to conflicts-of-interest and disclosure,[30] or more committed participation in the strategy and tactics of institutional change, are surely not beyond the range of our professional interest. There is no canon against our caring enough about the future of the system to seek to nourish the seeds of adaptive regeneration that have always been at work within it.

Notes

Chapter 1: The Setting and the Problem

1 James Willard Hurst, *The Growth of American Law*, (Boston: Little, Brown, 1950), p. 62.

2 For a brilliantly corruscating analysis, see Glendon Schubert, *The Public Interest*, (Glencoe: Free Press, 1960).

3 *The Federalist*, Modern Library Edition, (New York: Random House, 1937), pp. 56-61.

4 "Many-Armed Bandit," *Newsweek*, XLI (April 1, 1963), 33.

5 The Governor made his comment in an interview over KNX (Los Angeles), June 29, 1961. See also *Santa Barbara News-Press*, May 1, 1963, quoting the Governor as saying "special interests" were out to "scuttle" his program.

6 KNX Station Editorial, "How to Succeed in Losing Money without Really Trying" (May 17, 1963).

7 William C. Havard and Loren P. Beth, *The Politics of Misrepresentation*, (Baton Rouge: Louisiana State University Press, 1962), p. 234.

8 Robert Luce, *Legislative Assemblies*, (New York: Houghton Mifflin, 1924), p. 421.

9 David Truman, *The Governmental Process*, (New York: Knopf, 1951). We adhere in what follows to Truman's distinction between "interests," "interest groups," and "political interest groups" (*op. cit.*, pp. 33-39). If no other designation is used, we are referring to "political interest groups," broadened to include corporations wherever the use is appropriate.

10 Jay Judkins, ed., *National Associations of the United States*, (Washington: Government Printing Office, 1949), p. viii.

11 The figures are derived from U.S. Congress, House, Select Committee on Lobbying Activities, 81st Cong., 2d Sess., *Lobby Index 1946-1949*, H. Rept. 3197 (1950), and subsequent Lobbying Act filings.

12 E. E. Schattschneider, *The Semi-Sovereign People*, (New York: Holt, Rinehart, and Winston, 1960), p. 31. Blaisdell notes that approximately 1,800 organizations "of importance for opinion-influencing purposes" maintained Washington offices in 1947-1948. Donald C. Blaisdell, *American Democracy Under Pressure*, (New York: Ronald, 1957), p. 59. Not all of these would meet most tests of "substantiality," however. A useful idea of the range and scope of national associations can be got from any *World Almanac* (e.g., 1961, pp. 525-540).

13 U.S. Congress, House, Select Committee on Lobbying Activities, 81st Cong., 2d Sess., *General Interim Report*, H. Rept. 3138 (1950), p. 8. In similar vein, see U.S. Congress, Senate, Special Committee to Investigate Political Activities, Lobbying, and Campaign Contributions, 85th Cong., 1st Sess., *Final Report*, Sen. Rept. 395 (1957), p. 194.

14 Alfred De Grazia, *Public and Republic*, (New York: Knopf, 1951), p. 143.

15 See Emmette S. Redford, *Administration of National Economic Control*, (New York: Macmillan, 1952), chap. 9.

16 Compare with Blaisdell, *op. cit.*, p. 67.

17 Richard W. Gable, "Political Interest Groups as Policy Shapers," *Annals*, CCCXIX (September, 1958), 91. See also Blaisdell, *op. cit.*, chap. 5, or Stuart Chase, *Government Under Pressure*, (New York: Twentieth Century Fund, 1945).

18 Paul Douglas, "Report from a Freshman Senator," *The New York Times Magazine* (March 20, 1949), p. 74.

19 In Chase, *op. cit.*, p. 2. The words are those of the late Raymond Clapper.

20 *General Interim Report* (note 13, above), p. 65. For a useful summary of relevant statutory provisions, see the McClellan Committee's *Final Report* (note 13, above), pp. 81-82.

21 *General Interim Report*, p. 65.

22 *Ibid.*, pp. 63-64. This thesis is more provocatively stated in Robert Lynd's introduction to Robert Brady, *Business as a System of Power*, (New York: Columbia, 1943).

23 Speaking for the Court in *United States v. Harriss*, 347 U.S. 612 (1954), at 625.

24 Ernest Griffith, *Congress: Its Contemporary Role*, (New York: New York University Press, 1951), pp. 106-107.

25 For a stimulating discussion of the costs and values of "chaos," see Morton Grodzins, "The Federal System," in *Goals for Americans*, (New York: Prentice-Hall, 1960).

26 *General Interim Report*, p. 66.

27 E. E. Schattschneider, *Party Government*, (New York: Rinehart, 1942), p. 200. This study remains a classic statement.

28 Emanuel Celler, "Pressure Groups in Congress," *Annals*, CCCXIX (September, 1958), 3.

29 Dissenting in *United States v. Harriss*, 347 U.S. 612 (1954), at 637.

30 Assembly Interim Committee on Legislative Representation, *Final Report*, (Sacramento: 1963), p. 10.

31 The statement was made by a young scholar to the House Select Committee on Lobbying Activities. U.S. Congress, House, Select Committee on Lobbying Activities, 81st Cong., 2d Sess., *Hearings*, Part 1 (1950), p. 54.

32 Chase, *op. cit.*, p. 8.

33 As they are by Truman, *op. cit.*, p. 503.

34 See below, Chapter 6, for discussion.

Chapter 2: The Origins of Regulation

1 Robert Luce, *Legislative Assemblies*, (New York: Houghton Mifflin, 1924), p. 367.

2 *Idem*, Finla G. Crawford, *State Government*, (New York: Holt, 1931), p. 146.

3 Karl Schriftgiesser, *The Lobbyists*, (Boston: Little, Brown, 1951), p. 5. See also Glyndon Van Deusen, *Thurlow Weed: Wizard of the Lobby*, (Boston: Little, Brown, 1947), for an engrossing account of the life and times of one of the first American political bosses.

4 Luce, *op. cit.*, p. 368.

5 Schriftgiesser, *op. cit.*, pp. 10 ff.

6 The merging is nicely suggested in Weed's remark about Harris, a senator from New York: "Do I know him personally? I should rather think I do. I invented him." See Frank M. Anderson, *The Mystery of a Public Man*, (Minneapolis: University of Minnesota Press, 1948), p. 177—a fascinating piece of historiography.

7 D.W. Brogan, *Politics in America*, (New York: Doubleday, 1960), p. 301.

8 Thomas Cochran and William Miller, *The Age of Enterprise*, (New York: Macmillan, 1947), pp. 79-80.

9 *Ibid.*, p. 81.

10 Louis Hacker and Benjamin Kendrick, *The United States Since 1865*, (3d ed.; New York: Crofts, 1941), p. 161.

11 J. Willard Hurst, *The Growth of American Law*, (Boston: Little, Brown, 1950), p. 63.

12 John D. Hicks, *The American Nation*, (Boston: Houghton Mifflin, 1941), p. 87.

13 See Miller and Cochran, *op. cit.*, p. 81, for the extraordinary terms of the charter.

14 Dayton D. McKean, *Pressures on the Legislature of New Jersey*, (New York: Columbia University Press, 1938), p. 189.

15 Paul S. Reinsch, *American Legislatures and Legislative Methods*, (New York: Century, 1907), p. 230.

16 Hacker and Kendrick, *op. cit.*, pp. 264-265.

17 Richard Hofstadter, *The American Political Tradition*, (New York: Knopf, 1949), p. 163.

18 Hacker and Kendrick, *op. cit.*, p. 161.

19 Matthew Josephson, *The Politicos*, (New York: Harcourt, Brace, 1935), p. 102.

20 Hurst, *op. cit.*, pp. 31, 38-39.

21 Luce, *op. cit.*, p. 432.

22 Notably, Maryland (1867), Virginia (1872), Pennsylvania (1873), and New York (1874).

23 Margaret A. Schaffner, *Lobbying*, Wisconsin Free Library Commission, Comparative Legislative Bulletin No. 2, (Madison: State of Wisconsin, 1906), pp. 17, 20, 21. The penalty in Rhode Island was forfeiture of a seat.

24 Although it has been said that the Pennsylvania provision of 1873 is essentially similar to that of Alabama, the Pennsylvania provision specifically classifies corrupt influence as "bribery." Schaffner, *op. cit.*, p. 20. See Francis N. Thorpe, *American Charters, Constitutions, and Organic Laws*, (Washington: Government Printing Office, 1909), V, 3129.

25 *Ibid.*, I, 153.

26 *Code of Alabama Recompiled* (1959), sec. 352.

27 Luce, *op. cit.*, p. 370.

28 *Code of Georgia, Annotated* (1936), sec. 2-205.

29 *Ibid.*, sec. 47-1000, 47-1001.

30 Constitution, Article IV, sec. 35, in *Statutes of California* (1947). The amendment further provided for the punishment and disqualification for office of legislators who had been corruptly influenced. Testimony in actions brought under the provision was to be compulsory, but with the proviso that it could not be used in subsequent proceedings against the person testifying.

31 Luce, *op. cit.*, p. 371.

32 Thorpe, *op. cit.*, VI, 4121, Wyoming Constitution of 1889, Article 3, sec. 12. Actually, this constitutional statement authorizes the legislature "to protect its members against violence or offers of bribes or private solicitation." It is the term "private solicitation" that dictates the present inclusion of the Wyoming provision, and the exclusion of articles from other state constitutions where the context indicates that the section is aimed at bribery alone. There are indeed few states that do not have, either as a part of their constitutions or statute law, some prohibition of outright bribery of legislators. See Thorpe, *op. cit.*, VI, 4356, in which some thirty-eight states are listed as having had such provision in their constitutions alone as of 1909.

33 The Alabama Constitution of 1901 prohibits any state or county official from accepting any fee, reward, or other thing of value "to lobby for or against any measure pending before the legislature or to use or withhold his influence to secure the passage or defeat of any such measure." *Code of Alabama* (1959), Constitution of 1901, Article 4, sec. 101. This provision is simply the current equivalent of the earlier provisions of the New Hampshire, Vermont, and Rhode Island constitutions, mentioned previously.

34 Reinsch, *op. cit.*, pp. 232-233.

35 For a somewhat contrary view, see A.F. MacDonald, *American State Government and Administration*, (New York: Crowell, 1940), p. 23.

36 Luce, *op. cit.*, p. 370, citing *Debates in Massachusetts Convention of 1853*, I, 785.

37 "Corruption in the Massachusetts Legislature," *Nation*, IX (July 1, 1869), 10; "Existence of the Lobby," *Nation*, IX (July 22, 1869), 64; see also Luce, *op. cit.*, p. 431.

38 Josiah Quincy, "Regulation of the Lobby," *Forum*, XIX (November, 1891), 353. Quincy was the drafter of this bill and of the subsequently successful one as well.

39 *Ibid.*

40 The committee report did not wholly blame the company, but rather agreed that it virtually "had to hire lobbyists for protection." See E.W. Kirkpatrick, "Bay State Lobbyists Toe Mark," *National Municipal Review*, XXXIV (December, 1945), 536. See also on this point, Logan, *op. cit.*, p. 86.

41 Quincy, *op. cit.*, p. 354. The moral of this story would appear to be: "Never underestimate the power of a determined legislature."

42 *Acts and Resolves of Massachusetts, 1890*, chap. 456, sec. 1.

43 *Address of His Excellency William E. Russell to the Two Branches of the Legislature of Massachusetts*, (Boston: Wright and Potter, 1891), pp. 22-23.

44 *Ibid.*

45 California, Nebraska, and Wisconsin.

46 *Annotated Code of Maryland* (1957), Article 40, sec. 4-13-11. There is no record of the authority granted having ever been invoked.

47 Quincy, *op. cit.*, p. 349.

48 *Ibid.*

49 Kansas, Kentucky, North Carolina, Rhode Island, South Carolina, South Dakota, and Illinois.

50 E.g., Louisiana and Texas.

51 E.g., Oregon.

52 Massachusetts continued to experiment after 1891. In 1895, the law was

further amended to require that paid lobbyists file authorizations to act, signed by their employers. In 1911, two further amendments were added. The first distinguished between "legislative counsel" and "legislative agents," with the former defined as persons whose legislative activities were confined to committee appearances, and the latter as persons engaging in all other lawful legislative activities. The second forbade members of state or distirct political committees from accepting employment as legislative agents (but not as counsel). Minor clarifications were also made in 1896, 1913, 1922, and 1939.

53 *Laws of Wisconsin*, 1899, chap. 243. There was some legislative activity *re* lobbying between 1891 and 1899. Tennessee declared lobbying to be a felony (*Acts of 1897*, chap. 117), and West Virginia provided for the exclusion of lobbyists from the floor of the legislature while it was in session (*Acts of 1897*, chap. 14). But no other state followed Massachusetts in requiring registration and financial reporting until Wisconsin so enacted in 1899.

54 *Annotated Code of Maryland* (1957), Article 40, sec. 4-13-11.

55 In addition to Massachusetts, Maryland, and Wisconsin, registration laws had also been passed by 1919 in Nebraska, Rhode Island, New Hampshire, Kansas, New York, Ohio, Georgia, Indiana, Kentucky, Maine, South Dakota, and Mississippi. For an incomplete chronology, see *Report of the Joint Interim Committee on Lobby Regulations*, (Sacramento: 1950), p. 25.

56 In Luce, *op. cit.*, p. 371.

57 Reprinted in P.S. Reinsch, *Readings on American State Government*, (Boston: Ginn, 1911), pp. 81-84. Emphasis supplied.

58 Although the governor spoke of "paid lobbyists" only, his proposal would have reached all persons who met the functional tests of "lobbying," since agency, at law, need not necessarily involve specific remuneration. For an illuminating discussion, see Luce, *op. cit.*, pp. 373-381.

59 Belle Zeller, "Pressure Groups and Our State Legislators," *State Government*, XI (August, 1938), 144.

60 *Report of the Joint Committee of the Senate and Assembly of the State of New York Appointed to Investigate the Affairs of Life Insurance Companies*, (Albany: 1906), X, 394 ff. See also Reinsch, *American Legislatures and Legislative Methods*, p. 250. The sums were indeed "enormous." In ten years, New York Life alone had paid out $1,117,697 for the "supervision of matters of legislation." See E.P. Herring, *Group Representation Before Congress*, (Baltimore: Johns Hopkins, 1929), p. 261; Belle Zeller, *Pressure Politics in New York*, (New York: Prentice-Hall, 1937), p. 252; Schriftgiesser, *op. cit.*, pp. 22-27.

61 *Report*, p. 396.

62 *Idem.*

63 *Ibid.*, p. 398.

64 Georgia, Indiana, Kansas, Kentucky, Maine, Maryland, Massachusetts, Mississippi, Ohio, Nebraska, New Hampshire, New York, Rhode Island, South Dakota, Wisconsin.

65 California, Connecticut, Illinois, Michigan, Montana, North Carolina, North Dakota, South Carolina, Texas, Vermont, Virginia.

66 *General Statutes of North Carolina* (1943), sec. 120-140, is the original law. The 1947 law is chap. 891, p. 1229, of *North Carolina Session Laws, 1947*.

67 The 1947 law served its immediate purpose, but it has otherwise been a dud. Four cause groups, all trivial, complied in 1947. The targets did not comply but

dissolved. No groups have complied since 1947, nor are many likely to. The approach of the law, however, deserves more serious consideration.

68 The word and the description were given the author by the former secretary of the commonwealth, the Honorable Thelma Gordon.

69 *Collier's Magazine*, August 13, 1949, pp. 11 ff; August 20, 1949, pp. 12 ff.

70 R.A. Collings, Jr., "California's New Lobby Control Act," *California Law Review*, XXXVIII (August, 1950), 479. For a breezy, but mildly terrifying, account of Samish, see Richard V. Hyer, "California," in Robert E. Allen, ed., *Our Sovereign State*, (New York: Vanguard, 1949), pp. 373-413.

71 Collings, *op. cit.*, p. 479. For information on Samish's contributions and on his ways before legislative committees, see United States Congress, Senate, Special Committee to Investigate Organized Crime in Interstate Commerce, *Third Interim Report*, 82nd Cong., 1st Sess., S. Rept. 307 (1951) pp. 102-103.

Samish had been the subject of investigation before. Among the findings developed in the Philbrick report of 1938 were the following: "Ample evidence has been produced by this investigation to show that corruption, direct and indirect, has influenced the course of legislation. . . . Corruption is not necessarily bribery. The term is a general one suggesting loss of integrity—a taint. The instances of bribery encountered in this investigation were relatively few. They were, also, relatively unimportant in the light of more widespread methods of corruption. A detailed dollars and cents record has been produced . . . to show that huge sums of money have been spent to influence legislation. The principal source of corruption has been money pressure. The principal methods of exercising money pressure have been through fees paid to lawyer-legislators and through expenditures of lobbyists.

"The principal offender among lobbyists has been Arthur H. Samish of San Francisco, through whose accounts has been traced a total of $496,138.62 during the years 1935-38. All of this money was provided by individuals, businesses, and organizations directly interested in legislation." Hyer, *op. cit.*, p. 395. For further comment on Samish and the Philbrick investigation, see Henry A. Turner and John Vieg, *The Government and Politics of California*, (New York: McGraw-Hill, 1960), p. 52.

72 For Warren's statement, see U.S. Congress, House Select Committee on Lobbying Activities, *Hearings*, 81st Cong., 2d Sess. (1950) part 1, p. 76.

73 1949 Extra Session, Assembly Bill 30, Senate Bill 7.

74 Collings, *op. cit.*, p. 479.

75 *San Francisco Chronicle*, December 23, 1949.

76 The description was that of Earl Behrens, the *Chronicle's* political editor, on December 22, 1949. See also Collings, *op. cit.*, p. 479.

77 *San Francisco Chronicle*, December 25, 1949.

78 *Report of the Joint Interim Committee on Lobby Regulations*, (Sacramento: 1950), p. 1.

79 *California Statutes, First Extra Session, 1950*, chap. 66.

80 David Truman, *The Governmental Process*, (New York: Knopf, 1951), p. 527.

81 See Belle Zeller, "The Regulation of Pressure Groups and Lobbyists," *Annals of the American Academy of Political and Social Science*, CCCXIX (September, 1959), 95-97 for comment.

82 Largely because the Richmond papers wondered abstractly what would happen if a financial report were not filed with the secretary of the commonwealth, the

legislature in 1945 added a section making it the duty of the secretary to inform the attorney-general of any violations coming to his attention: See *Acts of Virginia, Exec. Session,* 1945, chap. 39, p. 37. On California amendments, see below, Chapter 5.

83 The Nebraska Law in 1945, the Wisconsin law in 1933, 1941, 1947, and 1957.

84 See below, Chapter 5, for details.

85 The details are given in *History of Lobbying,* a paper prepared for the Wisconsin Institute for Trade Association Executives, dated February 11, 1949.

86 Told the author by then senator, later governor, Gaylord Nelson, Democrat. Also in 1949, the Senate Judiciary Committee killed a bill sponsored by Governor Rennebohm which would have made lobbyists' employers responsible for the acts of their employees. See *Madison Capital-Times,* November 9, 1949.

87 Zeller, *op cit.,* pp. 96-97.

88 For example, *Acts of Ohio, 1929,* p. 784; *Acts of Kentucky, 1930,* chap. 547; *Virginia Acts and Joint Resolutions, 1948,* p. 1332. The 1958 Illinois law makes such lists available at the request of legislators. Act of July 10, 1957, as amended by Acts of May 9 and July 25, 1961.

89 For a partial survey of recent efforts, all unsuccessful, to amend or study various state laws, see *Book of the States, 1954-55,* (Chicago: Council of State Governments, 1954), p. 131.

Chapter 3: The Statutory Basis of State Regulation

1 See for example, Edward B. Logan, "Lobbying," *Annals of the American Academy of Political and Social Science,* CXLIV (July, 1929), 65; James K. Pollock, "The Regulation of Lobbying," *American Political Science Review,* XXI (May, 1927), 340; Belle Zeller, "Pressure Groups and Our State Legislatures," *State Government,* XI (August, 1938), 147.

2 Article IV, sec. 35.

3 *Code of Alabama, Recompiled* (1959), title 14, chap. 55, sec. 352. This and following references to state laws refer to the last complete revision and not to the latest supplement, against which all references have been checked. References are to sections only except where title or chapter identifications are necessary for locating the law within the code.

4 See "The Federal Lobbying Act of 1946," *Columbia Law Review,* XLVII (January, 1947), 102-103. See also Robert Luce, *Legislative Assemblies,* (New York: Houghton Mifflin, 1924), p. 432 ff. for an illuminating discussion of the development of antibribery laws.

5 See "Control of Lobbying," *Harvard Law Review,* XLV (May, 1932), 1242.

6 *Utah Code Annotated* (1953), sec. 76-28-26. There is an identical provision in Mississippi. *Mississippi Code Annotated* (1942), sec. 2264.

7 *Deering's California Political Code* (1962), sec. 9054, cited hereafter as *California Political Code.*

8 *Arizona Revised Statutes, Annotated* (1956), sec. 41-1223.

9 *Revised Codes of Montana* (1947), sec. 94-2913.

10 *Nevada Revised Statutes* (1947), sec. 197.100. *Revised Code of Washington* (1956), sec. 9.18.110. The Washington law and, until the last revision, the Nevada law were titled "Grafting." This was the bluff and honest Old West.

11 *Tennessee Code Annotated* (1956), sec. 39-820.

12 *Vernon's Texas Penal Code Annotated* (1925), title 5, chap. 2, article 179. The provision was repealed by a registration law passed in 1957. *Acts, 1957,* 1st C.S., p. 17, chap. 9, sec. 16.

13 *Louisiana Revised Statutes* (1959), title 24, sec. 51.

14 Idaho, Kentucky, Louisiana, North Dakota, Oklahoma, and South Dakota. Section 313 of the Oklahoma Law states outright that "if any person . . . shall in any manner privately attempt to influence the act or vote of any member of the State Legislature . . . he shall be deemed guilty of Lobbying." This section, standing by itself, would be an absolute bar to all personal communications with legislators. In section 314, however, it is held to be "against public policy, and against the best interest of the people of the State of Oklahoma" to lobby except by the means specified, i.e., committee appearances, briefs, etc. These qualifications are practical limitations to an absolute interpretation of section 313, and the courts would undoubtedly so hold. Yet the sweeping literalities of section 313 remain on the books. *Oklahoma Statutes* (1961), secs. 313-316.

15 *Above,* note 10.

16 See Samuel Maxwell, "Necessity for the Suppression of Lobbying," *American Law Review,* XXVIII (March-April 1894), 211; "The Evils of Lobbying and Proposed Remedy," *American Law Review,* XXX (May-June, 1896), 398; "The Evils of Lobbying and Suggestions of a Remedy, "*American Law Review,* XXXIV (March-April, 1900), 224, for contemporary comment.

17 "Control of Lobbying," p. 1243.

18 *Kentucky Revised Statutes* (1959), title 2, sec. 6.260.

19 Illinois, Kansas, Montana, North Carolina, North Dakota, Rhode Island, South Carolina, South Dakota, and Wisconsin.

20 By this interpretation, agents of the Anti-Saloon League customarily avoided registration in these states, claiming in entire good faith that their employer had no pecuniary interest in any legislation. Peter Odegard, *Pressure Politics,* (New York: Columbia University Press, 1928), p. 105.

21 *Oregon Revised Statutes* (1961), sec. 162.520. The Louisiana law requires that personal interest in measures which are the subject of citizen petitions must be "fully disclosed" by the petitioner. Several other states also make disclosure of interest a prerequisite for contacts with legislators concerning pending measures.

22 See, for example, *Connally v. General Construction Co.,* 269 U.S. 385 (1926).

23 *Wisconsin Statutes* (1959), sec. 13.62.

24 *Code of Virginia* (1950), sec. 30-20. Similar language is used in Indiana, North Carolina, Rhode Island, South Carolina, and South Dakota.

25 *Florida Statutes* (1959), chap. 11, sec. 11.05.

26 See, for example, *Revised Statutes of Maine* (1954), title 1, chap. 10, sec. 34.

27 In Maryland, the two phrases both relate to the efforts to influence. In Mississippi and Ohio, "directly or indirectly" relates to the employment of persons, and "in any manner" to their functions.

28 *Annotated Laws of Massachusetts* (1961), title 1, chap. 3, sec. 39. Indiana, Kansas, Maine, Maryland, Rhode Island, South Dakota, and Vermont also use this distinction.

29 *Michigan Compiled Laws* (1948), secs. 4.401, 4.402.

30 Michigan seems to make a small specialty of innocuous legislation in the area of citizen-legislator contacts. Following disclosures of widespread corruption

involving a score of members, the legislature passed an act in 1945 that solemnly forbids payments for services to legislators "in excess of the reasonable value of such service if the same was performed by a person not a member of the legislature." *Ibid.*, sec. 750.4116.

31 *California Government Code,* title 2, chap. 8, sec. 9903, cited hereafter by section.

32 Zeller, "Pressure Groups and Our State Legislators," p. 147.

33 Allen, *op. cit.,* p. XXXVI.

34 *Ibid.,* p. XXI.

35 "Improving the Legislative Process; Federal Regulation of Lobbying," *Yale Law Journal,* LVI (January, 1947), 316.

36 Zeller, "Pressure Groups and Our State Legislatures," p. 147.

37 Alaska, California, Connecticut, Georgia, Indiana, Illinois, Kansas, Kentucky, Maine, Maryland, Massachusetts, Michigan, Mississippi, Montana, Nebraska, New Hampshire, New York, North Carolina, North Dakota, Ohio, Rhode Island, South Carolina, South Dakota, Texas, Vermont, Virginia, and Wisconsin.

38 *Baldwin's Ohio Revised Code* (1958), sec. 101.71.

39 *Code of Georgia, Annotated* (1936), sec. 47-1001 to 1006.

40 Kentucky, Kansas, North Carolina, North Dakota, Rhode Island, South Carolina, South Dakota, and Vermont.

41 *Vermont Statutes, Annotated* (1959), title 2, sec. 251.

42 *Mississippi Code, Annotated* (1942), sec. 3370.

43 *Baldwin's Ohio Revised Code* (1958), sec. 101.72. The phrase "not otherwise connected" has never been clarified.

44 For example, *Michigan Compiled Laws* (1948), sec. 4.404.

45 *Baldwin's Ohio Revised Code* (1958), sec. 101.72. The Virginia and Mississippi provisions are identical.

46 *California Government Code,* sec. 9906. The Illinois exemption was added to the original 1959 law in an act approved May 9, 1961.

47 Newspaper freedom has its obverse which only two states have recognized. The Indiana Provision is probably unenforceable but it recognizes the dimensions of the problem:

"It shall be unlawful for any proprietor, editor or publisher of any newspaper, journal, periodical or other publication, printed or circulated in this state, to receive any compensation whatsoever, or thing of value in the nature of an award from any source, either directly or indirectly, for the printing of any article, editorial, news-item (so-called), or advertisement, either for or against any bill or resolution pending, before either house of the general assembly of this state, without indicating in such article, editorial, news-item (so-called) or advertisement, at whose instance the same was printed, and the compensation or thing of value received therefor."

Burns' Indiana Statutes, Annotated (1949), sec. 34-306. The Wisconsin provision is similar but requires reporting rather than prohibition. There is no record of such reports having been filed in either state. *Wisconsin Statutes* (1959), sec. 13.72.

48 This exemption was picked up in slightly modified form in the relatively new (1957) Texas law. *Vernon's Texas Penal Code, Annotated* (1952), Article 183, sec. 4(c).

49 California, Connecticut, Illinois, Kansas, Maine, Massachusetts, Michigan,

Mississippi, Nebraska, New York, North Carolina, North Dakota, Rhode Island, South Carolina, South Dakota, Texas, and Virginia.

50 *South Dakota Code* (1939), sec. 55.0705.

51 *General Statutes of Kansas, Annotated* (1949), sec. 46-210.

52 The appearance of a vice-chancellor of the University of California (an attorney) for the California Retailers Association, and the hiring of a lobbyist by the Golden Gate Special District were the major *casus belli. California Statutes, 1961,* chap. 1966, sec. 1. For comment, see *San Francisco Chronicle,* May 23, 1961, and *Sacramento Bee,* January 28, 1961.

53 *United States Code,* title 18, sec. 201.

54 Note 19, above. Montana and Wisconsin use the phrase in defining "principals," or employers of registered lobbyists, but lobbying is defined broadly in both statutes and the phrase does not limit their applicability.

55 Act of July 10, 1957, as amended, sec. 1.

56 The 1947 revision of the Wisconsin law redefined "lobbying for hire" to include "activities of any officers, agents, attorneys or employees of any principal who are paid a regular salary or retainer by such principal and whose duties include lobbying." *Wisconsin Statutes* (1959), sec. 13.62. This is the only applicability section in any state law which in terms reaches "multifunctional" officers or employees.

57 *Revised Statutes of Maine* (1954), title 1, chap. 10, sec. 35, requires only employers to register within 48 hours; employees must register before acting as such.

58 California, Connecticut, Georgia, Indiana, Kansas, Michigan, New Hampshire, New York.

59 Massachusetts, Mississippi, and Ohio.

60 *Baldwin's Ohio Revised Code* (1958), sec. 101.71.

61 *California Government Code,* sec. 9906.

62 *Burns' Indiana Statutes, Annotated* (1949), sec. 34.301.

63 *Acts of Indiana,* 1955, chap. 238, sec. 1; *Alaska Compiled Laws, Annotated* (1949), sec. 35-2-181. Alaska registrants are additionally required to list their "party affiliation, if any." These days, you just can't be too careful.

64 *Wisconsin Statutes* (1959), sec. 13.61; *Revised Codes of Montana* (1949), sec. 43.802.

65 *Final Report of the Joint Interim Committee on Lobby Regulations,* (Sacramento: 1950), p. 10.

66 *Baldwin's Ohio Revised Code* (1958), sec. 101.71.

67 *North Dakota Century Code, Annotated* (1959), sec. 54-05-03.

68 *Wisconsin Statutes* (1959), sec. 13.67; *Revised Codes of Montana* (1949), sec. 43-805. It should be noted that the Wisconsin Legislature only infrequently complies with its statutory duty to publish.

69 *Michigan Compiled Laws* (1948), sec. 4.404. Other state legislatures have occasionally passed resolutions requesting the secretary of state to submit lists of registrants. These are generally limited to the life of a single legislature. See, for example, *Laws of Kentucky, 1930,* chap. 547; *Laws of Ohio, 1929,* p. 784. A Virginia resolution of 1948 was similarly limited, but lists are still regularly submitted. *Virginia Acts, 1948,* H.J. Res. 3.

70 Act of July 10, 1957, as amended by Act of July 22, 1959.

71 *California Government Code,* sec. 9906. See below, Chapter 5, for discussion.

72 *Baldwin's Ohio Revised Code* (1958), sec. 101.71, 101.72. Indiana, Mississippi, Montana, and Wisconsin also issue certificates.

73 The holding was by the legislative counsel early in the law's history. See *Assembly Journal*, 1951, p. 1496.

74 In Alaska, a resident counsel pays $10.00 for each resident employer and $5.00 for each additional resident employer, and $25.00 for each nonresident employer. Nonresident agents pay $100.00 for *any* employer, $5.00 for each additional resident employer, and $25.00 for each nonresident employer. Employers are called "contributors" in the Alaska law.

The question of whether the legitimate exercise of the right of petition can be taxed has never been litigated in Georgia. It would seem to be a sitting duck, however.

75 Kentucky, Maryland, Massachusetts, Montana, North Carolina, North Dakota, Rhode Island, South Carolina, South Dakota, Virginia, and Wisconsin.

76 In one case of which the writer has personal knowledge, a legislator in a midwestern state regularly introduces a bill to impose a one-cent tax on bottled soft drinks. A lawyer is just as regularly paid off by a large manufacturer of these drinks to "influence" the legislator to withdraw his bill. He does, and cuts the payoff with the lawyer. Robert Luce has written of similar situations, including an alleged purchase of his own vote. See Luce, *op. cit.*, p. 388.

77 *Wisconsin Statutes* (1959), sec. 13.62(3).

78 *Florida Statutes* (1959), chap. 11, sec. 11.05, states the penalty; the comment is from Harvard and Beth, *op. cit.*, p. 238.

79 *Oklahoma Statutes* (1961), title 21, secs. 313-315. Senate Rule 57 spells out the procedure for handling applications.

80 *Idaho Code* (1948), sec. 18-4707. See statement by Professor Zeller, U.S. Congress, House, Select Committee on Lobbying Activities, 81st Cong., 2d Sess. (1950), *Hearings*, part 1, p. 72.

81 Colorado, House Rule XLIV; Florida, House Rule 75; Iowa, House Rule 62.

82 House Rule VII, sec. 41. The disclosure statute, specifying registration with the chief clerk of the legislature, became effective in 1959.

83 *Baldwin's Ohio Revised Code* (1958), sec. 101.76.

84 See, for example, *Revised Statutes of Nebraska* (1960 reissue), sec. 50-304. Connecticut, Georgia, and New York have similar provisions. Maine and Vermont go their own Yankee way by barring employment for "compensation dependent upon a contingency." The language is probably broad enough to span committee action.

85 See "Lobbying Contracts," *Central Law Journal*, III (January 21, 1876) 34, for early cases on the point. See also Luce, *op. cit.*, pp. 374-381 for illuminating discussion of the development of decisional law on contingency.

86 *Kansas General Statutes, Annotated* (1949), sec. 46-207 is typical.

87 Among the states with docket systems: Georgia, Kansas, Kentucky, North Dakota, North Carolina, South Dakota, Virginia, and Wisconsin. Also Missouri, Louisiana, Texas, West Virginia.

The value of this ban is well illustrated by the following comment of a New York Assemblyman in 1927: "I well remember last year when this house was voting on a very important bill that a certain lobbyist stood behind the clerk's desk and checked the vote in order to make sure that the bill was passed." *New York Times*, January 26, 1927.

In 1949, the New York Senate "banished" lobbyists from the floor to the galleries. Also in 1949, a North Dakota lobbyist was held in contempt of the Senate for lobbying on the floor. Professor Zeller reports that a bill to restrict lobbying on the floor was defeated. Belle Zeller, "State Regulation of Lobbying," in *Book of the States, 1950-1951,* (Chicago: Callaghan, 1950), p. 134. North Dakota already restricts such lobbying. *North Dakota Century Code, Annotated* (1959), sec. 12-09-18. The Kentucky Senate voted for strict enforcement of the rule during the closing hours of the 1960 session. *Cincinnati Enquirer,* March 11, 1960. Two lobbyists were ejected from the Ohio Senate gallery in 1960, although there is no provision otherwise barring lobbyists on the floor or elsewhere. *Cincinnati Enquirer,* March 15, 1961. The Political Editor of the *Atlantic Constitution* observed: "Perhaps the most stringent regulation against them (lobbyists) is 'reading the rule' on the House and Senate floors which allows only members and the press in the chambers. When the hall becomes too full of lobbyists, they are read off the floor." Letter to writer (1962).

88 But see *Campbell* v. *Commonwealth of Kentucky,* 229 Ky. 224, 17 SW (2d) 227 (1929) where this provision was held to apply only to registered lobbyists.

89 Josiah Quincy, "Regulation of the Lobby," *Forum,* XIX (November, 1891), 350-351.

90 "The Federal Lobbying Act of 1946," p. 101.

91 The laws with this distinction do not appear to have been more effective in operation than those without it. See below, Chapter 4. That several laws make professional exemptions is suggestive to some observers of the inutility of requiring counsel to register at all, to say nothing of registering separately. ("The Federal Lobbying Act of 1946," p. 101.) This is strange logic. Because two provisions conflict, there is no reason to condemn both of them.

92 Kentucky, Nebraska, North Dakota, Oklahoma, South Dakota.

93 Notably, Idaho, Louisiana, Tennessee.

94 *Kentucky Revised Statutes* (1959), sec. 6.260(4).

95 "Control of Lobbying," p. 1246.

96 Act of August 10, 1945, repealing *Revised Statutes of Nebraska* (1943), sec. 50.301.

97 *Wisconsin Statutes* (1959), sec. 13.70. Montana picked up the sense of the Wisconsin revision in its new act of 1959.

98 *Annotated Laws of Massachusetts* (1961), chap. 3, sec. 43.

99 *Burns' Indiana Statutes, Annotated* (1949), sec. 34-306. Elsewhere in the same section, the publication of paid material bearing on legislation without adequate labelling as to source and payment is prohibited.

100 *Wisconsin Statutes* (1959), secs. 13.73, .3.74.

101 Kansas, Maine, Michigan, Montana, North Dakota, and Vermont.

102 *McKinney's Consolidated Laws of New York* (1952), Legislative Law, no. 66.

103 *Burns' Indiana Statutes, Annotated* (1949), sec. 34-303.

104 *Kentucky Revised Statutes* (1959), sec. 6.300.

105 In North Carolina, for example, reporting is required of every "person, corporation, or association whose name appears on the legislative docket." This could, of course, mean either agents or employers; in practice, it means the former. Agents also file in Kentucky (despite the express language of the law), New Hampshire, Rhode Island, South Carolina, and Virginia. Employers file in Connecticut, Georgia, Indiana, Maryland, Massachusetts, and New York.

106 Indiana, Kentucky, Maryland, Massachusetts, Mississippi, New Hampshire, North Carolina, Ohio, Rhode Island, South Carolina, South Dakota, Virginia, and Wisconsin. The latter state requires only that employers file within thirty days.

107 Connecticut, Georgia, and New York.

108 *Wisconsin Statutes* (1959), secs. 13.67, 13.68.

109 *California Government Code*, sec. 9903. The section reads "principally to aid, or the principal purpose of which person is to aid" in influencing legislation "directly or indirectly." This language borrows the most contentious and unnecessary phrase of the Federal Regulation of Lobbying Act. For a closely reasoned analysis of its origin and meaning, consult Norman Futor, "An Analysis of the Federal Lobbying Act," *Federal Bar Journal*, X (October, 1949), 366-390.

110 Sec. 9906.

111 Sec. 9903.

112 347 U.S. 612. See below, Chapter 5.

113 *Final Report*, p. 10. A similar objection was transmitted in the report of the Special Assembly Committee on Legislative Representation seven years later. *Lobbying*, (Sacramento: 1957), pp. 10-12.

114 *Burns' Indiana Statutes, Annotated* (1949), sec. 34-305.

115 *Ibid.*, sec. 34-303.

116 See Chapter 5 below for an analysis of the California experience. The Nebraska law can be read as literally requiring groups to report their income; it states that all counsel and agents and all employers of counsel and agents shall report "all money directly received or promised" in connection with legislation. *Revised Statutes of Nebraska* (1942), sec. 50-305. The writer has been told by legislators—and he believes them—that this was a drafting error; the law, revised in 1945, was not intended to require groups to account for their income, but only for that of their employees. That this may have been poor judgment changes nothing.

117 *Annotated Laws of Massachusetts* (1961), sec. 48. This provision was added in 1913, the date of the fourth of six revisions.

118 *Code of Laws of South Carolina* (1952), sec. 30-156; *General Statutes of North Carolina recompiled* 1955), sec. 120-46.

119 *Michigan Compiled Laws* (1948), sec. 4.406.

120 *Ibid.*, sec. 4.407.

121 *California Government Code*, sec. 9906.

122 *Annotated Code of Maryland* (1957), Article 40, sec. 12.

123 Alaska, Connecticut, California, Florida, Indiana, Kansas, Kentucky, Michigan, Mississippi, Montana, Nebraska, New York, North Carolina, Ohio, Oklahoma, South Carolina, Texas, Virginia, Wisconsin.

124 *New Hampshire Revised Statutes, Annotated* (1955), title 1, chap. 15, sec. 15:5.

125 *Florida Statutes* (1959), chap. 11, sec. 11.05.

126 The Kentucky law punishes lobbyists with five years imprisonment for any violation; corporate officers are imprisoned for only one year, however, when guilty of failure to register or report for legislative agents employed by the corporation. *Kentucky Revised Statutes* (1946), sec. 6.990.

127 Robert Allen disagrees, noting with disgust that "the penalties for violation are solicitously mild." Allen, *op. cit.*, p. xxxvi.

128 It is probably no accident that the penalties are lower in these states. In

North Carolina and Virginia especially, the laws are relatively recent in origin—both were passed in the 1930's—and this doubtless reflects some realization of the inappropriateness of overstringent penalties.

129 Both are possible in Kansas, Kentucky, Nebraska, New York, North Carolina, Ohio, Virginia, Texas, and Wisconsin. Either fine or imprisonment is possible in Connecticut, California, Indiana, Michigan, Mississippi, Montana, South Carolina.

130 Kentucky, Maine, Mississippi, Nebraska, New York, North Dakota, Rhode Island, South Dakota, Wisconsin.

131 *Kentucky Revised Statutes* (1959), sec. 6.290.

132 *Revised Statutes of Maine* (1954), sec. 39.

133 California, Kansas, Maryland, Massachusetts, Montana, North Dakota, Rhode Island, South Dakota, and Wisconsin. The Wisconsin law provides for the revocation of licenses. This suspends the lobbyist's privileges as defined in the law, until such time as his license may be reinstated. *Wisconsin Statutes* (1959), sec. 13.63(3). The Massachusetts provision prohibits the *employment* as lobbyists of those convicted of violations. *Annotated Laws of Massachusetts* (1961), chap. 3, sec. 43. The Maryland provision is similar. *Annotated Code of Maryland* (1957), Article 40, sec. 8.

134 *California Government Code*, sec. 9908(b). Violation of disbarment is made a felony; other violations are misdemeanors.

135 Assembly Interim Committee on Legislative Representation, *Report,* (Sacramento: 1961), p. 27.

136 *General Laws of Rhode Island* (1956), sec. 22-10-7.

137 In addition to Rhode Island, California, Indiana, Kansas, Maine, Maryland, Massachusetts, Michigan, Montana, New Hampshire, North Dakota, South Dakota, Vermont, and Wisconsin. The Ohio law merely states that the attorney-general or a designated assistant may appear before any grand or petit jury before which a prosecution under the law is being heard. *Baldwin's Ohio Revised Code* (1958), sec. 101.77.

138 "The Federal Lobbying Act of 1946," p. 101.

139 "Improving the Legislative Process: Federal Regulation of Lobbying," p. 315. See also, Pollock, *op. cit.,* p. 340; Truman, *op. cit.,* p. 528; Zeller, *Pressure Politics in New York,* p. 257.

140 *General Statutes of Connecticut* (1958), title 2, sec. 2-45.

141 *Code of Virginia* (1950), sec. 30-28.

142 "The Federal Lobbying Act of 1946," p. 102.

143 Some observers believe that this has happened in California, which has a much more open and theoretically responsible system of legislative supervision. See below, Chapter 5.

144 The provision was added in 1945 after some press criticism that the law had no teeth. The criticism was abstract; a capitol reporter wondered what would happen if a registrant failed to file a report, a rare event in Virginia. The use of this statutory authority is described in the *Richmond News-Leader,* March 7, 1947, and April 30, 1948.

145 *Wisconsin Statutes* (1959), sec. 13.63(2). For discussion of actions brought under this section, see Chapter 5 below.

146 *Final Report,* Joint Interim Committee on Lobbying Regulations, (Sacramento: 1950), p. 19.

147 *Ibid.*, p. 20.

148 *California Government Code*, sec. 9909.

149 This has twice been proposed by Assembly Committees on Legislative Representation—in 1957 (*Report*, p. 8), and 1961 (*Report*, pp. 23-24, 29-30). Assembly Bill 1816, embodying this proposal, was defeated in 1961.

150 Among the many discussions, see W.P. Hard, "Consider the Ethics of Lobbying," *Nation's Business*, XVII (October, 1929), 50-52; W.W. Musser, "Legal Ethics of Lobbying," *Oklahoma Bar Association Journal*, XII (April 26, 1941), 597-600; "Ethics in Government," *Report of the Governor's Committee on Ethics in Government*, (St. Paul: 1959); "Ethical Standards in American Public Life," *Annals of the American Academy of Political and Social Science*, CCLXXX (March, 1952), 82-104; George A. Graham, *Morality in American Politics*, (New York: Random House, 1952), chaps. 6, 7.

The comment about avoidance applies—almost *a fortiori*—to the United States Congress. The work of the Douglas Subcommittee in 1951 is unique for having touched the problem of the legislator's involvement in the ethics of lobbying, although it was more sparing of legislative sensitivity than the facts might have warranted. See "Ethical Standards in Government," United States Congress, Senate, *Report* of the Subcommittee on the Establishment of a Commission on Ethics, 82d Cong., 1st sess. (1951).

151 Truman, *op. cit.*, p. 159.

152 Schattschneider, *Party Government*, p. 200.

153 Havard and Beth, *op. cit.*, pp. 223, 236.

154 For details, see the *Cleveland Plain Dealer*, July 31 and August 3, 1959. Havard and Beth also write: "And inevitably the story is heard that one lobby in 1953 operated a call-girl setup with imported (that is, not local) prostitutes." Havard and Beth, *op. cit.*, p. 236. Late in the 1963 California session, San Francisco newspapers charged that "Nevada gambling interests" had established several doxies in Sacramento hotel rooms and were handing out keys to legislators who promised to vote "right" on a racing measure. See, for example, *San Francisco Examiner*, September 2, 1963. An investigation by Attorney General Mosk's office came up dry.

155 For details, see "Many-Armed Bandit," *Newsweek*, XLI (April 1, 1963), 34.

156 KNX Editorial, "Storm Signals at Sacramento," April 18, 1963, p. 2.

157 See *New York Times*, November 21, 29, December 2, 12, 26, 1961.

158 Havard and Beth, *op. cit.*, p. 233.

159 *Wisconsin Statutes* (1959), sec. 13.62.

160 For commentary, see Leon Epstein, *Politics in Wisconsin*, (Madison: University of Wisconsin Press, 1958), pp. 117-120.

161 *Michigan Compiled Laws* (1948), sec. 750.411b. The provision is not properly a part of the Michigan disclosure law, but it is appropriately discussed here since it was part of the episode that culminated in the registration statute two years later. The complex story is well summarized in the *Detroit News*, January 3, 1947. The "joke" comment is in Allen, *op. cit.*, p. xxxvii.

162 Opinion 83, in *Michigan State Bar Journal*, XXIX (May, 1950), 106.

163 *California Government Code*, sec. 9906.1.

164 *Ibid.*, sec. 9910.

165 Loth's comment may be in point: "In politics alone, the pimp enjoys a higher moral standing than the prostitute." David Loth, *Public Plunder, A History of Graft in America*, (New York: Carrick and Evans, 1938), p. 15.

166 "TRB from Washington," *New Republic*, CXLVIII (January 12, 1963), 2, "TRB" is reputedly Richard Strout of the *Christian Science Monitor*. See Arthur S. Schlesinger, Jr., *The Politics of Hope*, (Boston: Houghton Mifflin, 1962), p. 53.

167 Cited in "Storm Signals at Sacramento," p. 2.

168 *Minnesota Laws, 1961*, Chap. 558.

169 The reader might verify this by a look at any state government text.

170 E.g., Truman's *The Governmental Process*.

171 E.g., John Wahlke *et al.*, *The Legislative System*, (New York: Wiley, 1962).

172 Truman, *op. cit.*, p. 528.

Chapter 4: Disclosure in Operation

1 Truman's *The Governmental Process*, *op. cit.*, pp. 527-528, is a major exception.

2 The landmark for this writer remains V.O. Key, *Southern Politics*, (New York: Knopf, 1949). Key's later *American State Politics: An Introduction*, (New York: Knopf, 1956) is also extremely valuable, as is Duane Lockard's *New England State Politics*, (Princeton: Princeton University Press, 1960). Malcolm Jewell's *The State Legislatures: Politics and Practice*, (New York: Random House, 1962), is a first-rate study in a particularly difficult area.

3 Among the best, in the present writer's view: Leon D. Epstein, *Politics in Wisconsin*, (Madison: University of Wisconsin Press, 1958); Hugh A. Bone and Daniel Ogden, *Washington Politics*, (New York: New York University Press, 1960); G.T. Mitau, *Politics in Minnesota*, (Minneapolis: University of Minnesota Press, 1960).

4 An experienced Atlanta reporter estimated that "there must be 100 lobbyists regularly working the legislative sessions." Letter to writer (1962).

5 *Southern Politics, passim.*

6 *The State Legislature: Politics and Practice*, pp. 10-11.

7 Truman, *op. cit.*, 325. For an example, see Havard and Beth, *op. cit.*, pp. 213-237.

8 E.B. Logan, "Lobbying," *Annals of the American Academy of Political and Social Science*, CXLIV (July, 1929), 71.

9 Letter to writer from Harold I. Goss, secretary of state of Maine.

10 Letter to writer from Henry L. Oakley, office of secretary of state of Michigan.

11 Letter to writer from Annamae Riiff, secretary of state of South Dakota.

12 Letter to writer from Harry E. Jackson, deputy secretary of state of New Hampshire.

13 Letter to writer from Helen E. Burbank, secretary of state of Vermont.

14 Letter to writer from Walter C. Herdman, assistant attorney-general of Kentucky.

15 Letter to writer from A. C. Gustafson, chief clerk of the Iowa House of Representatives. Mr. Gustafson did not offer any of the facetious details.

16 *Columbus Citizen*, January 26, 1949, *Columbus Citizen* and *Columbus Evening Dispatch*, February 9, 1949.

17 It would appear to have improved too much to suit a few legislators. On March 31 there was introduced a bill which would have set the registration fee at $100. This measure, reminiscent of the Georgia tax, was quietly shelved, but it suggests how formidable a barrier the legislature itself can be to the intelligent use of disclosure. A bill to bar registered lobbyists from the floor of the legislature was also killed during the same session.

18 In 1959, a Franklin County (Columbus) Grand Jury investigated charges that a Cleveland senator's hotel bill was picked up by an Ohio Coal Producers Association lobbyist. The Grand Jury also toyed inconclusively with charges that call girls had been paid by lobbyists to visit legislators. For details, see the *Cleveland Plain Dealer*, July 31, August 4, August 14, 1959.

19 *Indianapolis Star*, March 2, 1949. A few names might have been added. The Lake County (Gary) Chamber of Commerce and the Studebaker Corporation had no registered lobbyists, although the latter was said to have been active against a proposed privilege tax. Several members of the assembly were described to the writer as "furloughed" Studebaker employees.

20 The episode is described in Melvin Pierce, "The Third House in Indiana," *National Municipal Review*, XL (October, 1951), 474. The law itself effects no such exemption. The attorney-general has ruled that a person who does not receive extra compensation for lobbying for his regular employer need not register. This, Pierce concludes, has "enveloped the law in a nebulous haze."

21 *Idem.*

22 *Raleigh News and Observer*, April 6, 1949.

23 *Ibid.*, April 7, 1949.

24 Told the writer by a Raleigh attorney, registered in behalf of two major trade associations.

25 The investigating committee also recommended that the registration law be "revised and extended," although the general terms of its recommendations would not likely have achieved the latter end. The legislature, on the point of adjournment, took no action on the report. The story is completely covered in *The New York Times*, March 28, 1953.

26 In Virginia in 1950, for example, the Southern Railway, the CIO, the Virginia Beer Institute, the Virginia Hotel Association, the Medical Society of Virginia, the Virginia State Bar, and several other major groups had no registrants in their behalf—a fact the more conspicuous by their having had registered representatives two years earlier.

27 On the Wisconsin act, see W.S. Carpenter, and P.T. Stafford, *State and Local Government in the United States*, (New York: Crofts, 1936), p. 47. Logan, *op. cit.*, p. 71, ascribes much of the success of the Wisconsin act to "the generally high plane of the state government." On the Massachusetts act, see E.W. Killpatrick, "Bay State Lobbyists Toe Mark," *National Municipal Review*, XXXIV (December, 1945), 543.

28 J.K. Pollock, Jr., "The Regulation of Lobbying," *American Political Science Review*, XXI (May, 1927), 339.

29 H. Zink, "Indiana Lobby Control Found Insufficient," *National Municipal Review*, XXVII (November, 1938), 544.

30 H. Walker, *Lawmaking in the United States*, (New York: Ronald, 1934), p. 295; F.G. Crawford, *State Government*, (New York: Holt, 1931), p. 148.

31 W.W. Crouch, and D.E. McHenry, *California Government, Politics and Administration*, (Berkeley: University of California Press, 1945), p. 71.

32 The registration figures for 1937 can be found in Belle Zeller, "*Pressure Groups and Our State Legislators*," *State Government*, XI (August, 1938), 1946-147.

33 For this information, the writer is indebted to Hugh Richardson, who as a Princeton junior in 1952, did an excellent piece of research on lobbying in Georgia.

34 Letter to writer from Harold I. Goss, secretary of state of Maine.

35 *Baldwin's Ohio Revised* Code (1958), sec. 101.71.

36 *Opinions of the Attorney-General*, 469, cited in *Annotated Laws of Massachusetts* (1944), sec. 41.

37 For a somewhat contrary view, see Belle Zeller, "State Regulation of Lobbying," *Book of the States*, 1948-1949, (Chicago: Council of State Governments, 1948), p. 126.

38 The national ratio is on the order of two and one-half lobbyists per legislator, the figure being significantly pulled down by some of the enormous New England legislatures. The writer refuses to guess what the "competence ratio" might be.

39 *Indianapolis Star*, January 14 and March 2, 1949.

40 Truman, *op. cit.*, pp. 353-362.

41 This explanation was given the writer by a registrant for a medium-sized statewide union.

42 Pierce writes: "Labor union lobbyists are registered in full force largely because they fear exposure if they fail to register. Some of them could rightly claim that lobbying is incidental to their regular employment, that they receive no extra compensation for it and therefore do not have to register. They feel that they have more to lose by not registering, however." Pierce, *op. cit.*, p. 474.

43 For an impressionistic but tremendously useful confirmation of some of these judgments, see John Gunther, *Inside U.S.A.*, (New York: Harper, 1947), pp. 253-254, 487, 646-648.

44 *Ibid.*, p. 32. Former Speaker Little was also registered under the Federal Lobbying Act for the same railroads.

That these things still happen in California is nicely demonstrated by this AP dispatch from California, dated August 8, 1962: "Assemblyman Walter I. Dahl, (R), Piedmont, has announced his resignation from the legislature effective September 1. Dahl, 53, said he will become a lobbyist for the California Pharmaceutical Institute."

45 Truman, *op. cit.*, p. 288.

46 From *The New Yorker*, November 13, 1960: "A kit of lubricants has been packed by a Milwaukee concern for use by householders, lobbyists, sportsmen, and Mechanics. Palm grease?"

47 *Raleigh News and Observer*, April 7, 1949. Where newspaper sources are not credited, the data are drawn from personal investigation and interviews.

48 *Providence Evening Bulletin*, March 7, 1962.

49 *Denver Post*, January 8, 1960.

50 *Houston Post*, January 13, 1959.

51 Mr. Wyatt was also registered under the Federal Regulation of Lobbying Act for a number of taxicab companies.

52 *Baltimore Sun*, May 3, 1961.

53 *Cleveland Plain Dealer*, August 5, 1959.

54 Epstein, *op. cit.*, pp. 195-196.

55 Told the author in confidence by the capitol editor of a Columbus paper.

56 Gunther, in *Inside U.S.A.* has a special feel for the "inside approach." Although fifteen years old, the book is still worth reading.

57 See Belle Zeller, *Pressure Politics in New York*, (New York: Prentice Hall, 1937), p. 258.

58 Professor Walker writes, "A small identification card carried in the wallet informs no one." Requiring the names of employers is simply a "repetition of the

obvious and well known." Harvey Walker, *The Legislative Process*, (New York: Ronald, 1948), p. 120.

59 D.D. McKean, *Pressures on the Legislature of New Jersey*, (New York: Columbia University Press, 1938), p. 244.

60 *Baltimore Sun*, May 18, 1960.

61 *Report*, p. 14. The figures also do not take into account unreported terminated employments.

62 See Pollock, *op. cit.*, p. 339 on Ohio; Zeller, *Pressure Politics in New York*, p. 256, on New York; and R.D. Wilson, "Registration of Lobbyists," *Nebraska Law Review*, XXVII (November, 1947), 125, on Nebraska, where reporting non-compliance was estimated at twenty percent.

63 Derived from Assembly Interim Committee on Legislative Representation, *Report*, (Sacramento, 1961), pp. 31-32.

64 A large part of the remaining noncompliance was by representatives of large, permanent associations; there is nothing *ad hoc* about such groups as the Ohio Railroad Association, Veterans of Foreign Wars, the Ohio Coal Association, NAACP, Ohio Manufacturers' Association, or Ohio Bankers' Association. The last two groups each had two noncompliant registrants.

65 *General Statutes of North Carolina* (Recompiled 1955), sec. 120-44.

66 Letter to writer, William T. Gleeson, deputy secretary of state.

67 *Revised Statutes of Nebraska*, 1943 (1960 reissue), sec. 50-305.

68 In North Carolina, 63 of 119 reports filed in 1949 were deficient in this respect.

69 *Burns' Indiana Statutes, Annotated* (1949), sec. 34-306.

70 *Annotated Laws of Massachusetts* (1961), chap. 3, sec. 48.

71 *General Statutes of Connecticut* (1958), title 2, sec. 2-45.

72 Wisconsin Statutes (1959), secs. 13.67 and 13.62, respectively.

73 The story was told the writer by a member of the Wisconsin Senate who bought his own. Apropos, Epstein observes (*op. cit.*, p. 119) that there were ten former legislators among the seventeen lawyer-lobbyists who spent most on entertaining legislators. He also notes (p. 103) that the free lunch is more important in the state capital than in "the more sophisticated atmosphere of Washington." The prohibitions of 1957 have however, cut into lobbyist entertainment considerably. See *Milwaukee Journal*, March 22, 1959.

74 Pollock, *op. cit.*, p. 339. For corroborating detail, see W.B. Graves, *American State Government*, (3d ed.; Boston: Heath, 1946), p. 333.

75 Truman, *op. cit.*, p. 528.

76 E.g., the Lorraine in Madison, the Claypool in Indianapolis, the John Marshall in Richmond, the Cornhusker in Lincoln, the Senator and El Mirador in Sacramento, and so on.

77 The compilation is printed as *Part Two* of the *Assembly Journal* for a legislative day—in 1961, June 16. *The Sacramento Bee* story appeared as a Sunday feature, September 10, 1961.

Studies made by the staff of the Senate Committee on Legislative Representation showed total reported expenditures of $1,046,983.60 for the months that the Legislature was in session during 1963. Special session reports brought the total to $1,343,503.14 for the first eight months of the year.

As to fees, salaries, and retainers, the Committee's estimate ran to an additional $2,000,000. Again, the figure is, if anything, conservative.

78 If there is any doubt as to what this means, note that Mr. Read regularly reports that his expenses are "paid direct by Committee on Legislation—California Medical Association."

79 Golden Gate Bridge and Highway District, Southern Counties Gas Company, Southern California Gas Company, California Music Merchants Association, and five water groups or districts.

80 Graves, *op. cit.*, p. 333.

81 The highest figure reported other than in California in 1961 was, to the best of the writer's knowledge, the $33,000 reported by former Judge Wyatt in Maryland. In Connecticut for the same year, attorney Joseph P. Cooney, former state senator and assistant U.S. district attorney, reported receipts of $18,915.90.

82 By far the best treatment of the subject remains Gordon Baker's *Rural versus Urban Political Power*, (New York: Random House, 1955).

83 Walker, *The Legislative Process*, p. 120.

84 *Idem.*

85 For a typical statement of the presumptive values of more frequent reporting, see "The Federal Lobbying Act of 1946," p. 120, where the author states that the Nebraska and Wisconsin monthly reports give "some warning that there has been objectionable lobbying before the session ends and makes legislative action on a measure irrevocable." This is an argument of logic, but not reality. The monthly reports in these two states are even more innocuous than the sessional ones.

Chapter 5: Enforcement, Administration, and Publicity

1 As in "The Federal Lobbying Act of 1946," p. 102; and "Control of Lobbying," *Harvard Law Review*, XLV (May, 1932), 1247.

2 Allen, *op. cit.*, p. xxxv.

3 The case occurred in 1949; the lobbyist was convicted and fined. The registration law prohibits going on the floor (*North Dakota Century Code* [1959], sec. 54-05-09). In several other states the prohibition is independent of the registration requirement, and is in any case irrelevant to it.

4 277 Mo. 194, 209 SW 863.

5 229 Ky. 264, 17 SW (2d) 227. Logan records the stir created by the *Campbell* case. Actually eight lobbyists who had violated the provision of the Kentucky law prohibiting uninvited appearances on the legislative floor were fined $250 and costs. Logan, *op. cit.*, p. 71. At the same time, cases against nine other lobbyists charged with the same offense were dismissed for lack of evidence. See *The New York Times*, September 4 and 5, 1928.

6 *Commonwealth* v. *Aetna*, 263 Ky. 803, 93 SW (2d) 840 (1936).

7 For interesting discussion and background, see *History of Lobbying*, mimeographed pamphlet of the Wisconsin Institute for Trade Association Executives, dated February 11, 1949.

8 Allen, *op. cit.*, p. xxxv.

9 *State ex rel. Arthur* v. *Superior Court*, 257 Wis. 430 (1950). See also *Madison Capital-Times*, June 18, September 27, 29, 1949.

10 The Milwaukee case is reported as *State* v. *Decker*, 258 Wis. 177, 45 NW (2d) 98 (1950); the Road Builders case as *State* v. *Hoebel*, 256 Wis. 549, 41 NW (2d) 865 (1950). For comment on these cases, see *Madison Capital-Times*, June 18, 28, July 13, December 2, 1949. Of Arthur's efforts, Allen, *op. cit.*, p. xxxv, writes: "He didn't get far."

11 "Pressure Politics in New York," p. 257.

12 See, for example, *Report* of the Joint Interim Committee on Lobby Regulations (1950), pp. 10, 18, discussed in greater detail below, this chapter.

13 *Richmond News-Leader*, August 30, 1948.

14 This has not always been the case. In Maryland in 1951, 30 of 123 principals never did comply. In Indiana, 43 of 87 principals were sent such letters in 1949, and all but one of them eventually complied.

15 "Control of Lobbying," p. 1247.

16 "The Federal Lobbying Act of 1946," p. 102, note 30, citing *Opinions of the Attorney General*, no. 1148 (1927), p. 2037.

17 McKean, *op. cit.*, p. 242.

18 Tentative steps were taken in New York in 1920 to bring the Anti-Saloon League before an Albany County grand jury for failing to comply with the New York law, but this action never materialized. Assemblyman Cuvillier estimated that the League would probably have owed the state some $70,000 in forfeits, although since their lobbyists had not registered it was problematical whether or not the forfeit provision could have been applied to them. Zeller, "Pressure Politics in New York," p. 257.

19 "Improving the Legislative Process: Federal Regulation of Lobbying," p. 315.

20 Walker, "Lawmaking in the United States," p. 295.

21 Several of these are discussed in Belle Zeller's "The State Lobby Laws," in *Book of the States, 1954-1955*, (Chicago: Council of State Governments, 1954), p. 131. The states involved were Maine, Vermont, Massachusetts, Rhode Island, Wisconsin, Kansas, and California.

22 *Sacramento Bee*, May 5, 6, 1953.

23 *Sacramento Bee*, July 6, 1953.

24 *Sacramento Bee*, July 7, 1951. Because of this deficiency, the *Bee* observed editorially that the law was "just a shade better than no law at all."

25 The prohibition was removed with the concurrence of the bill's author, Assemblyman Lanterman of Los Angeles. *Sacramento Bee*, May 31, 1961.

26 Pollock, *op. cit.*, p. 340.

27 Rex A. Collings, Jr., "California's New Lobby Control Act," *California Law Review*, XXXVIII (August, 1950), 493.

28 The latter is nicely demonstrated by a remark made to one of the writer's students by the secretary of a southern state: "Lobbying is a sin, but my hands are tied."

Among the more interesting "gimmicks" is Walker's proposal that a special grand jury sit concurrently with the legislature and conduct a running investigation of lobbying. "Lawmaking in the United States," p. 297. Something like this happened in Ohio in 1959, when a Franklin County (Columbus) grand jury conducted a generally inconclusive inquiry. See *Cleveland Plain Dealer*, August 3, 1959.

29 *California Government Code*, sec. 9909.

30 Printed in *Assembly Journal* (1951), pp. 2457-2464.

31 In *Assembly Journal* (1951), p. 1496. For comment, see *San Francisco Chronicle*, July 16, 1951.

32 Senator Burns asserted that the man had a "subversive record dating back to 1940" with the Senate Fact-Finding Committee on Un-American Activities. *Sacramento Union*, April 3, 1962. The president of the Federation declared that

the representative "had the complete trust and confidence of the Federation." *Sacramento Bee*, April 5, 1962.

33 Perhaps the strangest comment was that made by John B. Long, general manager of the California Newspaper Publishers Association, who thought the act should be repealed on the ground that "the man that is capable and fit to be a State Senator or an Assemblyman should have the courage to stand up under any kind of pressure." Of course he should. *Lobbying*, Report of the Special Assembly Committee on Legislative Representation, (Sacramento: 1957), p. 12.

34 *Report*, Assembly Interim Committee on Legislative Representation (Sacramento, 1961). The intern was James Heaphy of the University of California, Berkeley.

35 *Report*, Special Senate Committee on Legislative Representation, (Sacramento: 1953); *Lobbying*, Report of Special Assembly Committee on Legislative Representation, (Sacramento: 1957); *Final Report*, Assembly Interim Committee on Legislative Representation, (Sacramento: 1963).

36 *Statutes, 1955*, chap. 713, extended the due date for monthly reports to the 15th instead of the 10th; *Statutes, 1957*, chap. 1470, added radio and television station personnel to those exempted from the registration requirement; and *Statutes, 1961*, chap. 1966, reduced the exemption so as to include only state officials acting in their official capacities, and any elected public official so acting.

37 These can be found in *Assembly Journal* (1951) pp. 1496, 4168; (1957), p. 6011; (1959), pp. 926, 1247, 4692; (1961), pp. 1175, 4695; and *Senate Journal* (1951), p. 515. Several others have been rendered but not printed. The attorney-general has also interpreted the contribution section of the act. 15 *Ops. Att'y Gen'l* 160.

38 The most important of these has read the law to require that individuals allocate general retainers or other receipts to legislative and nonlegislative categories. *Assembly Journal* (1959), p. 926.

39 The testimony is described in *Lobbying*, p. 13. Three organizations complied in 1951, and an average of two every biennium have since reported under section 9903.

40 *Report*, pp. 22-23. The Committee's proposal was based on the argument that the present language was "extremely confusing, and possibly uncomprehensible" (sic). Over six hundred groups have apparently been so confused by the identical section of the Federal Regulation of Lobbying Act that they have complied with it, however.

41 *Ibid.*, p. 29.

42 *Santa Barbara News Press*, April 16, 1963.

43 The treatment accorded the Teachers Association representatives whose credentials were withheld contrasted sharply with that accorded the Sacramento representative of the Public Health League, following allegations that he had covertly planned tactics with members of the legislature at luncheons paid for by him. For details, see *Los Angeles Examiner*, February 24, 1961; *San Francisco Chronicle*, February 27, 1961.

44 "Improving the Legislative Process: Federal Regulation of Lobbying," p. 329.

45 *Ibid.*, p. 330.

46 Truman, *op. cit.*, p. 50. This assertion he continues, "flies in the face of all that we know of the behavior of men in a complex society."

47 State legislatures occasionally pass resolutions requesting the secretary of

state to provide periodic lists of registrants. For an example, see *Virginia Acts and Joint Resolutions, 1948,* Joint Resolution 3 (p. 1332).

See William Miller, "The Legislature: Lobbying," *Governor's Committee on Preparatory Research for the New Jersey Constitutional Convention* (May, 1947), p. 4. See also, Belle Zeller, "State Regulation of Lobbying," *Book of the States, 1950-1951,* (Chicago: Council of State Governments, 1950), p. 134.

48 Wilson, *op. cit.,* p. 124.

49 Hugh Bone reports having gone to Annapolis, Md., with a group of students and finding that the secretary of state "had no idea" of where a list of registrants could be found, although he "knew of its existence." He was told that a search would be conducted and the material made available if the group would drop back "in a week or so." Hugh A. Bone, *American Politics and the Party System,* (New York: McGraw-Hill, 1949), p. 251.

50 To the best of the writer's knowledge, such handouts are written and distributed only in New York, and there only in recent years, during the incumbency of Mrs. Caroline Simon as secretary of state.

51 Well, almost unfailing. The chief clerk of the New York Department of State once responded to the writer's request for certain information (number of registrants, number filing reports, etc.) with a letter stating that it was "against the policy of this Department to give such information."

52 Wilson, *op. cit.,* p. 124.

53 In a letter to the writer.

54 Again, in a letter to the writer.

55 The coverage is principally through a special assessment arrangement with the Associated Press, which runs down the basic data that the *Sun* and a few other papers carry as "Legislative Routine."

56 The states would be Colorado, Connecticut, Georgia, Indiana, Iowa, Massachusetts, Nebraska, North Carolina, North Dakota, Rhode Island, and Virginia. Most of the papers that do a fairly thorough job (relatively speaking) with the filings have been mentioned in the text and notes. The list might be extended to include the *Denver Post, Houston Post, Bismarck Tribune,* Barre, (Vt.) *Daily Times, Hartford Courant, Indianapolis Star, Richmond Times-Dispatch and News-Leader, Raleigh News and Observer, Lincoln* (Neb.) *Star.*

57 For the details, see the *Seattle Post-Intelligencer* and the *Spokane Spokesman-Review,* March 3, 4, 5, and 25, 1951. A $16,000 report filed in April, 1963, however, drew some legislative fire. *Santa Barbara News-Press,* April 19, 1963.

58 *Report* of the Joint Interim Committee on Lobby Regulations (1950), p. 18.

59 *Ibid.,* p. 10.

60 *Ibid.*

61 *Ibid.* Cf. Truman, *op. cit.,* p. 528.

62 Bert C. Goss, "The Lobby Probe and Public Relations, "*Public Relations Journal,* VII (May, 1951). Compare with the writer's "The Lobby Probe Revisited," *Public Relations Journal,* VII (October, 1951), 14-16. For the argument against disclosure in its baldest form, see the testimony of Mr. Leonard Read of the Foundation for Economic Education, before the House Select Committee on Lobbying Activities of the 81st Congress. *Hearings* (1950), part 8, pp. 114-120.

63 This could, among other things, help to lay the notion of equal group competition, an interesting statement of which can be found in *Final Report of the*

New York State Joint Legislative Committee on Legislative Methods, Practices, Procedures, and Expenditures, Legislative Document no. 31 (1946), p. 27.

64 "Mass Media" is here meant in a broad sense. If a disclosure system were working as it should, it would be working through other media than the newspaper alone.

Chapter 6: Disclosure in Perspective

1 Truman, *op. cit.,* p. 528.

2 E.E. Schattschneider, *The Semi-Sovereign People,* (New York: Holt, Rinehart, and Winston, 1960), p. 31.

3 Luce, *op. cit.,* p. 421.

4 Hurst, *op. cit.,* pp. 63-64.

5 The Senator also declared that "the legislatures of America—local, state, and national—are the greatest menace to the successful operation of the democratic process. . . . This is where the vested-interest lobbies run riot, where conflict of interest rides unchecked, where demagoguery knows no bounds, where political lag keeps needed action a generation behind the time." In *The Elite and the Electorate* (pamphlet), (Santa Barbara: Center for the Study of Democratic Institutions, 1963), p. 14.

6 *Final Report* of the Assembly Interim Committee on Legislative Representation, (Sacramento: 1963), p. 16.

7 Robert Carr and Marver Bernstein, *American Democracy in Theory and Practice,* Essentials Edition, revised, (New York: Holt, Rinehart and Winston, 1961), pp. 122-123. Karl Schriftgiesser makes essentially the same distinction in *The Lobbyists,* (Boston: Little Brown, 1951), p. 90, referring to the "availability of the information to all citizens as well as to interested members of Congress."

8 Bertram Gross, *The Legislative Struggle,* (New York: McGraw-Hill, 1953), p. 46.

9 Truman, *op. cit., p.* 528.

10 "Improving the Legislative Process: Federal Regulation of Lobbying," *Yale Law Journal,* LVI (January, 1947), 316.

11 Belle Zeller, "The Regulation of Pressure Groups and Lobbyists," *Annals,* CCCXIX (September, 1958), 103. The language is from the preamble of S.2191, introduced in the 85th Congress, 1957.

12 George B. Galloway, "A Report on the Operation of Title III of the Legislative Reorganization Act of 1946," in U.S. Congress, Senate, Special Committee on Investigating Political Activities, Lobbying, and Campaign Contributions, *Final Report,* 85th Cong., 1st Sess. (1957), p. 200.

13 *United States* v. *Harriss,* 347 U.S. 615 (1954).

14 T.V. Smith, *The Legislative Way of Life,* (Chicago: Chicago University Press, 1938), p. 9.

15 Truman, *op. cit.,* p. 528.

16 Gross, *op. cit.,* p. 46. On the point of complexity, Blaisdell has observed that the "same opinion, both official and private, has held that federal and state lobby regulation laws have failed and have been ineffective because of the sheer mass of data filed." Donald Blaisdell, *American Democracy Under Pressure,* (New York: Ronald, 1958), p. 90. No; there is not too much data but too little use made of it.

17 In U.S. Congress, House, Select Committee on Lobbying Activities, 81st Cong., 2d Sess., *Hearings,* part 1 (1950), p. 45.

18 U.S. Congress, Senate, Committee on Labor and Public Welfare, Subcommittee on the Establishment of a Commission on Ethics in Government, *Ethical Standards in Government*, 82nd Cong., 1st Sess. (1951), p. 37. See also George Graham, *Morality in American Politics*, (New York: Random House, 1952), pp. 245-252.

19 *Ethical Standards in Government*, p. 38.

20 Gross, *op. cit.*, p. 26.

21 The phrase is Gross's, *ibid.*, p. 25.

22 The reference to "lifelines" is in Stuart Chase, *Democracy Under Pressure*, (New York: Twentieth Century Fund, 1945), p. 8. Hugh Bone refers to disclosure laws as "essentially futile" means of "coping with the undue power exercised by special interest groups." *American Politics and the Party System*, (New York: McGraw-Hill, 1949), p. 252. The majoritarian argument has been best advanced by E.E. Schattschneider, most recently in *The Semi-Sovereign People*, above, note 2.

23 V.O. Key, *Politics, Parties, and Pressure Groups*, (3d ed.; New York: Crowell, 1952), p. 180.

24 Harvey Fergusson, *People and Power*, (New York: Morrow, 1947), p. 101.

25 As they are, in Truman, *op. cit.*, pp. 525-535.

26 Gross, *op. cit.*, p. 25.

27 Truman, *op. cit.*, p. 51.

28 Schubert, *op. cit.*, p. 223.

29 Hurst, *op. cit.*, pp. 37, 39.

30 For an excellent example, see the study drafted by Professors Bernstein and Manning for the New York City Bar, *Conflict of Interests and Federal Service*, (Cambridge: Harvard University Press, 1960).

Index

Abshire, Vernon, 160

Administration: statutory requirements for, 87-91; in California, 162-168; proposals for, 168-169. See also Disclosure; Enforcement

Administrative agencies, lobbying with, 10. See also Interest groups; Lobbying

AFL-CIO, 122

Alabama: constitutional prohibition of lobbying in, 26; lobbying statute of, 26-27, 48

Alaska: lobbying statute of, 63, 65, 70; operation of law in, 123, 125, 158

Albany Times-Union, 172

Allen, Robert, 99, 155

American Federation of Teachers, 164

American Hypnotists Association, 119

American Mutual Alliance, 125

Ancient Order of United Workmen, 116

Arizona: constitutional prohibition of lobbying in, 29; statutory prohibition of lobbying in, 49

Armstrong Insurance Investigating Committee, 36-37

Arthur, Robert, 156-157

Associated General Contractors of California, 148

Associated Public Works Contractors of Wisconsin, 150

Association of American Railroads, 10

Atlanta Constitution, 171

Attorneys: as lobbyists, 62; registration compliance by, 124-127

Attorneys-general, provisions for enforcement by, 87-89, 161

Bailey, Stephen K., 186

Baltimore Sun, 172, 173

Beth, Loren P., 5, 94, 96

Boston, Hartford, and Erie Railroad, 31

Bowie Race Track, 129

Bricker, John, 129

Brogan, Dennis W., 20

Bromley, Elmer, 148

Brown, Edmund G., 4, 165

Burns, Hugh, 164

Business groups, reported spending by, 150-151

Butler, Monroe, 148

California: lobbying methods in, 8, 95-96, 145-146; lobbying expenditures in, 8, 144-146; constitutional prohibition of lobbying in, 28, 48; passage of lobbying act in, 40-43; statutory requirements in, 55, 59-61, 63, 65, 67-70, 78-82, 85, 89, 99-101, 138; conflict-of-interest problems in, 104; operation of law in, 108, 110-111, 117, 119, 122, 134-135, 144-146, 183; former legislators as lobbyists in, 128, 148; report forms in, 141; proposed amendments in, 160-161; administration of law in, 162-168; Committees on Legislative Representation in, 163-165; press coverage of law in, 170, 172

California Association of Highway Patrolmen, 145

California Beverage Distributors Association, 145

Californians against Capital Punishment, 147

California Railroad Association, 10, 150

California Real Estate Association, 145

California State Bar Association, 145, 151

California State Brewers' Association, 41, 145

Campbell v. *Commonwealth,* 155, 159

Celler, Emanuel, 13

Charleston News and Courier, 172

Chase, Stuart, 14
Cincinnati Enquirer, 173
Clark, Joseph, 181
Cleveland Plain Dealer, 173
Cochran, Thomas, 21
Collier's, 41
Colorado: registration by legislative rule in, 57, 72; former officials registered in, 128
Columbus Citizen-Journal, 172
Communist Party of California, 164
Compliance: by lobbyists, 112-118, 133; by groups, 134-135, 142
Conflicts-of-interest, 95-96, 104. *See also* Ethics
Connecticut: definition of lobbying in, 54; statutory requirements in, 63, 70, 85, 89; operation of law in, 110, 111-112, 122, 126, 138; balance of interests in, 123; former officials registered in, 128, 129; report forms in, 139
Contingent fees, prohibitions of, 73
Crawford, Finla G., 18

De Grazia, Alfred, 8
Del Mar Turf Club, 145
Disbarment provisions, 86-87
Disclosure: definition of, 15; purposes of, 16, 32-33, 174-175; origins of, 40, 177; legislative antipathy to, 43-45, 160-161, 182-183; values and limitations of, 183-189. *See also* Administration; Enforcement; Publicity
Donnelly, Hugh, 161
Douglas, Paul, 94
Douglas Committee, report of, 186-187

Eastern Railroads Presidents Conference, 6
Enforcement: statutory requirements for, 87-91; prosecutions, 155-157; evaluation of, 158-162. *See also* Administration
Entertainment, expenditures for, 140-141, 145-146. *See also* Lobbying
Epstein, Leon, 129
Equitable Life Assurance Society, 36
Erwin Bill, 42
Ethics: lobbying and, 92-97; legal remedies and, 97-101; public and legislative attitudes on, 102-105

Farm groups, reported expenditures by, 151
Federal Administrative Procedure Act, 10
Federalist Papers, 1-2
Federal Regulation of Lobbying Act, 7, 80; and California Lobbying Act, 55, 175
Florida: definition of lobbying in, 54; *ad hoc* registration in, 57, 71, 84; registration by legislative rule in, 57, 72; lobbying methods in, 94
Florida Power and Light Company, 96
Ford Motor Company, 122
Friends Committee on Legislation, 147

Garibaldi, James, 145, 148
Garland, Gordon, 145, 148
General Motors Corporation, 122
Georgia: constitutional prohibition of lobbying in, 27; statutory requirements in, 27, 50, 58, 63, 70, 84; operation of law in, 108, 117, 133
Ginn and Company, 145
Gould, Jay, 6, 24
Governmental Process, The, 6
Graves, W. B., 146
Gross, Bertram, 184, 186, 189

Hacker, Louis, 22
Havard, William C., 5, 94, 96
Hofstadter, Richard, 23
Hollywood Turf Club, 145
Holmes, Oliver Wendell, Jr., 190
Huntington, Collis, 10, 23
Hurst, J. Willard, 1, 21, 179, 192

Idaho, lobbyist regulation in, 71-72
Illinois: lobbying act of 1958, 34, 44, 60, 68, 70; operation of law in, 112
Indiana: statutory requirements in, 65-66, 70, 77, 81-82, 85; operation of law in, 108, 110, 117, 119, 121-122, 126, 134, 158; control of legislature in, 112; press coverage of disclosed data in, 170